To dear +Lila
+ best love from Mummy.

June 1983

2

၁၉၇၀-ခုနှစ်
ေထာင်ရွေ့

THE INSIGHT GUIDES SERIES
RECEIVED THE
1980 SPECIAL AWARD FOR EXCELLENCE
AWARDED BY
THE PACIFIC AREA TRAVEL ASSOCIATION

ISBN 9971-925-08-7 English edition, softcover
ISBN 9771-925-09-5 English edition, hardcover

Typesetting:
Innovative Media Inc., Honolulu
Color Separations:
Laserscan Co. Pte. Ltd., Singapore
Colourscan Co. Pte. Ltd., Singapore
Printed by Singapore National Printers Pte. Ltd

burma

Directed and Designed by Hans Johannes Hoefer
Written by Wilhelm Klein
Photographed by Gunter Pfannmüller
Edited by John Gottberg Anderson

Published by Apa Productions (HK) Ltd
Second Edition July 1982

Burma. The hidden country behind the horseshoe mountains. The last refuge of an age-old lifestyle shielded for decades from Western eyes, and only now opening its door a little wider for the outside world to peek within.

Burma's isolation has been almost legendary in international travel circles. Apa's Singapore-based staff had covered most of the rest of Southeast Asia in its highly acclaimed *Insight Guides* series, but had temporarily shelved the idea of a Burma book because of the bureaucratic obstacles involved. So imagine the surprise of publisher Hans Hoefer when Austrian author Wilhelm Klein approached him at the 1980 Frankfurt Book Fair, with a completed German and English-language manuscript and more than 1,000 beautiful color photographs!

Burma is the only *Insight Guide* to have been conceived, and essentially written and photographed, outside of the Apa editorial fold. Klein, former co-editor of a German political magazine and one-time publisher of books on international affairs through his Mega Press, has traveled to Asia on a regular basis since the early 1960s. Long fascinated by the unique blend of ancient Buddhism and modern socialism found in Burma, he was disappointed that no thorough photographic guide to this exotic land existed. So in 1978, he approached his friend, Bangkok publisher Suk Soongswang, with a proposal for just such a volume. Soongswang agreed to back him, and the project was launched.

Klein's first step was to find a photographer — one with sufficient sensitivity to catch the mystery and diversity of Burma on film. He found him in Gunter Pfannmuller, a graduate of Germany's Darmstadt Academy of graphic design. "Pfanny," as he is known to friends, travels extensively as a free-lance photographer for Gruner und Jahr, the publishing company known for *Geo*, *Stern* and *Brigitte* magazines. He had never been to Burma, but upon hearing Klein's wondrous tales from this extraordinary land, he and his Nikon needed no further convincing.

A one-week time restriction on tourist visas to Burma was but a minor aggravation in the preparation of the book. Klein and Pfannmuller overcame that obstacle by sheer persistence. Two years and many week-long visits later, they had thoroughly canvassed all areas of Burma regarded as accessible to visitors.

Klein then turned to Martin Pickering, an instructor of German language in Kirkcaldy, Scotland, to translate the basic manuscript to English. Pickering became so enthralled with Burma that he and his wife made immediate

Hoefer

Klein

plans to visit the Asian country themselves.

At first, the book was scheduled to go to press at Soongswang's DK Bookhouse in Bangkok in the fall of 1980. But Klein and Pfannmuller, longtime admirers of the philosophy behind Apa's *Insight Guides,* had purposely modeled their work upon the publishing principles and artistic execution of this series. So when Klein — who had first met Hoefer four years earlier — showed his work to Apa's chief executive in 1980, a publishing agreement was quickly reached. Soongswang released his rights to the book, and a new *Insight Guide* was born.

Hoefer, a Baulfaus-trained designer-photographer, had come to Singapore from his native Germany in 1968 and soon thereafter established Apa Productions. Beginning with an award-winning title on Bali in 1970, Hoefer had directed *Insight Guides* on Java, Singapore, Malaysia, Thailand, Korea, the Philippines, Hawaii and Hong Kong; new volumes on Nepal, Sumatra, Florida, Mexico, Southern California and Northern California were being prepared by Apa editorial teams.

Klein and Pfannmuller were delighted to be associated with this celebrated series. They returned to Burma twice more early in 1981 to collect additional information. This time, they outdid themselves — getting off the usual visitor routes and traveling to such fascinating locations as the Kyaik-tiyo "Golden Rock," the Irrawaddy Delta capital of Bassein, and the little-known lost cities of Arakan. Their trip to Arakan, in particular, was a

Pfannmüller

Anderson

triumph of perseverance: for three years, they had petitioned Tourist Burma for the opportunity to visit this state, normally off-limits to visitors. Finally, they were given the okay "as a trial for future tourism." Pfannmuller's pictures of Arakan are the first to appear in a Western publication in more than two decades.

With the text and photos compiled and translated, it remained for *Burma* to be shaped into true Apa style. The editing job was handed to John Anderson, a former newspaper reporter and editor in Honolulu and Seattle who had himself spent time in Burma during extensive Asian travels in the mid-1970s. At the time he was chosen *Burma* editor, Anderson was one of six American journalists immersed in a Gannett Foundation fellowship in Asian studies at the University of Hawaii. He previously had assisted on Apa's *Insight Guide: Korea* and the forthcoming *Insight Chronicle: The Hula*.

Anderson recruited Sherry Cox, a University of Hawaii graduate degree student in Burmese music, to prepare a section on "Survival Burmese." Cox is one of very few young Westerners fluent in the Burmese language, having studied it in California as well as during a period of residence in Rangoon.

While Pfannmuller took the vast majority of photographs for *Burma*, other important shots were taken by Kal Muller, Jan Whiting, Ronni Pinsler, John Anderson and Whilhelm Klein. *Burma* also owes special thanks to Mi Seitelman, who provided a series of World War Two photos from the U.S. Army archives, and Leo Haks, who gave permission to reproduce a number of 19th Century photographs from his collection.

Burma's magnificent selection of color maps and charts was drawn by cartographers Everett Wingert and Jane Eckelman of Honolulu. April J. Siegenthaler used pen and ink to recapture a 19th Century Burmese cosmic concept of the world. Nedra Chung prepared the index.

Several Burmese assisted in making *Burma* a reality. They include U Bokay in Pagan, Win Myint in Taunggyi, Freddie Khin Maung and Ba Ky in Rangoon, U Tin Htway in Heidelberg, and U Gye Myint in Bonn. Other persons and institutions who contributed to *Burma* in one or many ways were Sabrina Will, Kurt Banse, Sam Oglesby, Leonard Lueras, Linda Carlock-Anderson, Renate Klein, Steve Petranik, Albert Moscotti, Raymond Boey, Alice Ng, Yvan Van Outrive, the late Walter F. Vella, the Embassy of the Union of Burma in Bonn, Tourist Burma, the Burmese Directorate of Information and Directorate of Archaeology, the U.S. Army, the Imperial War Museum in London, *The Asia Record*, the University of Hawaii Center for Asian and Pacific Studies, and many others.

To all, *cei zu tin ba de.*

— Apa Productions

TABLE OF CONTENTS

TABLE OF CONTENTS

Cover
— by Gunter Pfannmüller

Cartography
— by Jane Eckelman and Everett Wingert

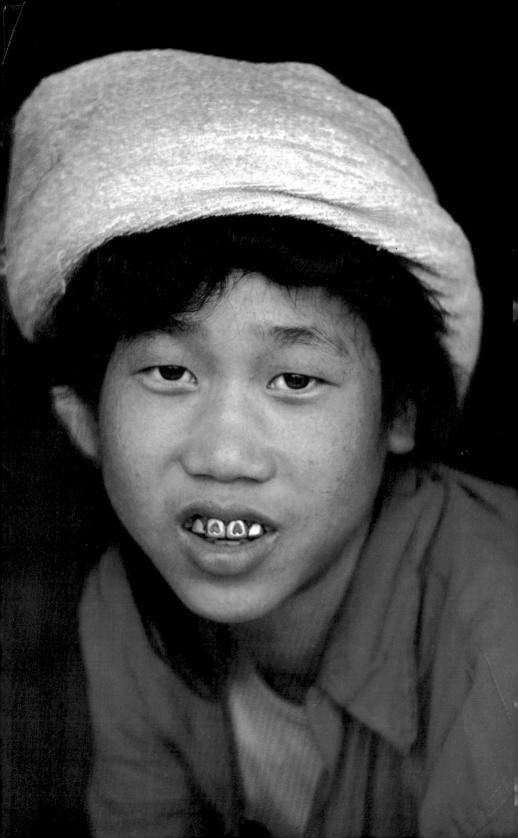

'A KIND OF SPELL'

The country casts a kind of spell over its friends which they cannot break if they would.
—*John F. Cady, A History of Modern Burma (1958)*

Any visitor arriving in Burma for the first time and visiting the Shwedagon Pagoda at sunset on the same evening will immediately appreciate the spell of which Cady writes. It is not just that wonder of the world, the Shwedagon; it is the atmosphere, the varied scents, the ambience ... and the feeling of another world, a world which one did not dare believe existed any longer, save in the pages of books.

Such a world is described in Aldous Huxley's *Island*—a world of harmony between the senses and the spirit. The visitor takes his first steps toward discovering this Burma as he approaches the main platform around the Shwedagon's golden stupa. A sign in good Burmese-English reads "Footwearing Prohibited," and the visitor, after years of confinement in the dictates and prejudices of Western society, sheds his shoes and feels the warmth of the marble slabs beneath his toes. As he climbs the pagoda stairs, he revels in his new-found freedom. As he wanders around the terraces, he is respectfully mindful of the many pious Buddhists who walk with the stupa always on their right, as they repeat their "Three Gems": "I take refuge in the Buddha. I take refuge in the Dharma. I take refuge in the Sangha."

Everything Is Change

The Shwedagon is a constant reminder of the transience of all things, a sign that Buddhism recognizes man's sorrowful plight. Yet in making its silent statement, it produces in devotees an almost imperceptible joy which can most readily be felt at the sunset hour among the pagoda's prayer halls and pavilions. Burma is a living fossil from another era, perhaps the last remnant of a world far from Coca-Cola, television and space travel.

The visitor will be greatly impressed on this first evening in Burma. He may expect the next week to offer similar splendors; he may feel this awesome initial attraction is here to whet his appetite for even more startling sights. Indeed, Burma can fascinate the visitor with one unexpected surprise after another, from the leg-rowers of Inle Lake to the pagoda-speckled plain of Pagan, from the *nat* dancers of tiny Taungbyon to the remarkable "giraffe women" of the Padaung tribe.

But too many preconceptions can lead to disappointment. Burma is a developing country in today's world, and is not among the richest. The traveler to Burma must be prepared to accept lower standards of living, even if he has managed to maintain his normal comforts elsewhere in the East. Foreign currency brought to Burma by visitors cannot be entirely reinvested for visitors' benefit; Burma's economic situation instead demands that these funds be used to finance projects which benefit the nation as a whole.

Students and Wanderers

Most Western visitors to Burma fall into two clearly defined groups. First, there are the backpack travelers, that worldwide brotherhood of latter-day wanderers. Comfort to them is synonymous with losing awareness of their senses. They want to feel the pulse of the host society, to be close to the people, their joys and anxieties.

Second are the students of culture who are well versed in advance on the country they visit. Theirs is a calculated risk, a knowledge that whatever they may sacrifice in physical comforts will be amply rewarded in terms of new stimuli, impressions and knowledge.

Those few visitors who belong to neither category of traveler can soon be recognized by their loud voices at hotel reception desks and restaurants. They feel at a loss in a country where the air-conditioning, although it does exist, is invariably out of order.

Despite their plaintive moans, Western visitors need not find Burma an unpleasant destination. All of the large towns have at least one

Preceding pages: Female workers march on Union Day, nurses hurry to a national celebration, 45 Buddhas gaze at a lone Sagaing monk, myriad spires rise from Rangoon's Shwedagon Pagoda, and two Arakanese monks travel by boat to mystical Myohaung. Left, a hill-tribe boy from the gem area of Mogok smiles a big ruby-and-jade smile.

hotel acceptable by Western standards, and persons who delight in new experiences will find a way to get by—though perhaps with a little more inconvenience than elsewhere. They certainly can't complain about prices: where else but in the Strand Hotel dining room could one pay a mere US $3 and be served two Lobster Thermidor halves in a genuine British colonial atmosphere?

One Tile in the Mosaic

To say that Rangoon is not Burma is a platitude. The city is like a single mosaic tile in a glittering work of art, the whole of which waits to be discovered. But in Rangoon, more than elsewhere, one can perceive the outside influences which have penetrated the barrier of isolation.

These "outside influences" will soon be evident in the provinces as well. The government is taking pains to modernize the country. Fertilizer factories, oil refineries, an automobile assembly plant, and the television channel planned for the 1980s all will leave their marks well beyond the environs of Rangoon, in areas where there is little or no evidence of modernity today.

Burma's colors, however, are still natural. Monks are clothed in a variety of shades from saffron to purple. Women, wearing pale yellow *thanaka*-bark makeup and smoking green or white cheroots, conjure images of the last century. The visitor to Burma is constantly reminded of past ages—indeed, of ages which may never have taken place. This, perhaps, is what makes Burma the thoroughly fascinating country it is.

Historians' Revenge

More than 100 years ago, in Mandalay, power was held by a king who wanted nothing to do with the modern era. He saw himself and his country bound eternally to the Buddhist historical concept of continual, cyclical change. The British ambassador residing at his court didn't fit into this concept; even King Anawrahta, 800 years removed, was considered more authoritative. The British were disgruntled, just as we would be today if someone did not accept our view of the 20th Century world.

But British historians took their revenge. For a full century, Burmese history—with very few exceptions—was written as the British saw it: the history of a barbarian race, a country lacking any kind of redeeming culture. And while the British wrote disparagingly about their colony, they tramped around Burma's temples and pagodas in their army boots, without regard to the sacred feelings of the Burmese people.

The British were neither better nor worse than any other colonial power in this respect. But their literature painted a negative picture of Burma which carried far beyond the colony's borders. Even such an engaging man as the famed author George Orwell—for years a police official in Burma—was not complimentary in his writing about the land. In his book *Burmese Days,* Orwell gave his readers an insight into what happened in Burma when the West tried to impose its ideals upon the Asians. Orwell's characters called the Burmese "a set of damn black swine who've been slaves since the beginning of history." How else could the committed counsels of His Majesty the British King have been conditioned to think?

It is, in fact, remarkable that Burma has managed to survive the last 150-plus years relatively unspoiled. A lot of the colonial damage has healed since Burma embarked on an almost involuntary isolation some 30 years ago. Now a national consciousness, so long suppressed, is gradually coming to the fore. Burma's maligned history is being put to rights at Rangoon University . . . but it will be years before the Burmese view of the nation's history is properly told.

Much of the historical material in this book has come from the British "scholars" of the colonial period. Because this is the only source currently available, it is a necessary evil—but the reader should be cautious in drawing any conclusions.

*   *   *   *   *

This book draws a distinction between the Burman people—the country's majority ethnic group as well as those people who speak a Tibeto-Burman language—and the Burmese, a term which represents all peoples of Burma. Indigenous terms used are from the Burmese (Tibeto-Burman) language, except for Sanskrit language words in religious contexts, or unless specifically noted.

A young Burmese boy wearing a socialist cap and *thanaka* bark powder (right) exemplifies the contradictions of growing up in contemporary Burma.

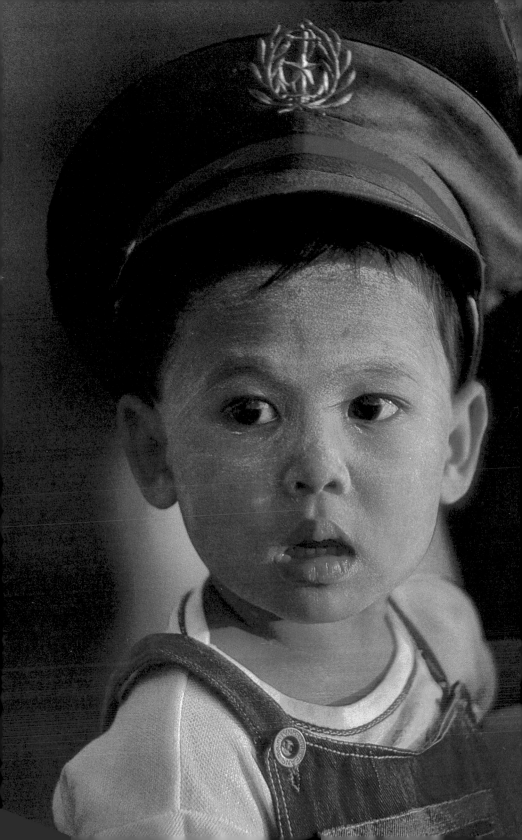

FASCINATION WITH AN ANCIENT LAND

Foreigners have been visiting Burma and recording their observations in journals and books since at least the 6th Century A.D. A survey of some of their comments serves not only to inform us about the country and its people through the ages, but also demonstrates how the perspective of the traveler has changed, often independently of the prevailing views of the time.

Among the first visitors to remark on Burma were the chroniclers of ancient China's T'ang dynasty:

When the P'iao (Pyu) king goes out in his palanquin, he lies on a couch of golden cord. For long distances he rides an elephant. He has several hundred women to wait on him . . . (The people) are Buddhists and have a hundred monasteries, with bricks of glassware embellished with gold and silver vermilion, gay colors and red kino.
—Chronicle of the T'ang Dynasty, 618–905 A.D.

Even so famed a world traveler as the Venetian merchant Marco Polo marveled at the treasures of Pagan, whose name he knew as "Mien":

The towers are built of fine stone; and then one of them has been covered with gold a good finger in thickness, so that the tower looks as if it were all of solid gold; and the other is covered with silver in like manner so that it seems to be all of solid silver. . . . The King caused these towers to be erected to commemorate his magnificence and for the good of his soul; and really they do form one of the finest sights in the world; so exquisitely finished are they, so splendid and costly. And when they are lighted up by the sun they shine most brilliantly and are visible from a vast distance.
—The Travels of Marco Polo, 1298

As the centuries wore on—and European visitors became more frequent—observations on the lifestyles of the people of Burma were more commonly recorded. Late in the 16th Century, one traveler commented on the system by which the king granted audiences to his subjects:

(The king) sitteth up aloft in a great hall, on a tribunal seat, and lower under him sit all his barons round about, then those that demand audience enter into a great court before the king . . . And if the king think it good to do to them that favor or justice that they demand, then he commandeth to take the presents out of their hands; but if he thinks their demand be not just or according to right, he commandeth them away without taking of their gifts or presents . . .
—Caesar Frederick, 1596

Two centuries later, the Briton Michael Symes was much kinder in his remarks about the Burmese than many of his countrymen would be in the decades to come:

POLO

The Burmans . . . are certainly rising fast in the scale of Oriental nations. . . . They have an undeniable claim to the character of a civilized and well instructed people. Their laws are wise and pregnant with sound morality; their police is better regulated than in most European countries; their natural disposition is . . . hospitable to strangers.
—*Michael Symes,* An Account of the Embassy to the Kingdom of Ava Sent by the Governor-General of India in 1795

Part of the reason for the low view of the Burmese generally taken by the British colonialists was, of course, their total disagreement on respective concepts of "the way things were." An example:

Major Phayre endeavoured to explain the solar system; but as the Burmese theory is that of a central mountain called Myen-Mo (Meru), several millions of miles high, around which are firmly fixed four great islands, on the southern of which Asia and Europe are situated, the sun which lights them revolving round the central mountain, the Envoy of course did not succeed in convincing the Minister of the truth of our view of the case. . . . The (Minister) somewhat indignantly said, 'It (Myen-Mo) is spoken of in our sacred books, and its height is given, and the inhabitants of each region are known exactly.'
—*Sir Henry Yule,* A Narrative of the Mission to the Court of Ava in 1855

But if the Burmese were not popular among the British, neither were the British popular among the Burmese:

The best thing a Burman can wish for a good Englishman, is that in some future existence, as a reward of good works, he may be born a Buddhist and if possible a Burman.
—*Shway Yoe (alias Sir James George Scott),* The Burman: His Life and Notions, *1882*

By the time of the Second World War, perhaps, the outside world was finally beginning to accept the Burmese way of life:

Burmese live every phase of their lives in accordance with a profound teaching, and cannot be considered uncivilized. It's wrong to ridicule them just because they don't have the kind of knowledge we do. They possess something marvelous that we can't even begin to understand.
—*Michio Takeyama,* Harp of Burma, *1946*

Since Burma's independence in 1948, scholars have been placing the highest premium on understanding Burma in light of her socialist government. Perhaps it is encouraging to note that Burma is now generally accepted as Burma, rather than through a comparison with something that it is not:

. . . The emphasis has been on the Burmese way to socialism; although new values and a new way of life are to supplant the old, the nation's social engineers have sought to create national unity and social harmony by finding a Burmese solution rather than importing one ready-made from abroad.
—*Josef Silverstein,* Burma: Military Rule and the Politics of Stagnation, *1977*

YULE

A LAND OF RICE AND RIVERS

Burma. The Irrawaddy. For millennia, the names of the nation and the river have been almost synonymous.

As the center of the rice culture on which Burma's economy has always been based, the Irrawaddy is the lifeblood of the land. Rising in the southern Himalayas, it traverses the country from north to south for about 2,170 kilometers (1,350 miles), emptying into the Andaman Sea through a nine-armed delta. Called "the Road to Mandalay" by British colonialists, the broad river has perennially been the land's major transportation route.

Were the traveler able to follow the Irrawaddy's entire course, he would find it possible to sample the full range of Burma's climatic zones. Beginning in the far north, he would travel through the rugged Kachin Hills, foothills of the mighty Himalayas. At Bhamo, the furthest point to which the Irrawaddy is navigable by steamer (1,500 kilometers, or about 930 miles, from the delta), the journeyer would enter the Shan Plateau region. Further downstream, he would emerge on the broad dry plain of central Burma, the center of classical Burmese civilization. He would cruise past sandbars to the ruins of Pagan and Sri Ksetra, then enter the moister southern stretch of the Irrawaddy's course. In its vast delta, 240 kilometers (150 miles) wide and 290 kilometers (180 miles) long, he would look out upon seemingly endless rice paddies—a region so fertile that Burma was until recent years the world's top exporter of rice.

The 'Kite' and Its String

Indeed, the Irrawaddy is the string controlling the "kite" that is Burma. Thinking of a kite is a good way to envision the country: it is roughly diamond-shaped, with long, narrow Tenasserim as its tail. A surface area of 678,033 square kilometers (261,789 square miles) makes Burma the largest Asian mainland country east of India and south of China. Despite its former colonial ties to India, it is usually grouped geographically with Southeast Asia.

Burma's population is estimated at about 31.5 million, of whom about 80 percent live in rural villages. After Rangoon, with its population of about 3.2 million, the major population centers are Mandalay (about 600,000), Moulmein (about 200,000) and Bassein (about 140,000).

Bounded by Bangladesh and India on the northwest, the People's Republic of China on the northeast, Laos and Thailand on the east, the Andaman Sea on the south, and the Bay of Bengal on the southwest, Burma is located between 10 and 28 degrees North Latitude. The Tropic of Cancer traverses the country 160 kilometers (100 miles) north of Mandalay.

The most agreeable season is the winter. From November through February, the average mean temperature along the Irrawaddy plain is between 21°C and 28°C (70°F and 82°F), although in the northern Kachin mountains and on the Shan Plateau the temperature can drop below freezing, making it cold enough to snow.

March and April are the hottest, driest months in Burma, with central Burma temperatures sometimes reaching a stifling 45°C (113°F). In May, however, the rainy season begins. This is a time of high humidity, somewhat more bearable in Mandalay than in Rangoon. From May through October, one must reckon with daily afternoon and early evening showers.

The 'Horseshoe Mountains'

This seasonal rainfall, as in all of South and Southeast Asia, is a result of the monsoon winds of the Indian Ocean, which move from the southwest in summer and from the northeast in winter. Burma gets its heaviest rains between June and August, but is protected by its "horseshoe mountains" from the very severe flooding which plagues much of the rest of the region.

Burma's central river system is ringed by a series of peaks—several over 3,000 meters (over 10,000 feet) in height—which create profound if predictable effects on the nation's climate. There are the Arakan, Chin, Naga and Patkai hills in the west, the Kachin hills in the north, and the Shan Plateau, extending to the Tenasserim Coast ranges, in the east.

The coasts of Arakan and Tenasserim receive 300 to 500 cm (120 to 200 inches) of rain per year, with the Irrawaddy Delta getting 150 to 250 cm (60 to 100 inches). On the leeward sides of the mountain ranges and on the Shan Plateau, annual precipitation ranges from 100 to 200 cm (40 to 80 inches), while central Burma's Dry Zone varies from 50 to

Preceding pages: A native craft glides down a tranquil Arakan river, rain saturates the central Burma paddies during the wet season, and a rice mill looks out on the Irrawaddy Delta at Bassein. Left, a woman rice-worker climbs a golden mountain of harvested paddy at a Hlegu workers' cooperative.

100 cm (20 to 40 inches). It is largely due to the protection of the 2,000 meter (6,500-foot) peaks of the Arakan Yoma that central Burma is Southeast Asia's driest region—and that Pagan's priceless buildings have remained so well preserved through the centuries.

The monsoon rains nourish Burma's rice crop. But it is the melting snows of the Himalayas, far to the north, which feed Burma's great rivers.

Two rivers besides the Irrawaddy are important to Burma's inland navigation and irrigation. One, the Chindwin, is a tributary of the Irrawaddy, joining the larger stream about 110 kilometers (70 miles) downstream from Mandalay. Readily navigable for about 180 kilometers (110 miles) upstream from its confluence—and for 610 kilometers (380 miles)

during the rainy season—it opens up remote stretches of the Sagaing Region.

In eastern Burma, the Salween River slices through the Shan State in a series of deep gorges. Like the Mekong, which comprises the Burma-Laos border, the Salween flows for long stretches through areas controlled by anti-government rebel forces. It has few tributaries between its source in the Himalayas and its exit to the Andaman Sea at Moulmein, despite a 2,816-kilometer (1,749-mile) course. It is navigable only for about 160 kilometers (100 miles) upstream because of its dangerously fast current and 20-meter (65-foot) fluctuations in water level. But it plays an important role in the Burmese economy as the route by which teak is rafted from the Shan Pla-

teau, where it is harvested, to Moulmein, its export harbor.

One other river has traditionally been of great importance in Burmese history. That is the Sittang, a relatively short stream which marks the lower boundary between the Pegu Region and the Mon State. But it has silted up badly in the past two centuries, to the extent that it is now navigable only by flat-bottomed boats, and then only on certain stretches.

High Peaks of the North

Geographically, Burma can be divided into several zones. In the far north, as noted, are the Kachin hills, reaching heights of 3,000 meters (about 10,000 feet). On the Tibetan border is Hkakabo Razi, the highest peak in Southeast Asia at 5,887 meters (19,314 feet). Deep valleys, many of them harboring subtropical vegetation and terraced rice, separate the mountain ridges. The chief inhabitants are the Kachin people, although tribes of Lisu are also common in the Chinese border region. The administrative center of Myitkyina (pronounced myit-CHEE-na) is the terminus of the railway from Rangoon and Mandalay.

Were future political events to allow a direct overland route between Europe and Southeast Asia, it would pass through the Kachin State. In ages past, the Ledo Road and several old caravan routes were of inestimable importance to commerce in the region. These roads, coupled with the more recent Burma Road, linked India's Assam with China's Yunnan, and were keys to war strategy during the Second World War and the preceding Japan-China conflict. Today they are closed except for use by the established minorities of this otherwise impassable region.

On their south, the Kachin Hills are linked to the Shan Plateau, a vast area averaging about 1,000 meters (3,200 feet) in elevation. Deep, incisive valleys intersect the undulating surface of the plateau, and the powerful Salween flows through it like an arrow on the east. Once popular as a site for "hill stations" where British colonials could escape the heat of central Burma, the region still offers the flavor of a bygone era in its administrative centers of Taunggyi, Maymyo, Kalaw and Lashio. A modern tourist center has developed around Inle Lake in the southwestern part of the plateau.

With an almost-European climate, fruits, vegetables and citrus crops thrive on the Shan

The monsoon-type rigging of boats in the Bay of Bengal (left) is much the same as in the 17th Century when pirates ruled the seas; the roadless jungles near Moulmein depend on a different conveyance—elephant—to deliver goods (right).

Plateau, as do timber crops. Burma is the world's leading exporter of teak, and most of that valued wood is harvested in the Shan State. Other crops include rice, peanuts, potatoes, tea, tobacco, coffee, cotton ... and opium. The notorious Golden Triangle encompasses much of the eastern part of the Shan Plateau.

To the east of the Gulf of Martaban, the Shan Plateau funnels into the Tenasserim coastal range which forms the natural border between southern Burma and Thailand. The long tongue of coastland which follows this range down the Isthmus of Kra—the "tail of the kite," as it were—is not easily accessible, and only in the coastal areas of Moulmein, Tavoy and Mergui does one come across more densely populated farming settlements.

Extending around the Irrawaddy, its tributary the Chindwin, and the Sittang, this is the settlement area of the Burman race. The region is generally subdivided into two parts—Upper Burma, that area surrounding Mandalay, north of the towns of Prome and Toungoo; and Lower Burma, focusing on Rangoon, and south of the Prome-Toungoo line. Not only do Upper and Lower Burma have distinctive climates; their historical development in colonial times was markedly different.

Upper Burma is a region of low rainfall, with farmers employing traditional methods of irrigated and dry cultivation in rice-growing. A complicated system of lakes and canals made it possible for the earliest Burmese civilizations to exist here. Today, 607,000 hectares (1½ million acres) of land are under irrigation

Strewn off the Tenasserim coast are the isles of the Mergui Archipelago, one of Southeast Asia's few remaining untouched island groups. Because of its isolation, it thrives as the center of the flourishing smuggling trade between Thailand and Burma—and for security reasons is therefore off-limits to most Burmese, let alone foreign visitors.

West of the Irrawaddy, on the seaward side of the Arakan Yoma, is the state of Arakan. This flat coastal strip is broken by numerous small rivers flowing out of the east-lying mountains—chief of which is Mount Victoria, elevation 3,053 meters (10,016 feet). Several long sandy beaches grace the coastline.

Then there is the central belt of the nation, or "Burma Proper," as the British called it.

and devoted to rice farming. But crop failures nevertheless occur with alarming regularity at least once a decade, and before rice was available from Lower Burma, famines were common in this region. Because the delta is now Burma's "breadbasket," about 1½ million hectares (3.7 million acres) of irrigated land in the Dry Zone are now devoted to the farming of cotton, tobacco, peanuts, grain sorghum, sesame, beans, chilies and corn (maize).

If Upper Burma's agricultural area is impressive, that of Lower Burma is astounding. The Irrawaddy Delta contains an estimated 3.6 million hectares (nine million acres) of irrigated rice farms, with a carrying capacity great enough to feed the entire population of Burma by itself. And the delta is expanding into the Andaman Sea at a rate of about five kilometers (three miles) a century, the result of silt deposits.

When the British arrived here in the mid 19th Century, the delta was uncultivated jungle and tall grass. The consistent monsoon rains attracted colonists from the Dry Zone, who cleared the jungle and planted it with wet-rice fields. For much of the 20th Century, until 1962, Burma was the world's largest exporter of rice. The population has grown faster than production, so that the annual amount exported—more than 3 million tons annually in the pre-war years—dropped to about 600,000 tons in 1976. The export tonnage improved to 1 million tons in 1981, but Thailand has surpassed Burma as the globe's No. 1 rice exporter. Rice still accounts for 60 percent of Burma's export income.

Other crops grown in Lower Burma, for export as well as for home consumption, include cotton, sugar cane, rubber, tea and jute. In addition to teak, two other hardwoods—ironwood and *pandauk* (Andaman redwood), are coveted export items.

A Fortune Waits in Minerals

Burma also has a tremendous untapped mineral wealth. Oil, found in the central Irrawaddy basin, is most important; in recent years, test drilling in the Gulf of Martaban and off the Arakan coast has been conducted with German and Japanese support. Iron ore, tungsten, lead, silver, tin, mercury, nickel, plutonium, zinc, copper, cobalt, antimony and gold are found in significant quantities in various parts of the country. Rubies and sapphires are mined in Mogok in western Shan State, and jade is extracted from the earth at Mogaung in Kachin State.

Burma's natural vegetation varies according to regional rainfall. Nearly half of the country's surface area is covered by vast unexploited forests; another 15 percent is given over to stands of teak and other hardwoods. In rainier districts, tropical rainforests climb the hills to about 800 meters (2,625 feet) above sea level; bamboo, used extensively in house construction, is common here along with teak. From this elevation to the snow line at about 3,000 meters (9,842 feet), oaks, silver firs, chestnuts and rhododendrons thrive. In the Dry Zone of central Burma, cacti and acacia trees are common sights. There are also extensive grasslands here, but because of the lack of adequate rainfall, pasture is rare.

The *taunggya* (slash-and-burn) cultivation through much of upland Burma has resulted in the depletion of a great deal of the original forest cover, now replaced by a second growth of scrub forest. In *taunggya* agriculture, large trees are felled and the jungle burned over to prepare it for planting—often with 40 or more different crops. When crops and torrential rains have depleted soil fertility in a year or two, the clearing is abandoned and left to the "elephant grass" for 12 to 15 years while the soil regains its fertility. Villages, therefore, often change their sites when the accessible land has been exhausted. About 2½ million of Burma's population still pursue this agricultural method.

Elephants, Tigers and Leopards

In the remaining virgin forests—of which there are many—a rich variety of wild animals makes their home. Elephants, tigers, leopards, wild buffalo and red deer are often hunted today, along with the Himalayan black bear, Malayan sun bear, civet cat, wild boar, several species of monkeys, mountain goats, flying squirrels, porcupines and even rhinoceros. There is a great variety of birds, insects and reptiles. But most dreaded of all are the snakes.

Burma has the world's highest mortality rate from snake bites. Its most highly infested areas are Dry Zone rivers and Irrawaddy Delta streams, especially during the winter. Deadliest of Burma's snakes is the *mwe-boai,* or Russel's viper, with a temper so nasty that it attacks to kill without aggravation. It reaches a length of about 170 cm (5½ feet). Also feared is the Asiatic King Cobra, which reaches 425 to 550 cm (14 to 18 feet) when full grown.

There is little domestication of animals in Burma, save for the beasts of burden—the oxen in the dry zone, buffalo in the wetter regions, and elephants in the mountains. Devout Buddhists do not kill animals. The Mon people of the southeast, however, have domesticated a number of animals, including cattle, swine, horses, dogs and poultry. The Karens also are noted for their domestic animals: some tribes, especially the Kayah, specialize in breeding horses.

No discussion of Burma's fauna could be complete without mention of the famed Burmese cat. This domestic breed, noted for its short brown hair, is actually from Thailand, not from Burma at all. In fact, the "fixed" characteristics of the pedigreed animal, according to Western cat breeders, was established only after a period of experimental cross-breeding with Siamese cats.

A typical Burmese bullock cart carries its driver high above the dust during the dry season—just as it keeps him well above the mud during the rains.

From Brahmâ to Burma: 2,500 Years of History

"The first inhabitants of the world."

That is what the name *Burma* means, and it is what the Burmans symbolically consider themselves to be.

According to *The Glass Palace Chronicle of the Kings of Burma*—19th Century history-mythology of the country—Burma's kings were descendants of the Buddha's family. They immigrated to the Irrawaddy Valley from India, established sovereignty over the tribes already settled there, and called their people *Brahmâ*. The word has taken many forms in past centuries—Mrâmmâ, Bamma, Mien, Myanma (as the nation now calls itself)—but always with the same meaning.

Ethnologists generally agree that the present inhabitants of Burma are the descendants of northern immigrants.

'The Land of Gold'

The Mons were the first group to reach Burma, several centuries before the birth of Christ. These people, whose language belongs to the Mon-Khmer family and who are still to be found in parts of Thailand and Kampuchea (Cambodia) today, probably came from Central Asia. They settled on the estuaries of the Salween and Sittang rivers. We know of their settlement area, which they called *Suvannabhumi* ("the land of gold"), from descriptions in Chinese and Indian texts.

Legend says it was the Mons who laid the foundation stone of the Shwedagon Pagoda some 2,500 years ago. While the pagoda has been altered so often in ensuing centuries that the legend would be difficult to prove, we do know the Mon race established the Buddhist tradition in Burma. In the 3rd Century B.C., the Mons already had close ties with the realm of King Ashoka in India through their port city of Thaton.

About 2,000 years ago, the Pyu people settled in Upper Burma. Unlike the Mons, they belonged to the Tibeto-Burman language family. They set up their first capital at Sri Ksetra, near present-day Prome, and today the brick ruins still display extensive evidence of their religious architecture—Buddhist, but with a strong Brahman influence.

About the 8th Century, the Pyus relocated their capital north to Halin, in the region of Shwebo. At approximately the same time, the Tai people were pressing southward from their ancestral home in Yunnan. As a part of the powerful Nan-ch'ao dynasty, they subjugated Upper Burma in the 9th Century, at-

tacking Halin in 832 and carrying the population off into slavery. From that time on, there are few mentions of the Pyus in history.

It was also in the 9th Century that the Mrâmmâ people, whom we know as the Burmans, first made their appearance. Originally from the China-Tibet border area, they moved down the Irrawaddy, overran the Kyaukse plain, and established themselves as the major power in the rice-cultivating region of the north. From Pagan, which they built into a fortified town, they could control the Irrawaddy and Sittang river valleys as well as the trade routes between China and India.

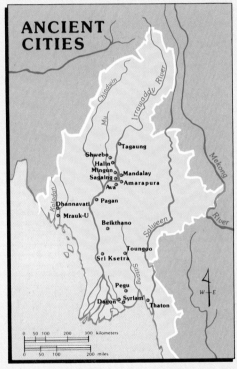

According to the *Glass Palace Chronicle*, Pagan had actually been founded in 108 A.D. But the town's first nine centuries of recorded existence are viewed with some skepticism because the *Chronicle* which tells its story, did not appear until 1829.

Anawrahta established the First Burmese Empire in 1057 when he suddenly and over-

Preceding pages: The temples of Pagan symbolize the dawn of modern Burmese history. Left, the Hindu god Indra mounts his elephant, Erawon, in a never-before-photographed relief at Myohaung's Htukkan-thein Pagoda. Above, ancient cities.

whelmingly conquered the Mon capital of Thaton. The first general to use elephants in war, he returned to Pagan with 30,000 prisoners, including the Mon royal family, many Theravada Buddhist monks, craftsmen and master builders. Other Mon and Pyu settlements submitted to Anawrahta's dominance over Burma, and the king reigned for 33 years.

Ironically, despite the Mons' defeat, their culture became supreme in the Burmans' capital. The Mon language replaced Pali and Sanskrit in royal inscriptions, and the Theravada Buddhist religion became predominant. Through the close relations maintained by the Mons with Ceylon—at that time the center of Theravadin culture—"the way of the elders" spread throughout the whole of Southeast Asia.

to power after his troops had crushed a Mon rebellion in which Anawrahta's son and successor, Sawlu, was killed.

Like Anawrahta, Kyanzittha was a highly religious man. He ordered the construction of the Ananda Temple, and sent a ship filled with treasures to Bengal to assist in the restoration of the famed Mahabodhi temple in Bodhgaya, place of Buddha's enlightenment. He gave his daughter in marriage to a Mon prince, and chose their son, Alaungsithu, as his successor to preserve the unity of the Burmese Empire.

Pagan's golden age came during the 12th Century, a time in which it acquired the name "city of the four million pagodas." The region's hundreds of monuments and their stories are discussed in another section. This civilization was supported by rice cultivation,

Under this new influence, especially from the monk Shin Arahan, Anawrahta became a devout convert to Theravada Buddhism. He commissioned the building of the Shwezigon Pagoda in Nyaung U (near Pagan), as well as other shrines on the dry plain.

Pagan's Golden Age

But it was under his second successor, Kyanzittha (1084–1113), that the golden age of pagoda-building began in earnest. Kyanzittha, whose name means "soldier lord," came

made possible by a highly developed system of irrigation canals.

But in the middle of the 13th Century, the empire began to crumble. The culturally sustaining power of Buddhism abated, and the Shans—descendants of the Tais—threatened from northern Burma. And then there arose the Mongol army of Kublai Khan.

Pagan as it must have looked when the Mongols invaded in the 13th Century (left), and a galleon typical of those on which the Portuguese arrived along the Arakan coast in the 16th Century (right).

The khan and his forces, whose homeland was in Central Asia, had occupied the Nanch'ao Empire in Yunnan. They now expected payment of tribute by the Pagan emperors. King Narathihapate, overestimating the strength of his own forces, refused. The result was the annihilation of the Burmese armies in the battle of Vochan, and the subsequent conquest of Pagan by the Mongols in 1287. The Mons, supported by the Shan leader Wareru, withdrew from the First Burmese Empire, and the Arakanese on the Bay of Bengal did the same.

After the fall of Pagan, Burma was divided into several states of varying sizes for almost 300 years. In Lower Burma, the Mons founded a new kingdom in the town of Pegu. They lost their grip on Tenasserim during a

It was in the 15th Century that Europeans began to make inroads into Burma. In 1435, a Venetian merchant named Nicolo di Conti visited Pegu and remained for four months. In 1498, the Portuguese seafarer Vasco da Gama discovered the sea route from Europe to India, and his countrymen were very quick to take advantage of his success.

The Portuguese Period

Affonso de Albuquerque conquered Goa in 1510, and within a year Malacca, the spice center of the Orient, was in his grasp. From these two ports, the Portuguese controlled all of their Indian colonies.

Antony Correa arrived in Martaban in 1519 and signed a trade and settlement treaty

mid-14th Century invasion by the Tais (Siamese) from Ayutthia, but managed to hold the rest of the realm together. In Upper Burma, the Shans established sovereignty over a Burmese kingdom with its capital at Ava. And in the west, along the Bay of Bengal, Arakan spread north to Chittagong in present-day Bangladesh.

Between 1385 and 1425, the Mons and Shans engaged in a long war. Despite the conflict, Theravada Buddhism underwent a revival in the court of Pegu. Monks and scholars from all over Southeast Asia flocked there.

with the town's viceroy, giving the Portuguese a port of trade with Siam without making the long sea journey through the Strait of Malacca. But Pegu's King Tabinshweti would not tolerate the Portuguese presence in his vassal state. In 1541, he laid siege to Martaban, and surprisingly was joined by 700 Portuguese who opposed their countrymen's decision to side with the viceroy of Martaban. When Tabinshweti was successful and solidified his grip on the Second Burmese Empire, the Portuguese maintained their hold on Martaban as a trading settlement until 1613. Mean-

WHEN THE EARTH SHAKES, 'GREAT CHANGES' ARE DUE

Earthquakes are as much a part of Burmese history as Buddhism. From earliest times, the Burmese people have lived with quakes—with rivers flowing upstream, entire coastal regions emerging from the sea, and golden *sikharas* tumbling from stupas and pagodas.

In contrast to the scientific Western mind, the Burmese see hidden meanings behind these "catastrophes." The Buddha told his followers that earthquakes occurred upon the conception of a future Buddha, at the time of a Buddha's birth, his enlightenment, his first sermon, and his death and entrance into nirvana. The coming of a *chakravarti* (universal monarch), his coronation and death were also believed to be signaled by great upheavals in the earth's crust.

In addition, Burmese cosmology dictates that the physical world and all planes of existence comprise a single indivisible unit. The shaking of the earth is a reminder that inhabitants of the Asian "island" constitute only a small part of the cosmic whole. In this framework, earthquakes are viewed as physical evidence of major occurrences on other planes of existence, and therefore indicative of great changes in the making.

Legend tells of an enormous tremor which may have occurred in the 5th Century B.C. (perhaps at the time of the Buddha's entry into nirvana). The soil on which Sri Ksetra was later to be built rose from the seabed; two new rivers began to flow; and Mount Popa, the sacred mountain of Burma, bulged from the central plain.

Another legend relates the fall of the 9th Century Pyu capital of Halin. It is said that the Pyu king's brother had a smile so wonderful, it was always followed by a shower of gold over the city. When the kingdom's coffers were exhausted, all it took was a smile to refill them. One day, the king needed gold and ordered his brother to smile. But the brother, having just heard of the imminent destruction of Halin, was only able to cry. The king shouted in anger. His rage was so great that it instigated an earthquake which swallowed up the whole city and its inhabitants.

Many major earthquakes have been recorded through the centuries. Whenever stupas were destroyed by movements of the earth, stone inscriptions erected on the renovated sites told the story of these quakes—and named the fortunate Burmese who gained merit by doing the repair work.

Not a temple or pagoda stands in Burma today that hasn't suffered some earthquake damage. Be it the Shwedagon, the Shwemawdaw, or the Ananda, all have lost their *htis* (upper "umbrellas") or have collapsed at some time during centuries past. It has been left to faithful Buddhists to restore the stupas and increase their karma at the same time.

In the 20th Century, there have been two major earthquakes whose scars are easily seen today. On May 5, 1930, a tremor shook the whole of southern Burma. Its epicenter was at the old Mon city of Pegu—and most of the community's ancient monuments, including the Shwemawdaw and Mahazedi pagodas and the Kalyani Sima, were utterly destroyed. It has taken five decades, but the Shwemawdaw and Kalyani Sima have been rebuilt, and reconstruction work on the Mahazedi is nearly complete.

The most recent of the major earthquakes occurred on July 8, 1975, when the jewel of Burma—the ancient city of Pagan—was shaken as never before. Initially, it was feared that the damage to the monuments had been so severe, reconstruction would be impossible. Fortunately, that was not the case.

Today—thanks to an international effort mounted by the United Nations Educational, Scientific and Cultural Organization (UNESCO)—most of the great buildings have been restored to their former splendor. The Burmese government gladly accepted any and all financial assistance from outside sources, but insisted in doing the repair work itself. No foreign architect or structural engineer was permitted to lay a hand on the monuments of Pagan. The ancient temples and pagodas were reconstructed with the same care and in the same Burmese fashion as when they had been built centuries ago.

while, the Portuguese also allied themselves with the king of Mrauk-U in Arakan, and thereby controlled the sea routes of the Bay of Bengal, often as pirates, for 100 years.

The most remarkable character from the Portuguese era in Burma was Philip de Brito y Nicote. De Brito came to Asia as a cabin boy and later accepted a post in the royal court of King Razagyi of Arakan after his conquest of Pegu. De Brito was entrusted with the job of running the customs administration in Syriam (then called Thanhlyn). Before long, de Brito had constructed fortifications, and placed the town under Portuguese sovereignty. After a trip to Goa, during which he married the viceroy's daughter, he returned to Syriam with supplies and reinforcements to withstand native sieges (as Burmans and Arakanese had

out of gunpowder. De Brito was captured and impaled: it took three days for him to die. The rest of the Portuguese and Eurasians in Syriam—called *Bayingyis*—were exiled to villages near Shwebo in Upper Burma, where they formed the basis of a foreign settlement.

Rise and Fall of an Empire

In the north of Burma, meanwhile, mountain tribes had attacked and burned down the Shan capital of Ava in 1527. The Burman population withdrew to the town of Toungoo, where Tabinshweti established his empire before moving it to Pegu. After his victory over Martaban, he extended his control down the Tenasserim coast to Tavoy, and west to Prome on the central Irrawaddy. His son-in-

already attempted), and proclaimed himself king of Lower Burma.

De Brito's superior naval power forced all seagoing trade to his port of Syriam. During his 13-year reign, 100,000 native people were said to have been converted to Christianity. But he displayed utter contempt for Buddhist monuments and relics, destroying and plundering them wherever he went. The Buddhist holy leaders condemned him to eternal damnation in the deepest hell of the Buddhist cosmos—and, indeed, he came to a horrific end.

In 1613, Anaukhpetlun of Toungoo stormed Syriam with a force of 12,000 men. The 400 or so Portuguese and their followers defended the town for 34 days until they ran

law and successor, Bayinnaung, overwhelmed the Shans and conquered the Tai kingdoms of Chiengmai and Ayutthia, thus extending Burma's boundaries to their maximum limits.

During the 17th Century, the Dutch, British and French set up trading companies in ports along the coast of Burma. When the country's capital was transferred back to Ava, it was retaken by the Mons in 1752 with the help of French arms. As a result, the Second Burmese Empire foundered and dissolved.

Soon afterwards, however, Alaungpaya, a Burman from Shwebo, founded the Third Burmese Empire. He defeated the Mons, de-

Above, a Burmese prince (left) and princess of Upper Burma's lengthy Konbaung dynasty period.

ported the French to Bayingyi, and burned down the British trading posts. Mon resistance ceased entirely, and the Mon people either fled to Siam or became assimilated with the Burmans.

Alaungpaya's second successor, Hsinbyushin, attacked Ayutthia in 1767 and returned to Ava with artists and craftsmen who gave a fresh cultural impetus to the Burmese kingdom. Bodawpaya, who took the throne in 1782, conquered Arakan, bringing the borders of his kingdom right up against the British sphere of influence in Bengal. On the advice of his soothsayers, he moved his capital to Amarapura, not far from Ava.

Because Burma and British India now shared a common boundary, the number of border incidents increased. Royal Burmese

feated. In the Treaty of Yandabo (1826), the Burmese were forced to cede Arakan and Tenasserim, plus Assam and Manipur border areas taken in 1819, to the European victors. The British thereby succeeded in making secure their exposed flanks on the Bay of Bengal, which had been their aim all along in fighting the war.

The Burmese were without a capable ruler through the first half of the 19th Century. Part of the reason for this was that no institutionalized system had been set up for transfer of power upon a ruler's death. When King Pagan ascended the throne in 1846, he—like so many of his predecessors—organized a massacre of all other potential heirs. His action was not unique in Burmese history. But for the first time, it was witnessed by European am-

troops frequently pursued rebels over the border and deep into Indian territory.

Serious conflict was sparked after King Bagyidaw came to the throne in 1819. The Raja of Manipur, who previously had paid tribute to the Burmese crown, did not attend Bagyidaw's coronation. The subsequent punitive expedition took the Burmese into the Indian state of Cachar, and this intrusion was used by the British as a pretext for what is now called the First Anglo-Burmese War.

The Burmese badly underestimated the strength of the British, and were soundly de-

bassadors, and did not enhance their faith in the Burmese crown.

In 1852, two British sea captains registered a complaint about unfair treatment in a Burmese court. The British Empire responded by sending an expeditionary force to Burma. In the Second Anglo-Burmese War, this force quickly conquered Lower Burma.

Burma's wars have varied as much in method as in result. Elephants were used in the 1767 invasion of the Siamese capital of Ayutthia (left); Burmese troops sought refuge behind Rangoon stockades during the First Anglo-Burmese War (right).

It was about this time that King Mindon (1853–1878) came to power in Amarapura. His was an enlightened rule. Mindon was the first Burmese sovereign to attempt to bring the country more in line with Western ideas. He sent young men to study in Europe, reformed his government structure, and made halting first steps toward industrialization.

Mindon's Marvelous Mandalay

In 1861, on the 2,400th anniversary of the preaching of the Buddha's first sermon, Mindon transferred his court to the new city of Mandalay. British sources say that when the town's foundation stone was laid, 52 people were buried alive under the gates and corner towers of the walls.

Mandalay Hill. The scriptures are so lengthy that a book version consists of 38 volumes of 400 pages each. But even this appeal for a return to the values of Buddhism, which would thereby sustain the Burmese state, could no longer alter the course of history.

Mindon was succeeded by the merciless King Thibaw, who wasted little time in alienating the British. When a smallpox epidemic struck Mandalay in 1880, soothsayers recommended the capital again be transferred—but Thibaw rejected this as unfeasible. Instead, he ordered 600 people to be buried alive. The result was a mass, panicked exodus from the city. Thibaw was forced to abandon his plan when the British protested vociferously.

The French, meanwhile, were negotiating an agreement with Thibaw for shipping rights

Mandalay, however, was sacred to the Buddhist faith, and in 1872 Mindon hosted the Fifth Great Synod of Buddhism. In the threatening shadow of British expansionism, this synod—the first such gathering in nearly 2,000 years—was staged as a means of unifying all Burmese people under a single creed. It was during the Fifth Synod that the text of the *Tripitaka*, the Buddhist scripture today recognized as authentic, was written. Some 2,400 scribes worked on the text, which was then chiseled on 729 tablets of stone. A pagoda was built over each of the tablets at the base of

on the Irrawaddy. They sought a direct route to China; but this was clearly contrary to British interests. When a British timber company became embroiled in a dispute with Thibaw's government, the king was issued an ultimatum. In no time, British troops had invaded Upper Burma, and with virtually no resistance overwhelmed the capital.

On Jan. 1, 1886, Burma ceased to exist as an independent kingdom. Thibaw and his queen, Supyalat, were forced to leave the country, and Burma was annexed as a province of British India.

In order to facilitate their exercise of power over the whole of Burma, the British permitted the autonomy of the country's many racial minorities. As early as 1875, they had enforced the autonomy of the Karen states by refusing to supply King Mindon with the arms he needed to put down a Karen revolt.

Throughout Upper and Lower Burma, the British themselves assumed all government positions down to the district officer level. In the bordering states where Chins, Kachins, Shans and other minorities predominated, the British relied on indirect rule, permitting the respective chieftains to govern in their place. Military forces were largely recruited from India and the northern hill tribes. Throughout the entire colonial period, Burmans were barred from admission to the armed forces,

which greatly intensified the already strained interracial tensions.

British interest in Burma was principally of an economic nature. So it is understandable that an economic upswing took place after 1886. The Irrawaddy Delta had been opened up for rice cultivation and colonized following the British occupation of Lower Burma in 1852, and a generation later this began to pay big dividends. This economic growth was to the advantage both of the British, who controlled the rice exports, and the Indian money lenders and merchants, who were far ahead of the Burmans in familiarity with a money economy. In particular, the *Chettyars*, a south Indian caste of moneylenders, profited from the agricultural expansion.

In the five years following annexation of Upper Burma, a quasi-guerrilla war tied up some 10,000 Indian troops in the country regions. The guerrillas were led by *myothugyis*, local leaders of the old social structure. But this resistance fell away after 1890, and the Burmese attempted to keep pace peacefully with the far-reaching social and economic changes taking place.

20th Century Nationalism

The first important nationalist organization of the 20th Century was the Young Men's Buddhist Association (YMBA), founded in 1906 when a group of London-trained lawyers merged with the Buddhist elite of Burma. It played an important role in the nation's politics in years to come.

Following the First World War, India had been granted a degree of self-government by its British sovereigns. But Burma remained under the direct control of the Colonial Governor. This led to extensive opposition within the country, highlighted by a lengthy boycott of schools beginning in December 1920. Finally, in 1923, the same condition granted India—known as the "dyarchy reform"—was extended to Burma as well.

A major revolt took place in the Tharrawaddy region north of Rangoon between 1930 and 1932. Saya San, a former monk, organized a group of followers called *Galons* (after the mythical bird), and convinced them British bullets could not harm them. In a subsequent battle, 3,000 of his supporters were killed and another 9,000 were taken prisoner, of whom 78 were executed.

Throughout the early 1930s, opinion was divided in Burma as to whether the country should be separated from British India or whether it should remain a part of that dominion. The question was resolved in 1935 when the "Gouvernement of Burma Act" was signed in London. Two years later, Burma became a separate colony with its own Legislative Council. This council dealt only with "Burma Proper," however, and not with the indirectly-ruled border states.

Even as Burma was gaining a greater degree of autonomy, however, the underground nationalist movement was gaining momentum. In 1930 at the University of Rangoon, the All Burma Student Movement emerged to defy the British system. The young men who spearheaded this group studied Marxism and called

Preceding pages: Rangoon as it appeared in the first half of the 19th Century. Left, the only portrait of King Mindon, founder of Mandalay, hangs today in the Kyauk-Tawgyi Pagoda. Right, a British soldier marvels at a Buddha in the Shwedagon.

each other *Thakin,* a title of respect (like the Hindi *Sahib*) previously used exclusively in addressing Europeans. In 1936, the group's leaders—Thakin Aung San and Thakin Nu—boldly led another strike of university and high school classes in opposition to the "alien" educational system. The success of their movement in bringing about major reforms helped give these young men the confidence in the following decade to step to the forefront of the nationalist movement.

Meanwhile, however, war was brewing. The Burma Road made that inevitable. Built as an all-weather route in the 1930s to carry supplies and reinforcements to Chinese troops attempting to repulse the Japanese invasion, it was of extreme strategic importance. As Allied forces moved to defend the road, the Japa-nese secretly picked out 30 members of the Thakin group—later known as the "Thirty Comrades"—to be trained by the Japanese on Hainan Island in the art of guerrilla warfare. Among the comrades were Nu and Ne Win.

Burma's Brutal Battlefield

In December 1941, the Japanese landed in Lower Burma. Together with the Burmese Liberation Army led by Aung San, they overwhelmed the British, drove them from Rangoon in March, then convincingly won battle after battle. British-Indian and American-Chinese troops suffered heavy casualties and were forced to withdraw to India.

While the Second World War raged in terrible fury in Europe and the Pacific, the fighting

nese made plans for an all-out attack on the Burmese heartland.

Burma's colonial government unexpectedly played into the Japanese hand when it arrested several leaders of the Thakin organization in 1940. Aung San escaped by disguising himself as a Chinese crewman on a Norwegian boat. He arrived in Amoy seeking contact with Chinese Communists to help in Burma's drive for independence. But the Japanese arrested him, and although his movement was highly opposed to Japan's wartime fascism, his release was negotiated on the grounds that he and other members of the Thakin organization would collaborate with the Japanese.

In March 1941, Aung San was returned to Rangoon aboard a Japanese freighter. He se-was nowhere so bitter as in the jungles of Southeast Asia. Hand-to-hand combat was a frequent necessity, and tens of thousands of Allied soldiers were killed, along with hundreds of thousands of Burmese. The 27,000 Allied graves in the Htaukkyan cemetery near Rangoon are but one testimony to the horror of the war.

The survivors of this no-holds-barred conflict emerged from the jungle with stirring stories of suffering, sacrifice and heroic deeds regarded with awe today. They made household words out of such names as "Vinegar Joe" Stilwell, "Old Weatherface" Chennault, Wingate's Chindits and Merrill's Marauders. These names acquired a Kipling-like ring of adventure which still stirs the imagination.

In February 1942, Joseph Warren Stilwell, a three-star lieutenant general, was sent by the U.S. government as the senior American military representative to the China-Burma-India theater. Within two months after his arrival, Stilwell was struggling through the malaria-infested hinterland of Upper Burma, a mere 36 hours ahead of Japanese troops, trying desperately to reach the safety of the British lines in India.

Stilwell's Retreat

There were 114 soldiers, mainly Chinese, in Stilwell's party. "Vinegar Joe" promised each one of them they would reach India. His retreat—which he called "eating bitterness," citing a Chinese proverb—involved 1,500 kilometers (over 930 miles) of trekking through formidable jungles and over arid plains with no hope of outside assistance. At about the same time, 42,000 members of the British-Indian army also began to withdraw. The Japanese were right on the tail of the Allied retreat. They burned every major town along the escape route to the ground. Hundreds of thousands of civilians were casualties, and only 12,000 British-Indian troops reached Assam safely. Some 30,000 did not.

All 114 of Stilwell's charges reached the haven of India, just as the general had pledged. But "Vinegar Joe" was riled. "I claim we got run out of Burma," he told a press conference in Delhi some days later. "It is humiliating as hell. I think we ought to find out what caused it, go back and retake it."

Stilwell's stirring words guided the Allied war effort in Burma from that point on. He and British General William Slim retraced their steps down the same difficult route—out of Assam, across the Chindwin River to Myitkyina, and down the Irrawaddy River to Mandalay. Rangoon was finally recaptured on March 3, 1945.

By that time, however, Stilwell had been relieved of his command because of his inability to get along with Chinese Generalissimo Chiang Kai-shek. Stilwell was obstinate and rude, keen to play the role of "Vinegar Joe." But at the same time, he was honest and reliable, and his personal courage was beyond question.

Wingate's Chindits

While Stilwell is perhaps best remembered for his retreat, others gained their greatest fame on the offensive. One of these men was General Orde Charles Wingate, a Briton whose deep penetration teams used guerrilla tactics to slip behind Japanese lines and block

the arrival of supplies. Known as Chindits—after the mythological *chinthes,* the undefeatable lions guarding temples throughout Burma—the troops were an amalgam of British, Indian, Chin, Kachin and Gurkha soldiers. They introduced to Southeast Asia the style of jungle warfare which has marked every military confrontation in the region since that time.

Wingate himself, an eccentric scholar, did not live to see the end of the war. His plane crashed into a mountain near Imphal, Manipur, on March 24, 1944.

The return to Burma of a large land force to combat the Japanese depended very much on a usable road. U.S. Army engineers undertook the task with a unit consisting mostly of black Americans. Called the Ledo Road, the new route was to reach from Assam to Mong Yo, where it would join the Burma Road and continue into Chinese Yunnan.

For more than two years, several thousand engineers and 35,000 native workers labored in one of the world's most inaccessible areas. The war was almost over by the time the 800-kilometer (500-mile) road was completed. Japanese snipers killed 130 engineers, hundreds more lost their lives through illness and accidents, and the Ledo Road became known as "the man-a-mile road." Built down deep gorges and across raging rapids, it traversed a jungle where no Western man had set foot before. Despite the great effort that went into building this vital link between India and Southeast Asia, today it is overgrown and unfit for motor traffic.

Flying 'The Hump'

Until the Ledo Road was completed, supplies had to be flown to the Allied forces in western China. The air link over "The Hump," as it came to be known, was one of the most hazardous passages of the war. Between Dinjan air base in Assam and the town of Kunming in Yunnan lay 800 kilometers (500 miles) of rugged wilderness. Planes had to fly over the Himalaya Range, with its 6,000-meter (about 20,000-foot) peaks, as well as the 3,000-meter-high Naga Hills, the 4,500-meter-high Santsung Range, and the jungle-covered gorges of the Irrawaddy, Salween and Mekong rivers. Yet the Air Transport Command flew with alarming regularity, carrying 650,000 tons of cargo to China.

About 1,000 men and 600 planes were lost during the operation. So many planes went down on one of the many unnamed peaks of

An exhausted member of Wingate's Chindits smiles in relief following a long jungle march (left).

"The Hump," in fact, that it was nicknamed "Aluminum Plated Mountain." The C-46, the workhorse of the transport operation, was quite overloaded most of the time, and its pilots, flying up to 160 miles per month, were overworked. During 1944, three men died for every 1,000 tons of cargo flown into Yunnan.

Chennault's 'Flying Tigers'

Another air unit which achieved fame in the Burma war was the "Flying Tigers" of Claire Lee "Old Weatherface" Chennault. Volunteer pilots from the U.S. Army, Navy and Marine Corps fought for only seven months under Chennault. But during that period they became so feared by the Japanese that a Tokyo

aircraft, possibly as many as 1,900, while losing 573 planes themselves. Before they were incorporated into the 14th U.S. Air Force, this ragtag band of air mercenaries—who made their planes look like airborne sharks and who painted Japanese flags on their planes' bodies for every enemy aircraft shot down—built a legend which lingers even today.

While the United States provided about 50 percent of the air strength to Allied maneuvers in Burma, there was only one U.S. ground unit involved in the theater. It had a colorless title: the 5307th Composite Unit. But behind this title was one of the toughest volunteer fighting teams the U.S. Army has ever assembled.

The troops called themselves "Galahad Force." But they were better known as "Merrill's Marauders," after their commander,

radio broadcaster called them "American guerrilla pilots" because of their unorthodox tactics.

These same tactics, masterminded by Chennault, put him in head-on conflict with General Stilwell. Whereas Stilwell pressed for an infantry-led reconquest of Burma, Chennault intended to win the war by means of air superiority. Ironically, both men had to leave the Asian theater before the war had ended. But Chennault left his unforgettable mark.

During their brief reign of terror, the "Flying Tigers" destroyed at least 1,200 Japanese

General Frank Merrill. Originally intended to join Wingate's Chindits, General Stilwell instead designated them for his own selected deep-penetration operations. From the border of Assam to Myitkyina, these tenacious soldiers went head-to-head with the Japanese 18th Division—the unvanquished conquerors of Singapore—in five major and 30 minor battles. It was a formidable task. By the

The war in 1944: Merrill's Marauders move toward Myitkyina via the Ledo Road in February (left), and General Joseph W. Stilwell discusses field tactics with American and Chinese officers in July (right).

time the unit was disbanded in the summer of 1944, there were 2,394 casualties out of its original strength of 2,830 men.

As the first American fighting force on the Asian mainland since the Boxer Rebellion at the turn of the 20th Century, "Merrill's Marauders" fought bravely and heroically. But their casualty figure tells a gruesome story, one which made the name of Burma synonymous with the brutality of the war.

The 'Thirty Comrades'

But there is still one more story of the Second World War in Burma which must be told. Aung San and the "Thirty Comrades" had joined the Japanese to help advance the Burmans' independence cause. Through the early

Aung San was named minister of defense, and Thakin Nu was chosen foreign secretary.

The *thakins,* however, were not at all pleased with the arrangement. In December 1944, Aung San established contact with the Allies, and in March 1945 he shocked the Japanese by transferring his 10,000-man army to the side of the Allies. His troops were now called the "Patriotic Burmese Forces"—and they helped the Allies recapture Rangoon. The Japanese surrender was signed in Burma's capital on August 28.

The war had completely devastated Burma. What had not been destroyed during the Allied retreat was laid waste during the reconquest. There was one, and perhaps only one, positive result of the war years for the Burmese: their experience of nominal self-gov-

1940s, Burmans joined the Liberation Army in great numbers. The minorities remained loyal to the Allies, and this led to warlike skirmishes in many parts of the country, especially between the Karens and Burmans in the Irrawaddy Delta region.

By 1943, however, it was evident that the Japanese wanted to see Burma's national government, which they had supported, placed under the administration of the army. Burma was declared "independent" in August of that year, with Dr. Ba Maw, former education minister, as head of the puppet state. Thakin

ernment. It was clear they could no longer resume living under the colonial constitution.

But the British, climbing back into the driver's seat after their wartime hiatus, had different ideas. They were planning a three-year period of direct rule.

As Great Britain plotted its moves, Aung San was quietly building up two important nationalist organizations. One of these was the Anti-Fascist People's Freedom League, a Marxist-oriented group better known by its acronym (AFPFL). As the military wing of this political league, Aung San founded the People's Volunteer Organization (PVO), which as early as 1946 claimed 100,000 (mostly unarmed) members.

Despite the growth of nationalist sentiment behind the AFPFL, the British remained firmly in control of Burma until September 1946. Then a general strike, first by police, then by all government employees plus railway and oil workers' unions, brought the state to a standstill. The colonial government turned to the AFPFL and other nationalist groups for assistance; a moderate national council was formed, and the strike ended in early October.

The AFPFL took advantage of the situation to seize political initiative. Thakin Aung San presented a list of demands to the British Labour Party government which included the

In February, however, Aung San met with minority representatives at Panglong in the Shan State. The result was a unanimous resolution that all ethnic groups would work together with the Burmese interim government to achieve independence for the minority regions more quickly. After 10 years, each of the major groups that formed a state would be permitted to secede from the union if desired.

Tragedy... and Independence

National elections for a Constituent Assembly were held in April 1947. Aung San and his AFPFL won an overwhelming majority of seats.

But on July 19, as the new constitution was still being drafted, tragedy struck. A group of

granting of total independence to Burma by January 1948.

A conference was promptly called in London in January 1947. Burma was awarded its independence as demanded. But there were several difficult questions to resolve in negotiations, especially concerning the ethnic minorities. The AFPFL representative insisted upon complete independence for all of Burma, including the minority regions; the British were concerned about the consequences of continual friction between the Burmans and other groups.

armed men burst in on a meeting of the interim government and assassinated nine people—including Aung San and six of his ministers. U Saw, right-wing prime minister of the last pre-war colonial government, was convicted of instigating the attack and was later executed. Today, the martyrs have their white marble mausoleum near the Shwedagon Pa-

Japanese officers arrive at Rangoon in August 1945 to sign their surrender to Allied forces (left); a solemn reminder of the war is this British soldier's grave, one of 27,000 in the Htaukkyan Allied War Cemetery a short way north of Rangoon (right).

goda in Rangoon, and Aung San, just 32 when he died, looks down on his country from portraits on the wall of every office.

Thakin Nu, one of the early leaders of the All Burma Student Movement and later of the AFPFL, was asked by the British colonial government to step into Aung San's shoes. Nu became prime minister when on Jan. 4, 1948, at the astrologically auspicious hour of 4:20 a.m., the Union of Burma became an independent nation. In so doing, Burma became the first former British colony to sever ties with the Commonwealth.

No sooner had Burma been thrust into solving its own problems, than it came face-to-face with the bitter realities of nationhood. The first three years of independence were marked by violent domestic confrontations

sumed all high-ranking military posts, and all Karens were discharged from active service. Under Ne Win, the army, after weathering sporadic challenges from the various rebel groups (whose diverse aims kept them from mounting a united front), gained an upper hand in the early 1950s.

Economic Disaster

In economic terms, the first years of independence were disastrous for Burma. Income from rice exports plummeted and tax revenue diminished, yet the expenditure needed to maintain the oversized military machine grew out of control.

U Nu (who had taken the honorary title "U" in 1950) and the AFPFL kept their grip on

and a militarization of daily life. No less than five separate groups took up arms against the newly founded state—including the Karens, who had been opposed to membership in the Union of Burma from the outset; two communist organizations; an armed wing of the PVO; and a faction of the Burmese armed forces.

Lieutenant General Ne Win became commander-in-chief of the armed forces, and soon thereafter minister of defense. The Burmans, who had not been allowed in the armed forces since the British took over in 1886, assumed all high-ranking military posts, and all

power during the 1951 national elections. But a schism within the party disrupted the government's program of economic development. The Eight Year Plan of 1953, produced by a team of American experts and called *Pyidawtha* ("Happy Land"), had to be abandoned in 1955 due to the intra-party disputes.

By 1958, the squabbling had become so serious that the government was virtually paralyzed. U Nu was forced to appoint a caretaker government, with General Ne Win at its helm. The 18-month Ne Win administration was stern, but made progress in cleaning up the cities, modernizing the bureaucracy, and establishing free and fair elections.

The elections were held in February 1960, and the U Nu faction of the AFPFL, now renamed the *Pyidaungsu* (Union) Party, succeeded in regaining power. Nu's campaign promises inspired skepticism, however. A deeply religious man, he sought to have the constitution changed to recognize Buddhism as the state religion. He also promised the Mon and Arakan people semi-autonomy. These promises spurred the Shans and Kayahs to demand the right of secession granted them in the 1948 constitution, and again the U Nu government was thrown into turmoil. There was little resistance when Ne Win swept himself into power in a nearly bloodless coup on March 2, 1962.

Ne Win's first move was to appoint a Revolutionary Council made up entirely of military personnel: 15 Army officers, one Navy man and one Air Force officer. On April 30, the council published its manifesto, titled: "The Burmese Way to Socialism." The manifesto declared that man would not "be set free from social evils as long as pernicious economic systems exist in which man exploits man and lives on the fat of such appropriation. The Council believes it to be possible only when exploitation of man by man is brought to an end and a socialist economy based on justice is established ... for an empty stomach is not conducive to wholesome morality ... "

For the next 12 years, Ne Win ruled by decree, with all power vested in the Revolutionary Council. Foreign businesses and land were nationalized, and the state took control of everything from banks to peddlers. The army was put in charge of commerce and industry. A foreign policy of self-imposed isolation and neutrality was pursued. Tourist visas were limited to 24 hours. Throughout this entire period, farmers and workers in all parts of the country participated in seminars, where they were educated in "The Burmese Way to Socialism" and made aware of their rights and duties.

At the time of the 1962 coup, Ne Win had imprisoned U Nu and other potential opposition leaders. Nu was released in late 1966, and for two years devoted himself to writing and meditation. But in November 1968, Nu was back in the political arena when he formed a National Unity Advisory Board, comprised of himself and 32 other formerly jailed politicians, to make recommendations to the Revolutionary Council on Burma's economic and political development.

The U Nu Revolt

Nu demanded a return to the parliamentary government that had existed prior to the coup. Ne Win, of course, rejected the proposal, and Nu left the country. By the summer of 1969, he was traveling to world capitals—Bangkok, London, Washington, Ottawa, Tokyo and Hong Kong—denouncing the Ne Win government as a "fascist regime." He raised money from several sources to help him regain power, then accepted an offer of permanent asylum in Thailand.

In May 1970, Nu announced the formation of a National United Liberation Front (NULF), an alliance between his followers and the Mons and Karens, as well as a smattering of Shans and Kachins. He claimed to have an army of 50,000, although that figure was probably exaggerated. In 1971, the rebels launched a series of successful raids across the Thai border, and for a while held territory inside Burma.

But Ne Win parried with successes of his own. Improved relations with some of the minorities and with the governments of China and Thailand, coupled with new steps to ease the economic bite, increased his strength at home. U Nu, meanwhile, resigned from the NULF, apparently at odds with minority members of the coalition on the issue of ethnic autonomy. Without its leader, the movement foundered, and U Nu fled to the United States.

General Ne Win poses as head of the Revolutionary Council in 1963 (left); modern Burma's founding father was Bogyoke Aung San, memorialized by a statue near Rangoon's Royal Lake (right).

After several months of lecturing on Buddhism in late 1973 and early 1974, he went into self-exile in India.

In Burma, meanwhile, Ne Win was reforming the government structure and introducing a constitutional authoritarianism. First, in an effort to civilianize the system, he dropped his military title. On March 2, 1974, the Revolutionary Council was officially disbanded and the Socialist Republic of the Union of Burma was born. Ne Win was seated as president of the nation and chairman of the Burma Socialist Program Party; 16 of the 17 ministerial posts were filled by various leaders of the armed forces.

All has not been smooth, however, and challenges to Ne Win's rule have not been lacking. In December 1974, for example, a major confrontation took place on the occasion of the funeral of U Thant, late Secretary General of the United Nations, who had died in New York the previous month. Sixteen persons were killed, hundreds wounded, and 45 arrested before the disturbance was quelled.

Six months later, there were new demonstrations, resulting in the arrest and sentencing of 203 students. Then in July 1976, a more serious challenge to Ne Win's reign arose. A coup attempt by 14 junior officers, unhappy with the government's one-party system and the failure of its economic policies, was discovered and nipped in the bud. The coup leader was sentenced to death, and hundreds of other officers were reportedly placed under detention.

Politics of Neutrality:
Burma in the 1980s

Threats to the government come not only from within Rangoon, but from outside as well. While Burma's central region (between Rangoon and Mandalay) is relatively secure and peaceful politically, battles with insurgents continue in the minority regions. The Shan State east of the Salween River, where communist and minority rebels have traditionally financed their insurrection through a thriving opium trade, is the major battleground. In 1978 and 1979, according to Burmese government figures, 150 government troops and 800 rebels were killed in clashes in this region. Foreign sources put the numbers in the thousands.

Further south, Karen and Mon rebels stage occasional attacks on buses and ships, although they are primarily concerned with their lucrative smuggling trade with Thailand. In the west, the militant Moslem Mujahid in the Arakan-Bangladesh border area continues to cause problems. All in all, it is estimated that 30 percent of Burma's population and 50 percent of the country's land area is controlled by armed rebels.

After years of decline and stagnation, Burma's economic situation has recently shown some signs of improvement. Since 1974, more foreign investment has been permitted, and privately owned businesses are now allowed in certain fields. Tourist visas have been extended to seven days, and tourist dollars now provide an additional source of income for the nation. A series of "Four Year Plans" have been introduced to stimulate agricultural production. The growth rate of the gross national product (GNP) since the mid-1970s has averaged five to six percent a year, as opposed to about two percent per annum in the preceding decade. The per capita GNP is only $148 a year, among the lowest in Asia; but there is sufficient rice, and the population isn't starving.

In foreign affairs, Burma shocked much of the world in September 1979 when it became the first country to withdraw from the 88-member Non-Aligned Movement. Impatience with "big powers engaged in a behind-the-scene struggle for exerting their influence on the movement" was the official government explanation for the decision to pull out.

Ne Win stepped down from the presidency in November 1981. U San Yu, a loyal disciple, was elected to succeed him, with Ne Win, nearly 71, continuing as Burma Socialist Program Party chairman. The Burmese leader was seeking a smooth transition to new leadership, to save Burma from a power struggle upon his death. In 1980, to appease opponents, he summoned a conference of Buddhist monks, freed many political prisoners, and declared a general amnesty to exiled former politicians. The latter action succeeded in drawing U Nu back to Rangoon; the former prime minister now spends his time translating Buddhist scriptures.

There are differing opinions on the relative successes or failures of the Ne Win regime. Burmese socialism is not built strictly on Marxist lines, as Marxism and Buddhism are not sufficiently compatible. The Revolutionary Council sought to plot a middle course, one that would steer the country away from hunger and exploitation, but would have a real chance of being accepted in a deeply Buddhist land. There have been no pronounced successes in turning the economy around or in quieting the rebellious minorities. But the course of isolation and neutrality did manage to keep Burma out of the wars which affected much of the rest of Southeast Asia through the 1960s and 1970s. And for many observers, that is quite a feat in itself.

A Capsule Chronology of Burmese History

623–544 B.C.	— Life of Gautama Buddha in India.
ca. 480 B.C.	— Founding of Shwedagon Pagoda.
3rd Cen. B.C.	— Establishment of Suvannabhumi, first Mon empire.
1st Cen. B.C.	— Pyus settle in Burma, build capital at Sri Ksetra.
108 A.D.	— First settlement at Pagan (traditional).
2nd Cen. A.D.	— Maha Muni Buddha probably cast in Arakan.
832	— Conquest of Pyu capital of Halin by Tais (Shans).
11th Century	— Building of Kyaik-tiyo Pagoda ("Golden Rock").
1057	— Anawrahta conquers Mons, establishes empire at Pagan.
1084–1167	— Pagan's Golden Age under kings Kyanzittha and Alaungsithu.
1287	— Mongols conquer Pagan, ending the First Burmese Empire.
1287	— Mons establish Talaing Empire at Martaban.
1315	— Sagaing founded as capital of independent Shan kingdom.
1364	— Ava founded as new Shan capital.
1369	— Talaing (Mon) capital shifted to Hamsawaddy (Pegu).
1385–1425	— 40-year war between Mons and Shans.
1433	— Arakanese capital of Mrauk-U founded.
1453–1492	— Reigns of Queen Shinsawbu and King Dhammazedi at Pegu.
1519	— Portuguese establish trade ports on the Burmese coast.
1541	— Second Burmese Empire founded at Pegu by King Tabinshweti.
1550–1581	— King Bayinnaung extends empire to Chiengmai and Ayutthia (Siam).
1613	— De Brito of Portugal executed after 13-year rule in Syriam.
1622–1638	— Golden Age of Arakan under King Thiri-thu-dhamma.
1635	— Burman (Toungoo dynasty) capital is moved to Ava.
17th Century	— British, French and Dutch set up trade in Burmese ports.
1752	— Mons rebel and conquer Ava, ending Second Burmese Empire.
1755	— Alaungpaya founds Third Burmese Empire at Shwebo.
1760	— Alaungpaya, after founding Rangoon, ousts Mons from Ava.
1767–1783	— Burmans conquer Ayutthia and Arakan, move capital to Amarapura.
1824–1826	— First Anglo-Burmese War, settled by Treaty of Yandabo.
1852–1853	— Second Anglo-Burmese War, giving British Lower Burma.
1861	— King Mindon (1853–1878) transfers capital to Mandalay.
1871–1872	— Fifth Buddhist Synod in Mandalay; *Tripitaka* recorded.
1885–1886	— Third Anglo-Burmese War, giving British colonial possession.
1923	— "Dyarchy reform" gives Burma degree of self-government.
1930	— All Burma Student Movement and union of *thakins* established.
1935	— Government of Burma Act separates Burma from India colony.
1937	— Burma Legislative Council established under British rule.
1941	— Japanese land in Lower Burma to begin conquest.
1943	— Burmese declaration of independence under Japanese military.
1945	— Allies recapture Burma.
1947	— London Conference grants independence effective January 1948.
1947	— Thakin Aung San, independence leader, assassinated.
1948	— Union of Burma becomes a nation, with Thakin Nu as prime minister.
1954–1956	— Sixth Buddhist Synod held in Rangoon.
1958	— General Ne Win named head of caretaker government.
1960	— U Nu regains power in general elections.
1962	— Ne Win stages military coup, establishes Revolutionary Council.
1962	— "The Burmese Way to Socialism" announced.
1969–1973	— U Nu stages unsuccessful rebellion from Thai border area.
1974	— New constitution creates "Socialist Republic of the Union of Burma."
1975	— Major earthquake causes serious damage at Pagan.
1976	— Coup conspiracy by junior officers stifled.
1979	— Burma withdraws from international Non-Aligned Movement.
1981	— Ne Win announces his retirement from the presidency.
1981	— U San Yu elected president.

By the old Moulmein Pagoda, lookin' lazy at the sea,
There's a Burma girl a settin', and I know she thinks o' me . . .
An' I seed her first a-smokin' of a whickin' white cheroot,
An' a wastin' Christian kisses on an 'eathen idol's foot . . .
—*Rudyard Kipling (1889)*

P. KLIER RANGOON

BURMESE IN FESTIVAL DRESS.

BURMESE BEAUTY 558 REGD.
P. KLIER. RANGOON.

68

A BURMESE MAN
438

P. KLIER RANG

A BURMESE VILLAGER. 500
P. KLIER, RANGOON

WELCOME TO BURMA

HOTEL & TOURIST CORPORATION

PADAUNG BELLE

A SIMMERING STEW OF ETHNIC DIVERSITY

Burma ... is peopled by so many races that truly we know not how many; nor who they are, nor whence they came. In no other area are the races so diverse, or the languages and dialects so numerous ...
—*C. M. Enriquez,* Races of Burma *(1933)*

The very name "Union of Burma" implies that the nation is a federation of many peoples. But it is an uneasy federation. "Burma Proper," chief settlement area of the Burman majority, is encircled by separate minority states for the Chins, Kachins, Shans, Karens, Kayahs (Red Karens), Arakanese and Mons. Through the centuries, there have been mistrust, antagonism, and frequent wars among the various races. The situation is no different today.

The current administrative divisions were built into Burma's 1948 constitution, based on the model devised by the British. During the colonial era, the British—with their principle of "divide and rule"—made a distinction between "Burma Proper" and "Outer Burma," the latter comprising the settlement areas of the ethnic minorities. "Burma Proper" was placed under the direct rule of British India, but the minorities were left with much greater autonomy under an indirect rule.

While the Burmans were denied a place in the colonial army, the various minorities were heavily depended upon for their fighting skills. The racial enmity between the Burmans and the minorities festered just beneath the surface until independence was granted. Since that time, more than a generation of violent domestic confrontations have played havoc with the nation's hopes of internal peace.

No less than 67 separate indigenous racial groups have been identified in Burma, not including the various Indians, Chinese and Europeans who make the country their home. A survey in the late British colonial period determined that 242 separate languages and dialects were spoken.

Traces of Prehistoric Man

Long before ancestors of the modern Burmese moved east and south from central Asia and Tibet, prehistoric man inhabited the area we now know as Burma. Caves and rock shelters in the mountains and fertile river valleys were home for these proto-Australoids. Not yet acquainted with agricultural techniques, they lived by hunting and gathering. Stone chips and other vestiges of their primitive culture have been found in western Shan State.

These aboriginal people mixed with Austronesians, and eventually moved on toward what is today Indonesia. No trace of them is found in the present-day population of Burma. The Andaman Islanders, who live in the middle of the Bay of Bengal south of Burma, and the Semang of the Malay Peninsula might be direct descendants.

In historic times, three separate migrations are important in Burmese history.

First to arrive were the Mon-Khmer people. They came from the arid, wind-swept plains

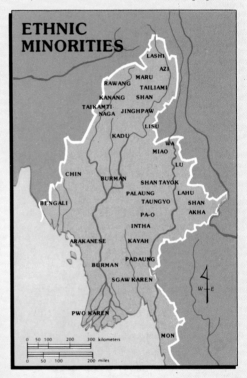

of Central Asia, and it is not difficult to imagine their motivation. Anyone who has seen the mountains of golden rice, piled high at harvest time, will understand why the first Mon-Khmer kingdom was called Suvannabhumi, the "golden land."

But then came a second wave of immigrants, the Tibeto-Burmans, who pushed the

Preceding pages: Two shaven-head Buddhist nuns engage in a contemplative twilight discussion. Left, a Padaung "giraffe" woman graces a poster in the Rangoon office of Tourist Burma. Right, map indicates location of ethnic groups.

Mon-Khmer people further to the south and east, away from the middle reaches of the Irrawaddy. First the Pyus, then the Burmans moved down the valleys of the Irrawaddy and Sittang rivers, establishing their marvelous empires at Sri Ksetra and Pagan.

Between the 12th and 14th centuries, the third migration took place. The Tais (known today in Burma as Shans), a Sino-Tibetan race who had settled in Yunnan in the 7th Century, began moving south down the river valleys. When they tried to force the Burmans out of the Irrawaddy Valley, centuries of warfare followed—with mixed success on both sides. In the end, the Burmans clung to their homeland. The Tais established themselves in the Shan Hills and the Menam (Chao Phraya) River valley in present-day Thailand.

Even today, there remains a tendency of mountain peoples to migrate toward the south. The Kachins were moving in that direction when the British assumed administration of northern Burma late in the 19th Century. The quest for better living conditions—and in very remote areas, the simple search for arable land—inspires such movement, and underlies the antagonism dividing the races of Burma.

The Burmans: In Control

As the majority racial group and the predominant landholder, as well as the group holding the reins of the present government, the Burmans bear the brunt of the hostility. Their settlement area is in the divisions of Rangoon, Irrawaddy (Bassein), Pegu, Magwe, Mandalay and Sagaing, as well as Arakan State, Mon State and Tenasserim. About 70 percent of Burma's people live here.

Most of the cultural forms described in later sections of this book are most representative of the Burmans, who typically live in thatched dwellings and work as wet-rice farmers. Perhaps their greatest cosmetic trademark is the yellow powder, made from *thanaka* bark, which they apply to their cheeks and foreheads as a protection against the tropical sun. Traditional dress is the wraparound *longyi*, or sarong.

The Once-Great Mons

Nestled mainly around the cities of Moulmein and Pegu are the Mons. Once the most powerful group in Burma, they have succumbed to Burman supremacy.

Today, the Mons—who number about 1.3 million—are largely assimilated in the mainstream of Burmese culture. Although they continue to use their own distinct language, and have had their own state within the union since Ne Win's 1962 coup, they are an integral part of the Burmese establishment.

The Mons are at home in the monsoonal plains of Burma's southeast. Far from being slash-and-burn agriculturalists, they prefer an area with plenty of rain to pursue wet-rice growing. They also produce yams, sugar cane and pineapples, catch fish and snare birds. Ardent Buddhists, they observe their own ceremonial calendar of Theravadin festivals.

Burmese Mons constitute only a small part of the Mon-Khmer race. Most of their "cousins" live further east on the Indochinese peninsula—in Thailand, Kampuchea (Cambodia) and Vietnam.

North of the Mon State, firmly ensconced in Shan territory, is another large group of Mon-Khmer speakers—the Palaungs. Unlike their southern cousins, they are hill dwellers and swidden dry-rice agriculturalists. Tea is their principal cash crop. Devout Buddhists and *nat* worshippers, their stockaded villages traditionally contain not only a monastery, but also spirit shrines.

The Padaung 'Giraffe Women'

Among the smaller minority groups belonging to the Mon-Khmer language family are the Padaungs and the Wa. Both have gained a certain fame—or notoriety—that far exceeds their meager numbers.

There are only about 7,000 Padaungs, all of whom live in the vicinity of Loikaw, capital of Kayah State. Their "giraffe women" have been highly publicized by various ethnogra-

Burman faces: a young girl smiles through her *thanaka*-bark makeup (left); and a weatherbeaten peasant takes a break from farming (right).

76

phers of the 19th and 20th centuries, as well as by *National Geographic* magazine recently.

Padaung women's necks give the appearance of having been elongated by nine kilograms (20 pounds) of copper or brass rings. Young girls receive their first neck rings—as well as rings for the arms and ankles—at the age of five or six. Year after year, new rings are added, until by the time of marriage, their necks are 25 centimeters (10 inches) long.

In fact, the womens' necks have not been elongated at all. Their collarbones and ribs have been pushed down. But the effect is the same. Since no muscles can develop where the heavy rings support the head, the rings become a necessity. If the rings are cut off—as they sometimes were in past times as a punishment for adultery—the head can flop over and

about them—except that they were headhunters who offered human skulls as sacrifices to their gods. They are believed to have halted that practice in recent years, but nobody really knows.

In the 1960s, due to the political turmoil raking Indochina, the Wa came into the focus of world attention. They were the main suppliers of raw opium in the "Golden Triangle."

Originally, the Wa had been dry paddy agriculturalists, using slash-and-burn methods to grow their staple rice crop. But their numbers outgrew their ability to support themselves. The opium poppy, until then a secondary product, became the principle cash crop.

After the post-World War II communist takeover in China, the Wa people were courted by many interest groups. The

suffocation can follow unless a neck brace is worn.

It is conjectured that this unusual custom dates from a time when the Padaungs were subject to frequent slave raids from larger tribes. By deforming their women in this manner, they were able to dissuade would-be captors from stealing them away. Some even claim the rings served as protection against tiger bites. As time passed, the original purposes became superfluous. But the custom has remained.

The Wild, Wild Wa

The other Mon-Khmer people of special note are the Wa, notorious frontier inhabitants of Burma's northeast flank.

About 300,000 Wa people live in remote habitats on both sides of the border with China. Until the 1940s, there was little known

Kuomintang (KMT), or Chinese Nationalists, who had to flee the new People's Republic; the American Central Intelligence Agency (CIA); and the communist rebels in Burma all sought to employ the Wa for their own purposes.

Because their settlement area was so secluded, the Wa were able to penetrate China's Yunnan province without detection, and thus were used by the KMT in anti-communist raids. The CIA bought their opium poppies to finance the mercenary units which fought during the Vietnam War. And last but not least, the Peking-supported Burma Communist Party recruited them to fight in their ranks against the Rangoon government.

Today, this is all changing. The KMT units have resettled in northern Thailand or have flown to Taiwan. Substitute cash crops like coffee and tea have been introduced in the Golden Triangle. The People's Republic of China has said it will stop its support for communist insurgencies in Southeast Asia, an apparently conciliatory gesture toward governments of the area.

All this means that difficult times are ahead for the Wa. Their methods of planting and harvesting are outmoded, and they will have to find new ways to survive.

The Shans: 'Free People' With a Feudal Past

Most of the Burmese Wa live in the eastern part of the Shan State. But their numbers are small compared to the 2½ million Shan people of this vast district.

Shan. Siam. Assam. All three geographical names have the same root meaning—an indication of the widespread migration and settle-

approximately equal to their revenues over a 15 to 25-year period.

Some of the *sawbwas* and their followers founded the Shan Independence Army, and in ensuing years attempted to wrest the Shan territory away from the Burmese government. Because of U Nu's apparent inability to deal with this problem (and others), Ne Win staged his military coup in 1962, and subsequently imprisoned all *sawbwas* and other Shan leaders who had not fled Burma. The *sawbwas* were released from prison in 1968, but by that time their era had definitely passed. Some of them are now in self-imposed exile; others, highly educated scholars, teach at universities in Rangoon and elsewhere; but none of them are permitted to return to their former homes in the hills, not even for a visit.

ment area of this race. The word means "free people," a theme which might have been the guiding force behind their medieval move down the alluvial plain of the Chao Phraya.

From the 15th Century—when they were pushed back onto the Shan Plateau after early success in establishing an Irrawaddy kingdom—until 1959, 34 *sawbwas*, or hereditary princes, ruled separate feudal principalities in medieval splendor, with serfs, slaves and harem girls. Their alliance of small states was recognized by the 1948 constitution, and was granted the right to withdraw from the Union of Burma after 10 years of membership therein.

But in 1959, the *sawbwas* were forced to sign a contract with the Ne Win caretaker government, renouncing all their hereditary rights and privileges. In exchange, they accepted a payment of 25 million kyats (over US $3 million at 1981 exchange rates), a sum

In the 1960s, a new rebel group appeared. These forces call themselves the Shan State Army, but they are disunited and pose no real threat to the government in Rangoon. This "army" controls the Thai border area, and with it about 10 percent of the opium trade in and out of the Golden Triangle. A highly profitable contraband business is also under this group's wing. But it lacks adequate support from Shan compatriots to mount a major rebellion against the government.

Most Shans are Buddhists. This in itself distinguishes them from animistic hill people, who generally occupy the mountaintops and steep slopes. Burma's 3.2 million Shans make their homes in valleys and on high plains. After the Shan State, the Shans' next largest concentration is in the Kachin State, but they can be found throughout the nation.

A Mon girl stares from her family's bamboo latticework house located near the Thai border (above).

OPIUM AND THE MINORITIES

Throughout the 1960s and into much of the 1970s, photographs in Western news media depicted caravans of 200 or more mules, stretching for miles through the roadless hills of Southeast Asia, carrying up to 20 tons of raw opium. We learned that this drug, destined for the high schools, military barracks and ghettoes of the industrial nations, was produced in a corner of the world beyond governmental control, unaffected by jet travel and satellite communication. This region was described as a hodgepodge of races and ideologies, fertile ground for continuous conflict.

This mountainous region is known as the Golden Triangle, and the largest part of it falls in Burma's Shan State. It also encompasses parts of Thailand, Laos, and China's Yunnan province. With an average elevation of more than 1,000 meters (3,280 feet), the Triangle offers ideal growing conditions for *papaver somniferum,* commonly called the Eurasian poppy. This is the raw material from which heroin is derived.

Opium, "the tears of the poppy," has been in local use as medicine and as a relaxant ever since the present inhabitants of Southeast Asia immigrated here from the plains of Central Asia.

Burmese kings prohibited the use of the drug, and punished its consumption by pouring liquid lead down the throats of offenders.

During the British administration, opium usage constituted no problem. The British fought two colonial wars in support of the sale of opium, and it was not until 1906 that the House of Commons in London declared the opium trade "immoral."

Southeast Asia's struggle for independence from colonial powers brought opium sharply to the focus of world attention in the mid-20th Century.

The Western nations' fear of communism in the 1950s and 1960s was so great, they gave tacit approval to anything which could stop the spread of the ideology. In order to pay local mercenary troops fighting for them, French and Americans encouraged a multi-million dollar opium business under the charge of Kuomintang (Nationalist Chinese) troops, who had settled in the Golden Triangle after fleeing the communist takeover of China, and Shan rebels, who used the revenues to support their struggle against Burma's new government.

By the end of the 1960s, it had become obvious that the only way to stop the cultivation and distribution of opium would be to alter the entire political landscape of the Golden Triangle region. The various tribes who had become involved as producers or middle men, including the Wa, Lisu, Lahu, Akha and Lu, had become so used to the easy money from this commodity that no other cash crop—not coffee, not tea—would be satisfactory.

The new governments of Indochina have outlawed the opium trade, and are fighting a rigorous war against hill tribes which have not complied with the new regulations. Laos is rapidly being lost as a source of raw opium and a haven for drug runners.

The Burmese government would raze every cultivated field it could find—if it could assert any political authority over the Golden Triangle region. Up until now, it has been totally unsuccessful in doing so because of the rebel activity.

The Kuomintang troops, once thought indispensable in the fight against communism, have lost much support since the Washington-Peking thaw. They have been ousted from Burma, but are still active in the distribution of opium and heroin from Thailand, although their power has waned.

They have been replaced by the Burma Communist Party as the kingpins of opium trade. Cut off from funding by Peking, these political rebels have taken the same path to financing as the KMT and Shans before them.

It is unlikely that the opium trade here will fade for a long time. A form of highly refined heroin, called No. 4 or Double Uoglobe, is produced at the laboratories in the Shan border region. This strain is so concentrated, it takes up about one-tenth of the space of raw opium—thus reducing logistical problems of shipment and transportation.

With residences at an average altitude of 1,000 meters (3,280 feet) above sea level, the Shans are the leading fruit, vegetable and flower growers of Burma. They also have developed stunning irrigation systems in the river valleys.

Shans are easily recognizable by their bath-towel turbans, worn by men and married women. Men generally dress in baggy, dark-blue trousers rather than *longyis,* perhaps indicative of their Western outlook and related dependence on the smuggling trade from Thailand. Girls wear trousers and blouses until the age of 14, at which time they don colorful petticoats. As they get older, their costumes get less colorful, until—at age 40—the women put away their bright garments and dress in black for the rest of their lives.

and the Bwe, whose subgroups include the Kayah (Red Karen), Karennet (Black Karen) and other remote mountain peoples.

The Pwo in particular are conspicuous in the Irrawaddy Delta, and are practically indistinguishable from the Burmans. They have to a high degree assimilated themselves into Burmese society, living in Burman-style houses and devoting their energies to wet-rice farming. Even so, the Karen Independence Movement has gathered a force of about 1,000 men in the delta region.

The Sgaw are less integrated into Burmese society than their Pwo cousins. Of all the many ethnic groups rebelling against the Burmese government, the Karen National Liberation Army is the best organized. Under the leadership of Bo Mya, the army has 8,000

The Many Faces of the Karens

The Karen people belong linguistically to the Tibeto-Burman-speaking majority of Burma. There are 2 to 3 million members of this race living in Burma. But although they have their own administrative division—the Karen (or Kawthule) State—only about one-third of the Karen population lives there. Other large numbers populate the Irrawaddy division around Bassein, as well as the Kayah State (actually the realm of the so-called Red Karens), the Mon State and Tenasserim.

There are three generally recognized groups of Karens: the Pwo, who prefer lowland or delta homes; the Sgaw, including the Paku (White Karen), Pa-O and other hill tribes;

well-equipped and trained soldiers. It controls a large area of Karen State, and has a more-or-less functioning administration, with schools, infirmaries and social services. This government is financed through control of most of the illegal imports into Burma, and by the raising of a 5 percent tax on all goods smuggled between Thailand and Karen country.

The border area controlled by the Sgaw Karens is inaccessible from within Burma. Any visitor to Thailand, however, can reach the Karen outpost of Wang Kha from Mae Sot.

Hill people: a group of animistic Nagas (left) from the isolated mountain country of northwestern Kachin State pose in ceremonial dress; and a Shan infant (right) from the Taunggyi area is tightly bundled for carrying on his mother's or sister's back.

In 1977, the Burmese government army waged a major offensive to try to halt this smuggling operation, which accounts for 40 to 50 tons of illegal goods arriving in Burma each day. The troops succeeded in devastating Wang Kha. But in a matter of weeks, the border village was reconstructed only a few kilometers away.

For the simple slash-and-burn hilltop peasants, the rebel activities have little effect on daily life. They fight a continuous battle against drought and food shortages. As their population increases, the soil they farm is becoming depleted of nutrients and unproductive. Many Karens now seek other jobs as *mahouts* (elephant riders) with woodcutters, or as miners in the tin mines. With few industries in the region, choices are slim.

Karens are said to have migrated to Burma by stages from an original homeland in the Gobi Desert region of Mongolia, where they lived about 4,500 years ago. In tribal legends, they still call the desert "the River of Sand."

Another ancient Karen legend helped make this race fertile ground for Christian missionaries. It is said the Karens' ancestors in the Gobi possessed a book of "holy scriptures." The book was lost during the migration, but they were told by "Y'we"—the creative power—that it would someday be returned to them by a "white brother."

Uncanny parallels between the Karen legends and Bible stories led many colonial era missionaries to believe they had found one of the lost tribes of Israel. The name "Y'we" is remarkably similar to that of the Hebrew God, "Yahweh." Included in the Karen scriptures were the story of a seven-day creation period, and of a serpent who persuaded the first man and woman to eat a forbidden fruit, after which they were subject to suffering, aging and death.

The missionaries found the Karens eager to embrace the Christian religion, and today the Karens are by far the largest Christian group in Burma.

Among the more unusual subgroups of the Sgaw Karens are the Pa-O. These people, who number about 200,000, make their principal home near Taunggyi in the Shan State, where they fled during Anawrahta's 11th Century attack on Thaton. Their language is an older, purer tongue than standard modern Karen; the written language of the Pa-O is unique.

The 'Red Karens' of Kayah State

The Kayahs, or Red Karens, have the smallest state in Burma, in terms of area as well as population. Virtually all members of this ethnic group—about 75,000—reside here. Dur-

ing the British colonial era, the Kayahs were never officially incorporated into the Burma colony, instead maintaining autonomy in several feudal principalities known as the Karenni States. Given the same hereditary rights as Shan princes according to the 1948 constitution, the Kayah princes—whose territory was united as Kayah State in 1951—relinquished their special rights at the same time as the Shans in 1959. They also suffered the same fate of exile or imprisonment following Ne Win's 1962 coup. During the 1960s, the feudal estates were split up and allotted to small farmers.

The Kayahs are primarily hill people, making their living through dry cultivation of rice, millet and vegetables. Probably nicknamed the "Red Karens" because that color is a fa-

vorite in the wardrobe of both men and women, the most startling aspect of their dress has nothing to do with color. Women tie their calves with many garters of cord or rattan, often to a thickness of two inches. These are then decorated with beads and seeds. Although walking and sitting thus become very difficult, this fashion is considered graceful.

The Kachins and Other Mountain People

Kachin State is the real hodgepodge of hill tribes in Burma. Throughout this large, heavily mountainous district in the nation's far north, Jinghpaws (Kachins), Shans and Burmans share space with Maru, Lashi, Azi, Lisu,

Rawang, Tailiami, Tailon, Taikamti, Tailay, Kadu and Kanang villagers without any recognizable settlement pattern.

The label "Kachin" is often indiscriminately applied to all inhabitants of this state. In fact, the only true Kachins are the Jinghpaw people. Traditionally hilltop dwellers, their lifestyle and social structure differ markedly from those of the Shans, who populate the valley floors.

This dominant Kachin group plants dry rice in a shifting cultivation scheme, alternating with buckwheat, millet and barley. When possible, they plant wet paddy in hill terraces, and trade with the Shans and Burmans for other necessities.

The Jinghpaws' religion is animistic, a trait they have in common with nearly all of

herits the father's position (including chiefdom). Jinghpaws maintain that the younger a son is, the greater the chance that he is of the same flesh and blood as his father.

As in most minority regions of Burma, Kachin State harbors rebel armies. The Kachin Independence Army, fighting for regional autonomy, and the Burma Communist Party have their bases in the wild country near the Chinese border. Scattered remains of the Kuomintang army of Nationalist China can also be found in the border region, supporting themselves by smuggling opium.

The Notorious Nagas

Another group of people who prefer high mountain terrain for their homes is the Nagas. While not strictly a Burmese race—they have their own state of Nagaland in eastern India—a sizeable number (perhaps 50,000) of the approximately 400,000 Nagas make their home in the upper Chindwin River area of Sagaing Region, as well as in the neighboring Kachin and Chin states.

In past decades they were notorious for warfare and headhunting. Today Nagas lead a more tranquil existence. Their agricultural and religious habits are similar to other highland peoples of Burma, and their social structure is archaic: there is no group hierarchy, and there are no legal institutions above the village level.

The main concern to the Burmese government in this region is that dissident Nagas from India, waging a guerrilla war of independence there, occasionally cross the border into Burma for training and weapons.

Putting the Chins Forward

The Chins are the least known of Burma's major ethnic groups, and the least affected by foreign influence. While the majority of Chins—about 800,000—live in India and Bangladesh, some 350,000 of them speak 44 mutually unintelligible dialects in Burma.

Over 60 percent of Burma's Chins live in the Chin State, with most of the rest settled in the Arakan Yoma and the Magwe division. Because of their relative isolation, they were largely overlooked by the medieval rulers of Pagan and other empires. By colonial times, however, they had developed a solid reputation as extraordinarily brave soldiers, and were heavily recruited for the British forces.

Burma's hill tribes. Their concept of the supernatural involves a hierarchical pantheon of gods who wield a mystic power over the lives of humans. The spirits must be propitiated with offerings and sacrifices, of which they consume the "breath," or essence, and leave the remainder for mortals to eat.

Witchcraft and sorcery are a part of the Jinghpaws' daily lives. Nothing "good" or "evil" can just happen. There is always a spirit behind every action who must be thanked or appeased, often by tribal shamans, who perform rites at village shrines.

Heredity is important in the kin-based clan structures upon which Jinghpaw society is based. But contrary to the norm elsewhere, the youngest son, rather than the eldest, in-

Urban immigrants: Mohamed Musa (left), South Indian manager of a biryani chicken restaurant in Rangoon, serves a customer; and affluent Chinese newlyweds (right) stand with in-laws at the Strand Hotel after a wedding before 2,000 guests.

The Chins are swidden agriculturalists, like other hill peoples, with their settlements built at an average elevation of 1,200 to 1,500 meters (4,000 to 5,000 feet). Northern Chins, who have an elaborate social hierarchy, construct permanent homes of wooden planks and raise corn (maize) as their staple crop. Southern Chins, whose clan system is less formal, build their homes of bamboo and rattan, frequently pulling up stakes and moving. Their principal crop is rice. Both groups of Chins are heavily animistic.

The Proud People of Arakan

It's a popular proverb among Burmans that if you meet an Arakanese and a snake at the same time, you should first kill the man from

Irrawaddy basin Burmans. True, Arakan gets far more rain and has higher humidity than the inland, due to its exposure to the monsoons. This has required that Arakan's entire transportation system be dependent on boats. Cultivated land is always situated only a short distance from navigable rivers, creeks, channels and tidal waters.

There are only a few roads in Arakan. The only motorable road across the Arakan Yoma is in no better than fair condition, and then in the dry season only. This isolation helps to keep interaction betwen the Arakanese and Burmans to a minimum, and helps to preserve a nationalistic consciousness.

Most Arakanese are devout Buddhists. But a fairly large number of people in the capital city of Akyab, and along the northern coast,

Arakan. The story is reflective of the 200 years of trouble Burmans have had with this coastal race since conquering their land in the latter part of the 18th Century. The Arakanese, for their part, still look back with pride and dignity on the many centuries of independence they enjoyed. They view the Burmans with distrust.

Although of the same Tibeto-Burman stock, Arakanese are slightly darker in complexion than the Burmans. The region's 2,000-year history of contact with Indian traders, sailors and Brahmin settlers has left its mark upon the physical appearance of the Arakanese people.

There are few major differences between the lifestyles of the coastal Arakanese and the

are Moslems of Bengali descent. The ancestors of most of these people settled in Arakan during the British era, when movement between India and Burma was not restricted.

In the 1970s, the population explosion in neighboring Bangladesh led to massive movements by illegal immigrants into Arakan. A militant Moslem faction, the Mujahid, began stirring up problems, and the Burmese national army swooped upon Arakan and forced more than 200,000 Bengalis across the Bangladesh border. Recently, however, about 187,000 Bengalis were readmitted to Arakan upon verbal statement that they were Burmese citizens.

In both city and country areas, Moslems and Buddhists lead separate lives and have little to do with one another. In Akyab, many Moslems have their houses along the Kaladan River and work as fishermen—a profession no devout Buddhist would ever take up, because it would involve taking life.

Rural and Urban Chinese

There are two groups of Chinese who inhabit Burma, with very different histories and lifestyles.

For millennia, Chinese have traveled overland into Burma, down the northeastern trade routes and along the great rivers. In centuries past, many Chinese settlements were established along these routes. The descendants of these early settlers still live in Upper Burma. One large group is known as Shan Tayok, or

Chinese Shan. They came over the border of Yunnan when the Shan principalities were under British administration.

The urban Chinese have an entirely different background. Most of them came to Rangoon by sea to work as small merchants and restaurant owners during the British colonial era. Working hard and diligently, sending their sons and daughters to Western-type schools and universities, they soon occupied the middle and higher strata of modern society. Despite the nationalization of private businesses under Ne Win, they remain strong, although some have turned to the arts or even vegetable farming as occupations.

Estimates of the number of Chinese in Burma today range from 100,000 to 400,000.

A sizable number left in 1967, when anti-Chinese riots took place in Rangoon. At the height of Mao's Cultural Revolution, many young Chinese in Rangoon undertook to import the revolution to Burma; with a minimum of instigation from the federal government, the Burmese reacted violently, thoroughly rampaging through the city's Chinese sector. Since then, the Chinese have kept a low profile in Burma, adapting themselves more strictly to local customs.

The Industrious Indians

The Indians and their culture have a 2,000-year history in Burma, predating even the majority Burmans.

But it was not until the 19th Century, when Burma became a part of the British India colony, that they began to settle in Burma in such quantity than a purely Indian community developed. They came in such great numbers, in fact, that by 1939 an estimated 58 percent of the population of Rangoon was Indian, and an estimated one million Indians were living in Burma.

The Indians were largely well educated, and occupied middle and higher levels of administration and business during the British era. Those not so well educated came to Burma as contract laborers for government projects, ranging from railway and road construction to the extension of urban areas. Many of them were from southern India, and brought with them the regional village social structure, with castes, Hindu deities and moneylenders.

These moneylenders (chettyars) quickly became so entrenched in Burmese society that they bought up more than half of the arable land in the Irrawaddy Delta region. Soon, however, the tide turned. Many were forced to return to India during the wartime Japanese occupation of Burma, and those who endured were soon faced with the land reforms of the new independent government of the Union of Burma. Businessmen who remained in Burma during the U Nu years staged a mass migration when Ne Win installed his nationalization program.

Today, there are fewer than a half-million Indians still living in Burma, perhaps only 100,000. Most are of the poorer classes and make their livings in menial jobs. Those born in Burma are generally Moslems, but have tried hard to adopt the Burmese lifestyle. Those born in India are mainly Hindus, and are employed in trades or professions.

An Arakanese woman (left) carries two pots of water from the Kaladan River to her kitchen. Right, Sister Luise-Marie, a lowland Karen, is a Catholic nun serving at St. Peter's Cathedral in Bassein.

84

COPYRIGHT.

THE 37 NATS

The 37 *nats* have changed their identities through the ages, but their number has remained constant. The *nats* represented in this collage, taken from Sir R.C. Temple's classic work, *The 37 Nats* (London, 1906), may not be the same 37 as Burmese worship today.

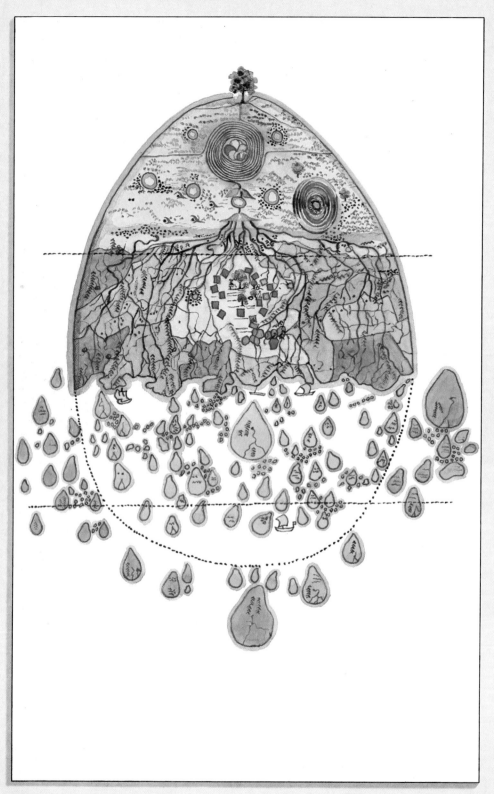

BUDDHA, JAMBUDIPA, AND THE 37 NATS

It has often been said that Burma is the most profoundly Buddhist country in the world. That may well be true. But the brand of Buddhism practiced in this isolated land is unique on the face of the globe.

Burmese Buddhism, theoretically, is Theravada or Hinayana Buddhism, that sect of Buddhism adhering most closely to the Buddha's teaching, and the dominant form of Buddhism throughout Southeast Asia. It was preceded in Burma, however, by the animistic beliefs of the hill tribes and by the Hindu-Brahmanism of early traders, which has had a profound effect on the cosmological concept of the land.

Burmese Cosmology: 31 Planes of Existence

Strictly speaking, Burmese cosmology is Buddhist cosmology. But it has been shaped by millennia of influences from other cultures, particularly that of the Brahmins.

According to the Burmese, the European-Asian continent is called Jambudipa. It is the southern of four islands situated at the cardinal points surrounding Mount Meru, the center of the world.

This southern island is the only place where future Buddhas can be born. This is because Jambudipa is a place of misery, compared to the other abodes of this universe. The inhabitants of the northern island, for instance, have lives of only joy and pleasure. There, everything one needs can be found growing on trees—the finest food already cooked, glittering garments waiting to be plucked from bushes. The northerner lives for 1,000 years in perfect, youthful shape. But because life for him is so pleasurable, there is no way he can gain merits.

Despite their lives of suffering, the Buddhist inhabitants of Jambudipa would not change places with the northerner. It is only in the land of humanity that one can gain sufficient merit in good deeds to rise through the vertical states of existence and attain the state of nirvana.

There are, in fact, 31 planes of existence on, above, and below Mount Meru. They can be divided into three main groups:

- The 11 planes of *Kama-Loka,* the realm of the sensuous world.

- The 16 planes of *Rupa-Loka,* the realm of subtle material matter.

- The four planes of *Arupa-Loka,* the realm of formlessness.

Of the 11 planes of *Kama-Loka,* four are beneath the human plane of existence. These are demon and ghost worlds, the animal world, hells and purgatories. This is the

sphere of punishment. A human being who collects demerits for bad deeds and who fails to counterweight them with meritorious deeds will be reborn in one of these four lower worlds.

Preceding pages: Buddhas are one face of Burmese religion; the 37 *nats* are another. Cosmology speaks of a physical world centered on Mount Meru (map drawing, left). An all-knowing *nat* stares from his alcove in a temple (above).

Still within the sensuous realm, but above the plane of humanity, are the six planes of sensual bliss on and above Mount Meru. Their inhabitants—*nats* and *devas, nagas, garudas,* and gods of many kinds—exist in the realm of pleasure. The duration of their lives is much longer than that of human beings. But these entities still need the inhabitants of Jambudipa to share in their merits, and thereby prolong their blissful existences. Once the power of the entities' merits—which led to their being reborn on this plane—has subsided, they must once again be reborn on Jambudipa to collect more merit for new opportunities in future lives.

The inhabitants of the 16 planes of *Rupa-Loka* are already free from sensual desire. They are born without the aid of parents, feed

on joy, and are luminous. This realm is sometimes called the "16 heavens of Brahma," because it is on this level that refined and beautiful beings exist. Indeed, the higher the plane of existence, the more refined and beautiful the beings become. The five uppermost *Rupa-Loka* planes are called the "pure abodes." Still, they belong to the material world.

It is different in the highest heavens, the four planes of *Arupa-Loka*. Here, the inhabitants are disembodied intellects. They no longer belong to the material world. These planes of existence are no longer places; they comprise (in order) the infinity of space, the infinity of consciousness, nothingness, and at the highest level, "neither perception nor non-perception."

The 31 planes of existence into which a human being can be reborn reach far beyond Mount Meru. The peak of the sacred mountain, in fact, is only the No. 7 plane (Jambudipa is No. 5) in this cosmic description.

The distance between the different worlds or heavens cannot be measured in earthly terms. According to the Burmese, heavens are millions of *yuzenas* (28,000 cubits, about nine miles) apart, and *kappas* separate worlds. A *kappa,* the duration of a single universe, lasts 4,320 million years. Single universes are destroyed and re-created on a regular basis; in fact, it is considered that precisely 10,100,000 universes of the same type as our own currently exist. These universes come and go, and at times when all other worlds have dissipated, only the four upper planes remain. Their inhabitants have lifespans of more than 20,000 *kappas*.

Within this cosmos, every aspect of life interacts with every other. Animals, man, *nats*, gods and demons—they are all bound to the wheel of life. They all exist and are a part of the Burmese Buddhist's world.

It is only the various Buddhas of history who are free from this wheel of *samsara*, or rebirth. The Buddha of our era, Gautama, left his Dharma, his teaching, for the inhabitants of Jambudipa so they could learn how to achieve enlightenment and escape the 31 planes of existence. Even the beings of the highest plane—that beyond consciousness—cannot directly reach nirvana. They must first be reborn in Jambudipa, our world of misery, the only world with a direct link to the state of "un-becoming."

The 37 Nats:
Respect and Honor, Or Else

Since long before the introduction to Burma of Buddhism, there has been a pronounced belief in animism among the native peoples. Even today, the 37 primary *nats* are an integral part of the religious beliefs of the Burmese people. Essentially demons and evil spirits, they make life difficult for those who do not accord them sufficient respect and esteem. The people of Burma appease and honor them with offerings of flowers, money and food, placed on special altars.

Originally, each village had its own spirits. Each tree and field was inhabited by a local *nat*. There were harvest *nats*, *nats* of the wind, and *nats* of the rain. Some of the iso-

Buddha images grace the Shwedagon terrace (preceding pages), where the shiny brass head of a Buddha (left) and the ethereal aura of Bo Bo Gyi, guardian *nat* of the pagoda (right), coexist.

lated tribes of northern Burma still have localized beliefs, manifested annually at the great Manao Festival in Myitkyina.

For most Burmese, however, there are specific *nats* recognized throughout the country for their individual powers. It has been so for more than 1,500 years.

According to the *Glass Palace Chronicle*, King Thinlikyaung (ca. 344–387 A.D.) united 19 villages in the vicinity of present-day Pagan to found the town of Thiripyitsaya. Within this coalition of communities, there arose the need for an inter-regional system of religious beliefs. So the king had a tree, which was reputed to be carrying brother and sister *nats* from the north of the land, fished from the Irrawaddy River. Two figures were carved from the tree; they were borne to the top of

Not all of the 37 *nats* worshipped today are the same 37 as those worshipped at Anawrahta's time. Some 15 of the original group have been replaced by historical figures through the centuries.

For the Burmese, these 37 *nats* serve nearly the same purpose as the saints of the Roman Catholic Church. In both cases, they are called upon in times of need. Theravada Buddhists cannot beseech the Buddha. When regarded from this perspective, the animism prevalent today within the framework of Burmese Buddhism is not as archaic as it may first seem.

The 22 *nats* originating from the pre-Pagan period are:

(1) Thagyamin, king of the *nats*, known as Indra in Hindu mythology, sometimes called Sakka.

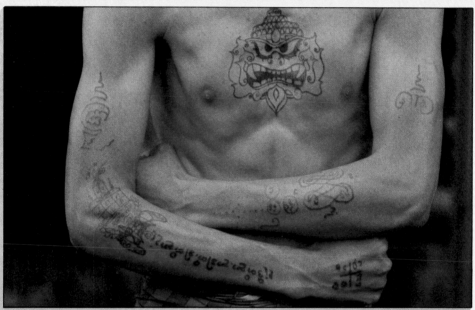

Mount Popa, where they remain in their own shrine to this day. They are known as the Mahagiri Nats.

King Anawrahta, founder of the First Burmese Empire, also devoted his attention to simplifying spiritual beliefs. When he introduced Theravada Buddhism into Upper Burma as the national religion, he was unable to eliminate the animistic beliefs of his people. Despite radical measures, 36 of the countless *nats* managed to survive in the people's daily activities. So Anawrahta introduced a 37th figure—Thagyamin—and made him king of the *nats*. He thereafter tolerated the popular worship of these 37 *nats*, once it had been established that they were also followers of the Buddha's teachings.

(2) Nga Tin De, or Min Mahagiri, the Lord of the Great Mountain.
(3) Shwemyethna, Princess Golden Face, his sister.
(4) Lady Golden Sides.
(5) Lady Three Times Beautiful.
(6) The Little Lady With the Flute.
(7) The Brown Lord of Due South.
(8) The White Lord of the North.
(9) The Lord With the White Umbrella.

"There are some young men who seem almost to make picture galleries of themselves," said Shway Yoe in 1882—and it's still true today (left). Many of the tattoos represent animistic deities. Right, a woman offers a prayer for relief from suffering at one of the Shwedagon's eight planetary posts.

(10) The Royal Mother (of No. 9).
(11) The Sole Lord of Pareim-ma.
(12) The Elder Inferior Gold.
(13) The Younger Inferior Gold.
(14) The Lord Grandfather of Mandalay.
(15) The Lady Bandy Legs.
(16) The Old Man by the Solitary Banyan.
(17) Lord Sithu.
(18) The Young Lord of the Swing.
(19) The Valiant Lord Kyawswa.
(20) Captain of the Main Army Aungswa.
(21) The Royal Cadet.
(22) His Mother, the Lady Golden Words.

The 15 *nats* who took their places after the reign of Anawrahta are:
(23) The Lord of Five Elephants.
(24) The Lord King, Master of Justice.
(25) Maung Po Tu.
(26) The Queen of the Western Palace.
(27) The Lord of Aungpinle, Master of White Elephants.
(28) The Lady Bent.
(29) Golden Nawrahta.
(30) The Valiant Lord Aung Din.
(31) The Young Lord White.
(32) The Lord Novice.
(33) Tabinshweti.
(34) The Lady of the North.
(35) The Lord Minhkaung of Toungoo.
(36) The Royal Secretary.
(37) The King of Chiengmai.

Each of the 37 *nats* has a tragic tale associated with him or her, in some way connected with the history of Burma. It is through these tales that the Burmese masses are introduced to their country's history and legend, myth and drama. The *nats*, in fact, essentially provide Burma with a national history comprehensible to one and all, splendid yet marvelously simplistic.

There is a widespread superstition in Burma that ailments can be cured and the future predicted by those with proper channels to the *nats*. Soothsayers, prophets and miracle healers are natural offshoots of this belief. With a tradition of thousands of years of *nat* worship, these beliefs are deeply ingrained in the lives of the country people even today, and a re-education program by the current government does not seem likely to succeed.

The Beatitudes of Buddhism

Theravada Buddhism is recognized as the principal religion of about 80 percent of all Burmese people. While there are significant numbers of Hindus, Moslems, Christians and primitive animists (among the northern hill tribes), it is safe to say that over 99 percent of

the Burmans, Mons, Shans and Palaungs are Theravadins.

Indeed, Buddhism permeates the everyday lives of Burma's people far more than does "The Burmese Way to Socialism." Every Burmese village supports at least one *kyaung* (a monastery, usually linked with a school); and the yellow, orange, or red-clad *pongyis* (monks, whose title literally means "great glory") are an established part of the street scenes in the villages and urban areas alike.

Another name for Theravada Buddhism is "Hinayana," "the lesser vehicle." This is not to imply that Theravada Buddhism is less powerful than its counterpart, Mahayana ("the greater vehicle"), dominant in most of East Asia. Rather, Theravada is a more conservative, more orthodox, form of Buddhism,

adhering strictly to the original Pali scriptures. It places a great emphasis on individual achievement, and allows fewer options to those seeking to attain nirvana (thus, "the lesser vehicle"). It does not, as Mahayanists sometimes claim, ignore the salvation of all but the individual; rather, it is through service to other beings that one enhances one's own status.

The division between Theravada and Mahayana, while developing for some time, actually occurred in 235 B.C., when King Ashoka convened the Third Buddhist Synod at Pataliputra, India. The Buddhist elders (Theravada means, "the way of the elders") held tight to their literal interpretation of the Buddha's teachings; they were opposed by a group which sought to understand the personality of the historical Buddha, and its relationship to one's salvation. This latter group became known as the Mahayana school. It established itself in Tibet, Nepal, China, Korea, Mongolia, Japan and Vietnam, where its further development varied greatly from region to region.

The Theravada school, meanwhile, has thrived in Ceylon, Burma, Thailand, Laos and Kampuchea (Cambodia). Buddhaghosa, the famous Indian monk, in 403 A.D. carried the Pali scriptures to Thaton (where a form of Buddhism was already practiced). Buddhaghosa had summarized and interpreted the *Tripitaka*—the "Three Baskets" of Theravada scripture, composed of the *sutras* (discourses), *vinaya* (rules and regulations of

the Sangha, the order of monkhood), and *abhidhamma* (interpretations of the Buddha's teachings)—and took this body of knowledge with him to the Mon capital.

In recent years, in synods at Mandalay in 1872 and Rangoon in 1954, there have been efforts to give Theravada Buddhism a new impetus. At the former synod, the entire *Tripitaka* was recited and recorded on stone tablets; and at the latter, an Institute for Advanced Buddhistic Studies was founded.

No God, No Self

There is no all-powerful god in Theravada Buddhism. In contrast to Mahayanism, even the Buddha himself cannot be invoked to intervene benevolently in one's life. It is up to the individual to work out his own salvation. Life and death are two sides of the same "coin" of existence. All living things, including plants and animals, are included in the perpetual round of *samsara*, or rebirth. According to Buddhist doctrine, this is an endless cycle of suffering from which there is but one escape: faithful adherence to the Dharma, the Buddha's teaching, and following the paths of *arhats* (saints) and *bodhisattvas* (future Buddhas) to reach nirvana.

In practice, Theravada Buddhism has developed a higher and a lower form of teaching. The pure form of Buddhism has largely been left to the monks. The masses engage in a hodgepodge of Buddhism and their ancient *nat* worship, coupled with cosmological beliefs; most Burmese Buddhists seem to be more desirous of making merit for a better rebirth in a higher heaven than they are in taking the direct path to nirvana to escape the cycle of suffering.

There are 227 rules by which monks must guide their lives, but only five precepts of Buddhist morality which are truly relevant to the masses. These are restrictions against killing, stealing, lying, adultery, and the consumption of intoxicating liquor.

As there is no true form of worship in Theravada Buddhism, the only ritual to which monks and laity submit themselves is the thrice-daily recitation of the "Three Jewels," the *Triratna*:

"I take refuge in the Buddha. I take refuge in the Dharma. I take refuge in the Sangha."

The formula of the "Three Jewels" offers solace and security. These are needed for strength if one understands the "Four Noble Truths" expounded by Gautama Buddha in his first sermon:

Life always has in it the element of suffering (1). The cause of suffering is desire (2). In order to end the suffering, give up desire, give up attachment (3). The way to this goal is the Noble Eightfold Path (4).

The Eightfold Path consists of right views, right intent, right speech, right conduct, right means of livelihood, right endeavor, right mindfulness, and right meditation.

This "path" is normally divided into three: views and intent are matters of wisdom; speech, conduct (action) and livelihood are matters of morality; and endeavor, mindfulness and meditation are matters of true mental discipline.

Despite a common code, monks are very individualistic. Left, a Mon monk dons a pair of bamboo spectacle frames purchased from a stall near the Kyaik-tiyo Pagoda. Right, an elderly monk rests between periods of meditation in a monastery.

The Buddha denied the existence of a soul. There is no permanence, he explained, to that which one perceives to be self—one's essence is forever changing. The idea of rebirth, therefore, is a complicated philosophical question within the structure of Buddhism. When a Buddhist (or any person, for that matter) is reincarnated, it is neither the person nor his soul which is actually reborn. Rather, it is the sum of one's karma, his good and evil deeds: one is reborn as a result of prior existence.

One popular metaphor used to explain this transition is that of a candle. Were a person to light one candle from the flame of another, then extinguish the first, it could not be said that the new flame was the same as the previous one; but its existence would be due to the previous flame's existence.

this life and the next—a goal which can be accomplished through participation in merit-making activities, and by avoiding demeritorious actions.

Sinful acts are those which violate the five precepts of Buddhist morality, as well as those which create greed, anger or delusion. Good Buddhists must keep the five precepts and strive above all for compassion, equanimity and wisdom.

Other activities earn additional merit. The single best deed is sponsorship of the construction of a pagoda or reliquary stupa. It is commonly believed that a person with the ways and means to build a pagoda will ensure his rebirth at the time of Maitreya, the Buddha of the future, and in Maitreya's presence will achieve enlightenment. This is why there

The Noble Eightfold Path, therefore, does not lead to salvation in the Judeo-Christian sense. By pursuing matters of wisdom, morality and mental discipline, one can hope to make the transition into nirvana, which can perhaps best be defined as extinction of suffering, cessation of desire. It is not heaven, nor is it annihilation. It is a quality of existence.

Popular Buddhist Practice

These, then, are the tenets of Theravada Buddhism. But the vast majority of Burmese Buddhists do not actively pursue the goal of nirvana in this lifetime. To them, "extinction" is not as desirable as a more pleasurable rebirth. They seek a reduction in suffering in

are so many pagodas in Burma. What's more, relics and many images of Gautama Buddha are believed to contain innate power that can be drawn upon by those who worship them; every pagoda builder hopes to obtain one of these "magic" relics for veneration at his own pagoda.

There are many other acts which earn lesser, but important, amounts of merit. Of these, becoming a monk and performing charitable acts for the Sangha are deemed most worthwhile. Worship, meditation, pilgrimage, preaching or listening to sermons on the Buddha's teachings, showing respect to elders and superiors, and sharing merit with others (through certain ritual acts) are other ways of earning merit.

It is estimated that Southeast Asian villagers may spend as much as 10 percent of their total cash income on merit-making activities. But in addition to advancing one's chances for a more prosperous future life, these acts can improve one's worldly prestige (pagoda builders earn a special title for life), as well as contribute to the gratification of physical pleasures—as at the annual temple festivals, where great feasting and pageantry abound.

The Sangha

There are no priests in Theravada Buddhism. But the faithful still need a model to follow on the path to salvation. This model is provided by the colorfully clad Southeast Asian monks.

In Burma, there are about 800,000 monks. Most of these are students and novices who are wearing the monk's robe only temporarily; nearly all male Burmese devote from a few weeks to several years of their lives to the monkhood. There are no vows such as those of Roman Catholicism. Indeed, the *pongyi* can leave the order at any time. Nevertheless, about 100,000 have dedicated their entire lives to the Sangha, a Buddhist brotherhood which has renounced our world.

There are three fundamental rules to which the monk must subscribe:

(1) The renunciation of all possessions, with the exception of the nine things required of a monk—three robes, a razor (for shaving), a needle (for sewing), a water container, a fan (for keeping cool), a belt, and an alms bowl.

(2) A vow to injure nothing and to offend no one.

(3) Celibacy.

The *pongyi* must make his livelihood by begging. He sets out two hours before dawn, begging for food from door to door. He does not thank the donor for alms received, for it is the donor who must be grateful: the monk has given him an opportunity to earn merit by doing a good deed for one in the Buddha's service. The food received at this time is the monk's only meal of the day.

The vow to injure nothing came about as a reaction to the animal sacrifices of Brahmanism. It is also valid, to a certain extent, for lay Buddhists. With few exceptions, Burmese fishermen and butchers are non-Buddhists.

The law of celibacy is based on the assertion that sexual union with a woman takes up a great deal of physical and psychic energy, which must instead be directed toward meditation. Women, therefore, are expected to avoid any contact with a *pongyi*. They should not touch his alms bowl, tread on his mat, or speak to him.

According to Buddhist belief, the fate of being born a woman is the price one must pay for having led a poor life in a prior existence. There is, however, an order of Buddhist nuns. They are easily recognizable with their pink robes and close-cropped heads. But they are not accorded the same respect as the monks.

A young Burmese begins his novitiate at around the age of nine. He is brought to a *kyaung* and handed over to the monks, who teach him the basic Pali scriptures and the 10 basic Buddhist rules of conduct. At the time of this initiation (called the *shin-pyu*), the boy is given an old Pali name and may only be addressed in revered tones, even by his parents. He is now a "son of Buddha," and addresses his father as "lay brother" and his mother as "lay sister."

For the majority of Burmese, their period of novitiate does not last long. Most have left the monkhood before their 20th birthday, which is the minimum age at which one can become a member of the Sangha and submit oneself to the 227 rules of the order. Those who become ordained have all the hair shaved off their bodies, then devote the rest of their lives to meditation, the study of the Pali scriptures, and the instruction of the laity.

Flowers, streamers, and miniature golden *htis* (left) are among the offerings made at planetary posts. Right, Rangoon monks pause during their daily alms collection rounds. Following pages: *pongyis* gaze from a Kemendine *kyaung*.

P.KLIER RANGOON

104

376
STERN OF BURMESE PADDY BOAT

PLACES

A journey through Burma is a journey through history. The visitor arrives in Rangoon, where contemporary and colonial Burma (19th and 20th centuries) continue to coexist decades after the British departure. Traveling north to Mandalay, he encounters living reminders of the Konbaung dynasty, which dominated in the 18th and 19th centuries here and in neighboring Amarapura. In Ava and Sagaing, the Burma of the Shan sovereignty (14th through 16th centuries) is predominant. And at enchanting Pagan, he can marvel at more than 2,200 stone buildings constructed during the First Burmese Empire (11th to 13th centuries).

Following the route just described—Rangoon to Mandalay to Sagaing to Pagan—the visitor can make a direct journey into the past. It is not an easy journey; it demands one to call constantly on one's imagination to make the ruins come to life, and it requires an advance historical perspective. The tourist who goes "temple-hopping" without these will wind up either exhausted or jaded . . . or both.

Pagan itself can be overwhelming. But if the tourist can make a careful selection of the temples he visits—and concentrates his limited time on those few—he will be able to trace the history of an incredible era. At the same time, he can observe in the structures of Pagan the development of a whole architectural style, one born 1,000 years earlier in India and which reached its unparalleled climax on the plain of Pagan.

The above-mentioned destinations are far from all Burma has to offer, either historically or scenically. Pegu, Tagaung, Myohaung and many other places are steeped in history, offering the visitor insights into past centuries. But the seven-day tourist visa and the travel restrictions within Burma itself—as well as the need to be selective so as not to be swamped by new discoveries—lead most visitors to concentrate on those places listed above.

There has been talk that the Burmese government might extend the visa period to 10 or even 14 days. But even if those plans are realized, little will have changed. Once the Western visitor has fallen under Burma's spell, he will always depart with the heavy heart of a lover who must leave his beloved behind.

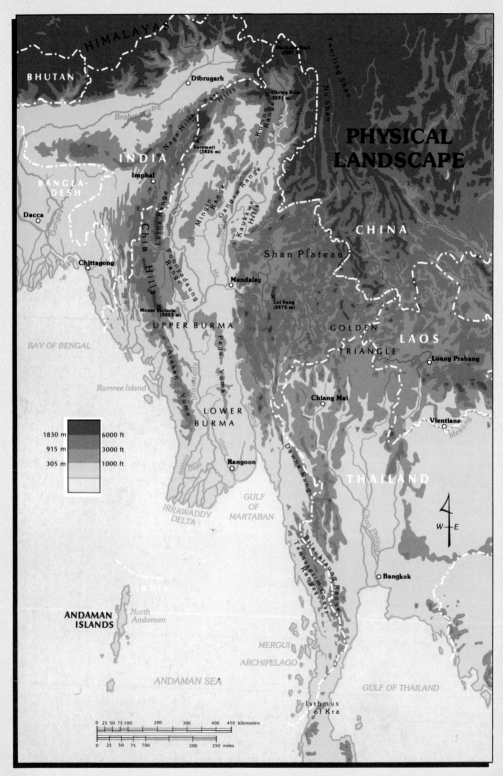

PHYSICAL LANDSCAPE

HIMALAYA

BHUTAN

BANGLA-
DESH

INDIA

CHINA

Dibrugarh

Naga Hills

Patkoi Hills

Imphal

Saramati
(3826 m)

Kumon Range

Hkrieg Bum
(2591 m)

Yan-ling Shan

Nu Shan

Nmai

Brahmaputra

Dacca

Ganges

Chittagong

Chin Hills

Letha Range

Mingin Range

Gangaw Range

Kaukkwe Hills

Irrawaddy

Shweli

Shan Plateau

Ponnyadaung Range

Mandalay

Chindwin

Mu

CHINA

Loi Sang
(2475 m)

Mount Victoria
(3053 m)

UPPER BURMA

Pegu Yoma

Inle Lake

Salween

GOLDEN

LAOS

BAY OF BENGAL

Arakan Yoma

Irrawaddy

TRIANGLE

Luang Prabang

Ramree Island

LOWER
BURMA

Sittang

Chiang Mai

Vientiane

Mekong

1830 m   6000 ft
915 m   3000 ft
305 m   1000 ft

Hlaing

Dawna Range

THAILAND

Rangoon

GULF
OF
MARTABAN

Bassein

Dagu

Chao Phraya

IRRAWADDY
DELTA

INDIA

ANDAMAN
ISLANDS

North
Andaman

Bilauktaung Range

Tenasserim Coast

Bangkok

W   E

MERGUI

ARCHIPELAGO

GULF OF THAILAND

ANDAMAN SEA

Isthmus
of Kra

0 25 50 75 100   200   300   400   450 kilometers

0 25 50 75 100   200   250 miles

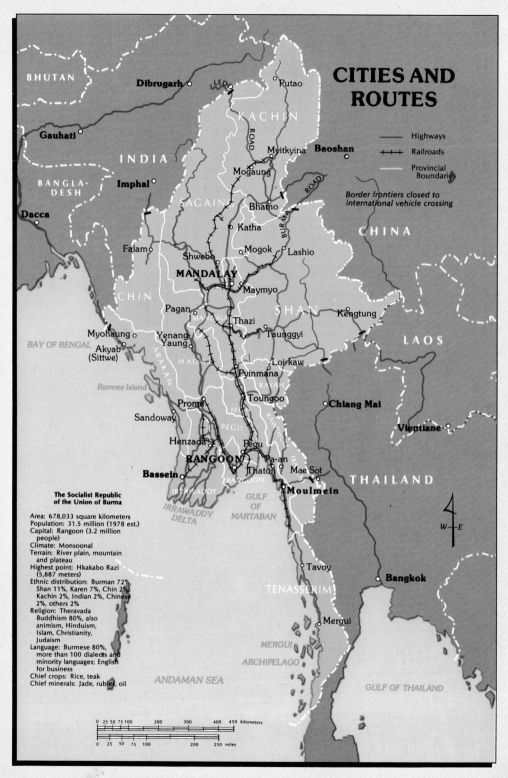

CITIES AND ROUTES

BHUTAN

Dibrugarh   LEDO   Putao

KACHIN

Gauhati

Myitkyina   Baoshan

INDIA

Mogaung

SAGAING

Bhamo

Imphal

Katha

Dacca

Mogok   Lashio

Falam

Shwebo

CHINA

MANDALAY

Maymyo

CHIN

Pagan

SHAN

Kengtung

Thazi

Myohaung   Yenang-   Taunggyi

BAY OF BENGAL   Yaung

LAOS

Akyab   (Sittwe)

ARAKAN   MAGWE

Pyinmana

Loi-kaw

Ramree Island

KAYAH

Prome   Toungoo

Chiang Mai

Sandoway

PEGU   Vientiane

Henzada   Pegu

RANGOON   Pa-an

Bassein   Thaton   Mae Sot

RANGOON   Moulmein

THAILAND

IRRAWADDY   GULF

OF

IRRAWADDY   MARTABAN

DELTA

	Highways
+++	Railroads
	Provincial Boundaries

Border frontiers closed to international vehicle crossing

BURMA ROAD

LEDO ROAD

W — E

The Socialist Republic of the Union of Burma

Area: 678,033 square kilometers
Population: 31.5 million (1978 est.)
Capital: Rangoon (3.2 million people)
Climate: Monsoonal
Terrain: River plain, mountain and plateau
Highest point: Hkakabo Razi (5,887 meters)
Ethnic distribution: Burman 72%, Shan 11%, Karen 7%, Chin 2%, Kachin 2%, Indian 2%, Chinese 2%, others 2%
Religion: Theravada Buddhism 80%, also animism, Hinduism, Islam, Christianity, Judaism
Language: Burmese 80%, more than 100 dialects and minority languages; English for business
Chief crops: Rice, teak
Chief minerals: Jade, rubies, oil

Tavoy   Bangkok

TENASSERIM

Mergui

MERGUI ARCHIPELAGO

ANDAMAN SEA   GULF OF THAILAND

0 25 50 75 100   200   300   400   450 kilometers

0 25 50 75 100   200   250 miles

Map 113

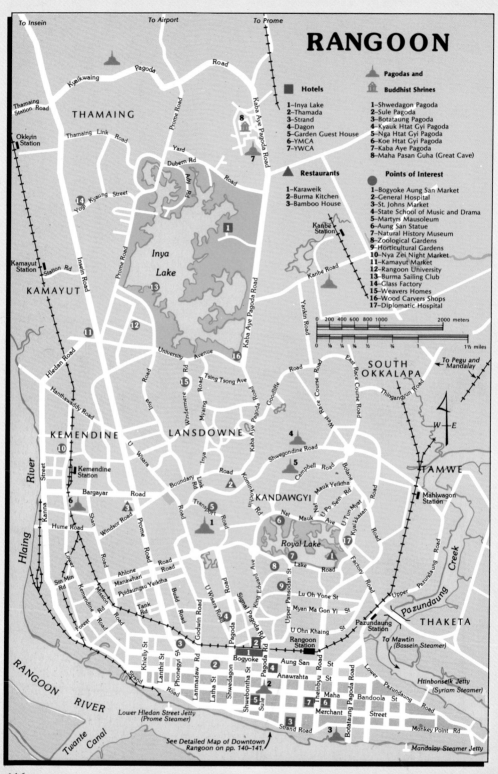

RANGOON

To Insein
To Airport
To Prome

■ **Hotels**

1—Inya Lake
2—Thamada
3—Strand
4—Dagon
5—Garden Guest House
6—YMCA
7—YWCA

▲ **Restaurants**

1—Karaweik
2—Burma Kitchen
3—Bamboo House

🛕 **Pagodas and**
🏛 **Buddhist Shrines**

1—Shwedagon Pagoda
2—Sule Pagoda
3—Botataung Pagoda
4—Kyauk Htat Gyi Pagoda
5—Nga Htat Gyi Pagoda
6—Koe Htat Gyi Pagoda
7—Kaba Aye Pagoda
8—Maha Pasan Guha (Great Cave)

● **Points of Interest**

1—Bogyoke Aung San Market
2—General Hospital
3—St. Johns Market
4—State School of Music and Drama
5—Martyrs Mausoleum
6—Aung San Statue
7—Natural History Museum
8—Zoological Gardens
9—Horticultural Gardens
10—Nya Zei Night Market
11—Kamayut Market
12—Rangoon University
13—Burma Sailing Club
14—Glass Factory
15—Weavers Homes
16—Wood Carvers Shops
17—Diplomatic Hospital

THAMAING

KAMAYUT

Inya Lake

KEMENDINE

LANSDOWNE

KANDAWGYI

SOUTH OKKALAPA

To Pegu and Mandalay

TAMWE

Royal Lake

THAKETA

PAZUNDAUNG

RANGOON RIVER

Hlaing River

Twante Canal

Pazundaung Creek

Lower Hledan Street Jetty
(Prome Steamer)

See Detailed Map of Downtown
Rangoon on pp. 140–141.

Htinbonseik Jetty
(Syriam Steamer)

Mandalay Steamer Jetty

0 200 400 600 800 1000   2000 meters

0 ⅛ ¼ ⅜ ½   ¾   1   1½ miles

RANGOON, 'END OF STRIFE'

Then, a golden mystery upheaved itself on the horizon—a beautiful, winking wonder that blazed in the sun, of a shape that was neither Muslim dome nor Hindu temple spire. It stood upon a green knoll. . . . 'There's the old Shway Dagon,' said my companion. . . . The golden dome said, 'This is Burma, and it will be quite unlike any land you know about.'

—Rudyard Kipling,
Letters From the East *(1889)*

It's nearly 100 years since Kipling sailed up the Rangoon River to the Burmese capital, but the glistening gold stupa of the Shwedagon continues to dominate Rangoon as perhaps no other single structure does in any other major city in the world. The massive pagoda not only is a remarkable architectural achievement, it is also the perfect symbol of a country in which Buddhism pervades every aspect of life. Indeed, it is hard to imagine a more stunning sight than watching the first rays of the dawn light bounce off the brilliant gold-plated pagoda and reflect in the serene waters of the Royal Lake.

But while the Shwedagon may dominate Rangoon from its post on Singuttara Hill three kilometers north of the city center, it is far from the whole show. If you can look beyond the dilapidated British colonial architecture of most of Rangoon's buildings—it seems as though little or nothing has been renovated or even painted since the British left in 1948—you will find a cosmopolitan city of 19th Century charm, with quiet, tree-lined avenues and gracious, fun-loving people.

Water on Three Sides

A burgeoning city of 3.2 million people (the population has tripled in two decades), Rangoon is surrounded on three sides by water. The Hlaing or Rangoon River flows from the Pegu Yoma (hills) down Rangoon's west and south flanks, then continues another 31 kilometers (20 miles) to the Gulf of Martaban. To the east of the city is Pazundaung Creek, a tributary of the Hlaing. North are the

Racecourse Road on Union Day (preceding page); and Mogul Street in colonial days (below).

MOGUL STREET RANGOON 538
P. KLIER. RANGOON.

foothills of the Pegu Yoma; it is here one finds the Shwedagon and the charming lakes artificially created by the British, now the centers of thriving residential districts.

Ceylonese chronicles indicate there was a settlement in the region of present-day Rangoon about 2,500 years ago. Probably a coastal fishing village or a minor Indian trading colony, Okkala, as the settlement was known, grew in fame after the construction of the Shwedagon. For centuries, its history was inextricably bound to that of the great golden pagoda.

'The Town With The Golden Pagoda'

We first hear of "Dagon, the town with the Golden Pagoda," from European travelers in the 16th Century. The English merchant Ralph Fitch in 1586 described the Shwedagon as "the fairest place, as I suppose, that is in the world." But it was the nearby town of Syriam, across the Pegu and Hlaing Rivers from Dagon, that was the most important European trading colony and Burma's main port well into the 18th Century.

King Alaungpaya essentially founded Rangoon and started it on its modern path in 1755 when he captured the village of Dagon from the Mon people. He called the settlement Yangon, or "End of Strife." With the destruction of Syriam the following year, Rangoon assumed its commercial functions. After the British conquered the town in 1824 during the First Anglo-Burmese War, its importance as a trade port flourished. But fire devastated the town in 1841 and 11 years later it was again almost completely destroyed in the Second Anglo-Burmese War.

Victorian Streets

In the heart of Rangoon is the Sule Pagoda, another gold-crowned stupa reputed to have been built in the 3rd Century B.C. The British used this landmark as the nucleus when they rebuilt Rangoon on a Victorian grid pattern. Although the street names have been changed to Burmese from English, the thoroughfares in the central city still intersect at right angles with mathematical uniformity.

Rangoon may have been a coastal village when the Shwedagon was built. But in 2,500 years, a vast delta has been created in Lower Burma by the Irra-

waddy and Hlaing carrying silt to the sea. Still, Rangoon's river is easily navigable to the capital and beyond, and a vast majority of Burma's import and export trade is still handled on Rangoon's docks.

Industrial suburbs have recently sprung up in the eastern and northern sections of the city, providing work for many of the immigrants flocking to the Rangoon area. There is a sizeable Indian community in the city—a holdover from the time when Burma was a part of the British India colony—as well as a large number of Chinese and indigenous ethnic minorities.

A stroll through Burma's capital is a unique experience. In what other modern city of more than three million people would the tallest structures be pagodas? There are no high-rises in Rangoon. In what other modern city would the streets be so free of the hectic madness of traffic? Because cars are so expensive, most people depend for transportation on jitney-type local buses, horse and bullock carts, trishaws or bicycles. And in what other 20th Century city would nightlife and commercialism be virtually nonexistent, save for the street markets? Welcome to Rangoon.

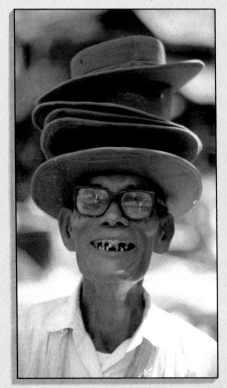

Rangoon's Indian quarter (left); and a happy hat peddler (right).

THE GREAT GILDED SHWEDAGON PAGODA

The Shwe Dagon rose superb, glistening with its gold, like a sudden hope in the dark night of the soul of which the mystics write, glistening against the fog and smoke of the thriving city.

—W. Somerset Maugham, The
    Gentleman in the Parlour (1930)

It has been said there is more gold on the Shwedagon Pagoda than in the vaults of the Bank of England. Given the way inflation has eroded the West's financial reserves in recent years, few would deny the possibility. The massive bell-shaped stupa, which soars nearly 100 meters (326 feet) above its hilltop surroundings, is a treasure-trove inside and out.

Inside, according to legend (see below), are enshrined eight hairs of the last Buddha, as well as relics of three previous Buddhas (who are said to come at 5,000 year intervals). And outside . . . well, the stupa is plated with 8,688 solid gold slabs, each worth more than US$400 today. The tip of the stupa is set with 5,448 diamonds and 2,317 rubies, sapphires and topaz. A huge emerald sits in the middle to catch the first and last rays of the sun. All this is mounted on and above a 10-meter (33-foot) *hti* (umbrella), built upon seven gold-plated bars, decorated with 1,065 golden and 420 silver bells. The golden stupa is surrounded by more than 100 other buildings—smaller stupas, pavilions and administrative halls.

It is here, of course—at the gem of gems for every Buddhist in a staunchly Buddhist country—that any tour of Rangoon should begin.

A Queen's Weight in Gold

While the origins of the pagoda are shrouded in legend, it certainly was well-established by the time Pagan dominated Burma in the 11th Century. Anawrahta visited the Shwedagon during one of his southern campaigns. In 1372, King Byinnya U of Pegu had the pagoda renovated, and 50 years later King Binnyagyan raised the stupa to a height of 90 meters (295 feet).

Binnyagyan's successor, Queen Shinsawbu (ruled 1453–1472), is still revered today for giving the pagoda its present

The Legend of Shwedagon

King Okkalapa of Suvannabhumi, land of the Talaings, lived in the region near Singuttara Hill in Lower Burma at the time Siddhartha Gautama was a young man in northern India. The hill was a holy place, because relics of three past Buddhas—a staff, a water dipper and a piece of garment—were enshrined atop the hill. Yet because nearly 5,000 years had passed since the last Buddha had walked the Earth, the hill would soon lose its blessedness unless the next Buddha appeared and offered a gift. So Okkalapa spent many hours atop the hill, meditating and praying that relics might be obtained.

In India, meanwhile, Gautama achieved enlightenment under the Bodhi tree in Bodhgaya. Soon he magically appeared before Okkalapa and promised that the king's wish would be granted. He thereupon meditated under the Bodhi tree for 49 days before accepting his first gift: a honey-cake offered by Tapussa and Bhallika, merchant brothers from the village of Okkala. To express his gratitude, Gautama plucked eight hairs from his head and gave them to the merchants.

The merchants' journey home was beset with problems. On the overland leg of the trip, the king of Ajetta robbed them of two of the Buddha's hairs; while crossing the Bay of Bengal, the seabed-dwelling king of the Nagas took two more.

But when they reached Okkala, King Okkalapa had a great feast prepared. The native gods and *nats* took part, and together they decided a place to erect a stupa for enshrining all the Buddha relics.

When King Okkalapa opened the casket containing the Buddha's hairs, he discovered that all eight hairs were miraculously in place, despite the robbery of half of them. As he did so, the hairs emitted a brilliant light that rose high above the palm trees and radiated to all corners of all worlds. Suddenly the blind could see again, the deaf could hear, the dumb could speak, and the lame could walk. The earth quaked, lightning flashed, the trees blossomed and bore fruit, and a shower of precious stones rained down.

A 20-meter (66-foot) high golden pagoda was erected over the shrine containing the relics. Smaller pagodas of silver, tin, copper, lead, marble and iron brick were built one over the other, within the golden pagoda, to enshrine the relics.

Preceding pages, the Shwedagon about 1900, and as it looks today. A *chinthe* guards the entrance (left).

shape and form. She established the terraces and walls around the stupa, and gave her weight in gold (40 kilograms, or 90 pounds, to be exact) to be beaten into gold leaf and used to plate the stupa. This act has been repeated by many rulers in the course of the Shwedagon's history, as thin layers of gold do not long withstand the region's heavy seasonal rainfall. Queen Shinsawbu's renowned successor, Dhammazedi, gave four times his weight in gold. Even today, it is an important event for Burmese families who make a pilgrimage to the pagoda to be able to buy a packet of gold leaf at a pagoda bazaar, and paste their offering to the Shwedagon or another stupa or Buddha image at the pagoda.

In 1485, Dhammazedi erected three stones on the Shwedagon's eastern stairway, telling the history of the pagoda from the time of its legendary founding in Burmese, Pali and Mon languages. The inscriptions can still be seen today.

Much of the ensuing history of the Shwedagon is the story of its bells. A bell weighing almost 30 tons, which Dhammazedi had donated, was plundered in 1608 by the Portuguese mercenary Philip de Brito y Nicote, who was based in Syriam. De Brito intended to melt the bell down to make cannons—but as he attempted to ferry it across the Pegu River, it dropped into the water and was never recovered.

The Pagoda's Great Bells

King Hsinbyushin of the Konbaung dynasty raised the stupa to its current height after a devastating 1768 earthquake brought down the top of the pagoda. His son, Singu, had a 23-ton bronze bell cast in 1779; known as the Maha Gandha bell, it can be found today on the northwest side of the main pagoda platform. The British pillaged the pagoda during their 1824 to 1826 wartime occupation and tried to carry the bell to Calcutta, but fell victim to the same fate as de Brito: This bell, too, sank into the river. The British failed in attempts to raise it. The Burmese said they would raise the bell on the condition it would be returned to its original resting place in the pagoda, and the British, thinking nothing would come of the attempt, agreed. But the Burmese had an ingenious plan. Divers tied countless bamboo poles underneath the bell and floated it to

The Maha Gandha Bell in 1825.

the surface. The undertaking helped to instill the Burmese with nationalism during the years of British occupation.

A third bell, this one weighing over 40 tons, was donated by King Tharrawaddy in 1841 along with another 20 kilograms (45 pounds) of gold-plating. This bell, called the Maha Tissada, today sits on the northeast side of the pagoda enclosure.

British Control, And King Mindon's Defiance

The Shwedagon was under British military control for 77 years between 1852 (the Second Anglo-Burmese War) and 1929. But the Burmese still had access to the pagoda. In 1871, King Mindon of Mandalay sent a new diamond-studded *hti* to the pagoda, leading to a festive procession by some 100,000 Burmese at the Shwedagon. The British were not pleased by the ruler's statement of independence, but were powerless to stop the action.

In the 20th Century, natural disasters have taken their toll. In 1931, two years after British troops left the pagoda, a serious fire broke out at the bottom of the western stairway and raced up and around the northern flank of the Shwedagon before being halted on the eastern stairway. It destroyed many ancient monuments in its path. A 1930 earthquake caused minor damage, and another quake in 1970—the ninth sizeable tremor since the 16th Century—led the Burmese government to undertake a special project to strengthen the pagoda's crown.

Despite its roller-coaster history, the Burmese people are convinced no lasting damage can befall the Shwedagon. Whenever the pagoda has been endangered, generosity has restored it to an even greater glory.

The Pagoda Monsters

The passage most commonly used by visitors to the Shwedagon is the **Southern Stairway** *(zaungdan)* **(1)**, which comes from the direction of the city center. Its 104 steps lead from Shwedagon Pagoda Road to the main platform. Running up both sides of the stairs is a bazaar, licensed by pagoda authorities to sell offerings—flowers and incense—and gilded remembrances to the Buddhist faithful. The entrance is guarded by two

Pagodas dwarf monks on the Shwedagon terrace.

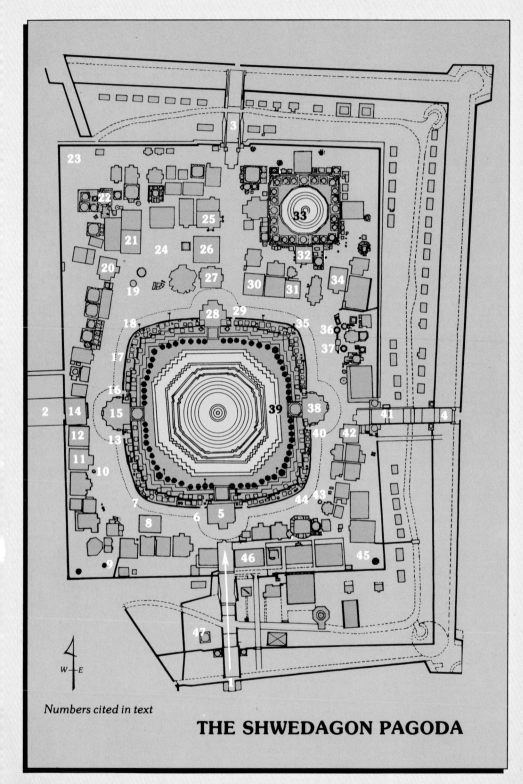

Numbers cited in text

W — E

THE SHWEDAGON PAGODA

mythological figures—a *chinthe* or leogryph, a half-lion, half-griffin beast; and an ogre, a man-eating monster often depicted as a giant. Their principal duty is to make sure each visitor to the pagoda removes his or her shoes and socks before beginning to climb the stairway.

As you climb the steps, you can still see a few older teak beams which survived the April 14, 1852, British assault, although the structure was rebuilt after the Second Anglo-Burmese War. About halfway up, the stairway crosses the former pagoda moat over a concrete bridge; until 1928, there was a drawbridge at this place. The richly embellished landing on the terrace was renovated in 1934 by a wealthy Chinese man. There is a lift at the foot of the south stairs for persons who might find the climb too strenuous.

Fire on the Stairway!

The **Western Stairway** (**2**), which leads up from U Wisara Road, was closed for almost 80 years during the British occupation. Originally erected by Ma May Gale, the wife of King Tharrawaddy, it was damaged during the Second Anglo-Burmese War and kept closed by a British

garrison. In 1931, a year after the stairway had been reopened, a stall at the foot of the stairs caught fire and the blaze spread through much of the pagoda area, causing severe damage to the precincts. This is the longest *zaungdan* with 166 steps. The landing on the platform bears the name "Two Pice Tazaung" (**14**) because of the contribution of two *pice* (a small copper coin) given daily by Buddhist businessmen and bazaar stall holders for the stairway's reconstruction.

The **Northern Stairway** (**3**) was built in 1460 by Queen Shinsawbu. It has 128 steps. The decorative borders to the steps are in the shape of crocodiles. Two water tanks can be seen to the north of the stairway; the one on the right bears the name *thwezekan,* which means "blood wash tank." According to legend, during King Anawrhata's conquest of the Mon capital Thaton, his commander-in-chief, Kyanzittha, used the tank to clean his blood-soaked weapons.

The **Eastern Stairway** (**4**) in a way is an extension of the Bahan bazaar, which lies between the Royal Lake and the Shwedagon. Souvenir, flower and book stalls are here, and there are a couple of tea shops on the stairway near the **Dhammazedi Stones** (**41**), placed there by the king in 1485. This stairway, 118 steps in length, also suffered heavy damage during the British attack on the pagoda in 1852.

'Fantastic Richness'

After the stroll up the stairs, you'll undoubtedly be stunned, as was Maugham, by your first glimpse of the upper terrace:

"At last we reached the great terrace. All about, shrines and pagodas were jumbled pell-mell with the confusion with which trees grow in the jungle. They had been built without design or symmetry, but in the darkness, their gold and marble faintly gleaming, they had a fantastic richness. And then, emerging from among them like a great ship surrounded by lighters, rose dim, severe, and splendid, the Shwe Dagon."

The terrace was created in the 15th Century when the rulers of Pegu leveled off the top of the 58-meter (190-foot) high Singuttara Hill. The terrace measures 275 meters (902 feet) from north to south and 215 meters (705 feet) from east to west. It is 5.6 hectares (14 acres) in

Father and daughter on the way to worship.

area and is supported by a 15-meter (49-foot) high retaining wall.

The main platform is inlaid with marble slabs. The slabs can be very hot under unaccustomed bare feet, so a mat pathway is laid out around the platform. As you walk, you'll discover various pavilions *(tazaungs)* and resting places *(zayats)* with traditional roofs of five, seven or nine tiers.

Method in the Madness: Eight Sides, 64 Stupas

At the center of the platform is the famed gold-covered stupa. Its circumference at platform level is 433 meters (1,421 feet). Its base is octagonal and on each of the eight sides are eight smaller stupas, making 64 in all. (Maugham was wrong; there was method in the madness.) The four stupas opposite the stairways are the largest. At each of the platform's four corners are *manokthihas* (sphinxes), each surrounded by several *chinthes.*

On top of the main platform are three rectangular terraces *(pichayas).* These are topped by octagonal terraces, which in turn are topped by five circular bands.

By means of this geometry, the vertical sides of the terraces merge with the swollen shape of the stupa's bell. The terraces account for 24 meters (79 feet) of the stupa's height.

The next 22 meters (72 feet) comprise the bell *(khaung laung bon).* This is 105 meters (344 feet) in diameter with a design of 16 petals on its shoulder. Above the bell is the 12½-meter (42-foot) high vaulted turban *(baungyit),* then an inverted bowl *(thabeik)* covered with lotus petals *(kyahlan),* which together measure 9½ meters (32 feet) in height. The slender, heavily bejeweled part of the stupa begins above this point with a 16-meter (52-foot) banana bud *(hnget pyaw bu).* The whole edifice is crowned with the 10-meter (33-foot) *hti.* Above it rises a 4.6-meter (15-foot) vane capped by a golden orb *(seinbu),* tipped with a single 76-carat diamond.

Now that you've savored the magnificent stupa, it's time to cast your eyes over the rest of the pagoda's treasures. From the top of the southern stairway, begin walking left, or clockwise, the direction to take at all Buddhist monuments.

Straight ahead at the top of the stairs is the **Temple of the Konagamana Buddha**

A leogryph is silent (left) as a Buddha gets a bath.

(5). Renovated in 1947, this is one of four *tazaungs* dedicated to previous Buddhas. In this temple are a great number of Buddha figures, probably among the oldest to be seen at the pagoda. The style and finish of these figures differ quite markedly from those produced today.

To the left and right of the Konagamana Temple is a **Planetary Post for Mercury (6)**. There are eight of these planetary posts around the stupa, and a gilded alabaster Buddha figure is to be found beside each one. Offerings of flowers and small flags are made here, and the figures are ritually washed. The planet Mercury is associated with a tusked elephant; its special day is *Bohddahu*, which runs from midnight to noon on Wednesday according to the eight-day Burmese week (see next page).

On the southwestern side of the stupa is the **Planetary Post for Saturn (7)** allied with the *naga* (mythological serpent) and Saturday. Opposite this post is the **Tazaung of the Chinese Community (8)**, a pavilion housing 28 small Buddha figures representing the 28 Buddhas who have so far lived on earth. Near the southwest corner of the platform is a **Commemorative Column (9)** inscribed in Burmese, English, French and Russian, a salute to the 1920 student revolt which sparked Burma's drive for independence from Great Britain. A short distance north, the **Guardian Nat of the Shwedagon (10)**, Bo Bo Gyi, is kept behind glass (he's on the right) with the figure of Thagyamin, king of the *nats*.

Entering Nirvana

Continuing down this side of the platform, one next comes to the **Arakan Tazaung (11)**. Next to this pavilion, built by two Arakanese, is an 8½-meter (28-foot) reclining Buddha. The Buddha's head is pointing north, indicating that he is in a state of transition into Nirvana. At his feet is a figure of Ananda, his favorite pupil, as well as figures of Shin Sariputta and Shin Moggalana, two of the Buddha's apostles who left this world before their teacher. Pictures on the rear wall of the Arakan Tazaung depict the legend of the founding of the Kyaik-tiyo Pagoda near Thaton. The pavilion is inlaid with beautiful, intricate wood carvings, as is the neighboring **Chinese Merchants' Tazaung (12)**. There are many Buddha images in a variety of positions here.

Monks at an open-air university.

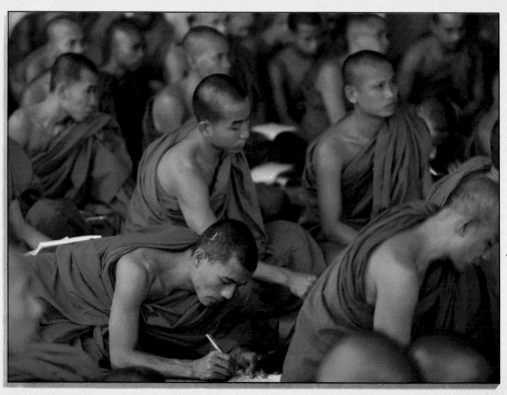

Opposite these two pavilions are **Statues of Mai La Mu and Sakka (13)**. These two legendary figures are said to be the parents of King Okkalapa, the founder of the Shwedagon. They are situated under white umbrellas, the symbol of royalty, on the first terrace on the southwestern side of the stupa. The homeland of Sakka, king of the *nats,* is in the heavenly province of Mount Meru, the center of the universe. Mai La Mu, considered the founder of a pagoda bearing her name in northern Rangoon, is said to have been born from the *La Mu* fruit.

Directly across the platform from the **Two Pice Tazaung (14)** is the **Temple of the Kassapa Buddha (15)**. Originally built by Ma May Gale in 1841, it was destroyed in the great fire of 1931 and later rebuilt. Flanking it is the **Planetary Post for Jupiter (16)**. This planet is allied with the rat and Thursday. Further to the north is a **Statue of King Okkalapa (17)**, situated under a white umbrella on the northwestern side of the stupa. In the northwest corner is the **Planetary Post for Rahu (18)**, the mythical planet allied with the tuskless elephant and Wednesday after noon.

In an open area to the northwest of the stupa is a small octagonal pagoda known as the **Pagoda of the Eight Weekdays (29)**. On each side is a niche containing a small Buddha image, with an animal above it corresponding to the eight Burmese weekdays (see below). Behind it is the **Maha Gandha Bell (20)**, the huge bronze bell King Singu had cast in 1779 and which was raised from the Rangoon River in 1825 after the British attempted to carry it off. The bell weighs 23 tons, is 2.2 meters (7 feet, 3 inches) high and has a diameter of 1.95 meters (6 feet, 5 inches) at its mouth. A 12-line inscription in Burmese requests that the donor (Singu) reach nirvana for performing this good deed.

When Sayadaws Talk, Monks Listen

Across from the bell pavilion is an **Assembly Hall (21)** containing a nine-meter (30-foot) high Buddha image. Lectures on Buddhist teachings are often held in this *tazaung*. The *sayadaws* (abbots), who often speak here in front of several hundred saffron-clad monks, are among the most respected men in Burmese so-

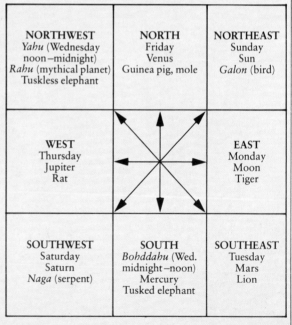

According to traditional Burmese astrology, there are eight weekdays with eight corresponding planets and animals. It is believed that the weekday on which a person is born is a determining factor in his or her life. Shway Yoe, who chronicled Burmese life in the 19th Century, said a man born on Monday would be jealous; on Tuesday, honest; on Wednesday, short-tempered but soon calm again, the trait being intensified on the so-called eighth day of *Yahu* (Wednesday noon to midnight); on Thursday, mild; on Friday, talkative; on Saturday, hot-tempered and quarrelsome; and on Sunday, miserly.

The animals associated with each of the days are keys to understanding interpersonal relations. For example, a marriage between people born on a Saturday and a Thursday would not have good results. The rat and the *naga* (serpent) do not get along well together.

Three systems are combined in the eight-weekday system: cosmology (cardinal point), astrology (planet) and psychology (animal sign). This constitutes the superstructure in which Burmese see themselves involved. The various planetary prayer posts at the Shwedagon are therefore approached by the faithful who seek to influence the appropriate powers.

Eight Days a Week

NORTHWEST *Yahu* (Wednesday noon–midnight) *Rahu* (mythical planet) Tuskless elephant	**NORTH** Friday Venus Guinea pig, mole	**NORTHEAST** Sunday Sun *Galon* (bird)
WEST Thursday Jupiter Rat		**EAST** Monday Moon Tiger
SOUTHWEST Saturday Saturn *Naga* (serpent)	**SOUTH** *Bohddahu* (Wed. midnight–noon) Mercury Tusked elephant	**SOUTHEAST** Tuesday Mars Lion

ciety. The Buddha figure gives the impression of watching the proceedings.

There are a number of small stupas in the northwestern corner of the terrace. In one of these is the **Wonder Working Buddha Image (22)**, virtually always decorated with flowers and surrounded closely by faithful. The gilded Buddha in the stupa's niche has the reputation of being able to fulfill wishes and work miracles. In the far northwest corner of the terrace are two **Bodhi Trees (23)** adorned with flowers and small flags. The smaller of the two trees is a cutting of the Bo tree in Bodhgaya, India, under which the Gautama Buddha gained enlightenment. It was planted by U Nu, first prime minister of Burma. The second tree is older, and was planted in 1903. Its roots surround several small altars.

Returning to the main part of the pavilion, you'll notice an especially busy location. This is known as the **Wish Fulfilling Place (24)**, where devotees kneel, facing the great Shwedagon stupa, and pray that their wishes will come true. In a nearby cluster of pavilions near the north entrance is a **Tazaung With Buddha's Footprint (25)**. Lifesized statues of Indian guards stand in front of this hall,

Lighting candles at a planetary post.

and a dragon stands guard over a representation of the Buddha as prince. In front of the "prince" is a *chidawya,* or footprint of the Buddha. This is actually a copy of the original, but is said to have been made by the Buddha himself from the footprint in the Shwesattaw Pagoda in Upper Burma. The footprint is divided into 108 sections, each of which has a special significance.

The building to the south is the **Library of the Zediyingana Society (26)**. More than 6,000 books, many of them rare texts on religion and Burmese culture, are housed in the library. The Zediyingana Society is one of seven societies responsible for maintaining the pagoda and making necessary improvements. Between the library and the stupa is the **Sandawdwin Tazaung (27)**, built in 1879 over the spring in which, according to legend, the Buddha's eight hairs were washed before they were enshrined. The spring is said to be fed by the Irrawaddy River.

On the north side of the main stupa is the **Temple of the Gautama Buddha (28)**. It is dedicated to the Buddha whose world dominion will last until the 45th Century. Beside it is the **Planetary Post**

for **Venus** (29), especially frequented by persons born on Fridays. Across the platform is the **Mahabodhi Pagoda** (30), a replica of the original pagoda of the same name in Bodhgaya, India. It is noticeably different from all other pagodas in the Shwedagon precincts which are built in Burman or Mon style.

A Burmese Oracle

Across from the northeast corner of the stupa is the **Kannaze Tazaung** (31). Legend says it was here that King Okkalapa prayed for relics of the Gautama Buddha. The Buddha figure in this shrine is therefore called Sudaungbyi, "Buddha grants the prayer of the king." In front of this is the "wish-granting stone," a sort of Delphic oracle. One bows before Sudaungbyi and lifts the stone, saying, "May this stone seem light to me, if my wish is to be fulfilled." If the stone still feels heavy, one has not been successful.

North of this pavilion is the **Shin Itzagona Tazaung** (32). Inside it is a Buddha statue with large eyes of different sizes. It is said to have been erected by or for Shin Itzagona, a *zawgyi* (alchemist) from Pagan's early period. According to legend,

his obsession with discovering the Philosopher's Stone, the mythical substance said to be able to change base metals to gold or silver, had plunged the country into poverty. When his final experiment was about to end in failure, he poked out both his eyes to satisfy the king. But in his final casting, he produced the Philosopher's Stone. He quickly sent his assistant to the slaughter house to obtain two eyes which would, with the stone's help, allow him to regain his sight. The assistant returned with one eye from a goat and another from a bull; from that time on, Shin Itzagona was known as "Monk Goat-Bull."

Just to the north is the **Naungdawgyi Pagoda** (33), situated in the place where the eight hairs of the Buddha carried by the merchants Tapussa and Bhallika were originally kept. The stupa, which looks like a smaller version of the great Shwedagon stupa, was reportedly erected by King Okkalapa and was later enlarged by King Bayinnaung. Nearby is the **Maha Tissada Bell** (34), commissioned by King Tharrawaddy in 1841. It weighs 42 tons, is 2.55 meters (8 feet, 4 inches) high and has a diameter of 2.3 meters (7 feet, 6 inches) at its mouth.

The **Planetary Post for the Sun (35)** is at the northeast corner of the great stupa. Its special day, of course, is Sunday; it is associated with the *galon,* the mythical bird (sometimes called *garuda* elsewhere in Southeast Asia) which guards one of the terraces of Mount Meru. Across the platform to the east are a **Replica of the Hti (36)** originally donated by King Hsinbyushin in 1774, and a **Replica of the Apex of the Pagoda (37)**, sent by King Mindon from Mandalay in 1871.

Keep Your Eye on the Hand

Opposite the Eastern Stairway is the **Temple of the Kakusandha Buddha (38)**. It was originally built by the wife of King Tharrawaddy, Ma May Gale, as was the Western Stairway. But the fire of 1931 destroyed it, and it was rebuilt in its original style in 1940. The Buddha figure in this *tazaung* is renowned for the fact that the palm of its right hand is turned upward—contrary to that of other representations of the Buddha. In front of the niche are four more sitting Buddhas, three of which are depicted in the same unusual posture. Behind this temple, in a niche on the eastern side of the upper platform, is the **Tawa Gu Buddha (39)**. This statue is said to be able to work miracles. As the upper platform of the pagoda is reserved for men, a five-kyat admission ticket can be purchased by men only at the administration building on the west side of the pagoda. On the upper platform, the visitor will come across very devout Buddhists, both monks and novices, deep in meditation.

Beside the Kakusandha temple is the **Planetary Post for the Moon (40)**, which is recognized as one of the eight planets in Burmese astrology. The tiger is its animal and Monday is its day. From here, one can turn around and descend the Eastern Stairway a short distance to the **Dhammazedi Stones (41)**. The *tazaung* which originally housed these stones was one of the last buildings destroyed by the 1931 fire before the blaze was finally brought under control. Because of these inscriptions, King Dhammazedi—himself a *zawgyi*—has gone down in Burmese history as the "master of the runes."

Next to the eastern entrance to the terrace is the **U Nyo Tazaung (42)**, which has wood-carved panels relating events in the life of the Gautama Buddha. Close to the southeast corner of the platform is

a **Hamsa Tagundaing (43)** or prayer pillar. Such pillars are said to guarantee the health, prosperity and success of their founders. At the top of the pillars is often found a *hamsa* or *hintha,* sacred bird of the Pegu dynasty. On the southeast side of the great stupa is the **Planetary Post for Mars (44)**. This planet is associated with the lion and Tuesday.

At the far southeastern corner of the terrace is a **Bodhi Tree (45)** which, like its cousin in the northwest corner, is said to be a cutting of the original at Bodhgaya. On the octagonal base which surrounds it is a huge Buddha statue. A **Curio Museum (46)** is situated to the east of the pagoda's south entrance. It contains a collection of small pagodas, statues and other objects.

Partway down the Southern Stairway is a **Pigeon Feeding Square (47)**. Pagoda pilgrims can buy food here to feed the dozens of pigeons, thereby earning merit for a future existence.

The Shwedagon is open daily from 4 a.m. to 9 p.m., giving pre-dawn and post-twilight visitors plenty of leeway. Buses and taxis make the run from downtown Rangoon up Shwedagon Pagoda Road in about 15 minutes.

Pagoda sweepers (left) earn merit; but onlookers (right) do not.

137

EXPLORING RANGOON

> Sule Pagoda Road, with its five theaters, was mobbed with people, dressed identically in shirt, [*longyi*], and rubber sandals, men and women alike puffing thick green cheroots, and looking (as they waved away the smoke with slender dismissing fingers) like a royal breed, strikingly handsome in this collapsing city, a race of dispossessed princes.
>
> –*Paul Theroux*,
> The Great Railway Bazaar *(1975)*

To stroll the streets of Rangoon is to know the "dispossessed princes" of which Theroux writes. In the downtown area, amidst the mildewing gray brick government offices built by the British colonialists, is the city's commercial center, its markets and cinemas. And it is here the true colors of Rangoon's diverse population can be seen.

Theroux again: "I walked aimlessly . . . slowing down at temples where children—still awake at 11 at night—wove ropes of flowers and laughed before Buddhas. Older people knelt in veneration, or set up displays of fruit, balancing a melon in a hand of bananas on a temple shelf and sticking a red paper flag into the melon. Elderly women leaned against flower stalls, the smoking cheroots in their hands giving them a look of haughtiness and self-possession."

A Synagogue, Cinemas, And Savory Spices

Walking through Rangoon like Theroux, you'll see the pagodas sending their golden spires skyward among an assortment of latter-day Chinese and Hindu temples, Islamic mosques, Anglican cathedrals and a Jewish synagogue. You'll see the movie theaters, where the citizens flock to watch Burmese, Indian and Japanese features, with an occasional European or American film. You'll see tiny residences opening directly onto the sidewalks, where vendors have spread a miscellany of spices and cheap domestic goods for sale to the highest bidder.

Occasionally, most frequently during the dry season, you'll stumble upon a night festival, featuring colorful shops and cafes lining the streets and a late-night performance of the *pwe*, Burmese dance drama. And any time of the year, day or night, you'll find loquacious Burmese with their "whickin' white cheroot" of which Kipling once wrote so eloquently.

Sule Pagoda: The Heart of the City

If the Shwedagon is the soul of Rangoon, then the **Sule Pagoda** is its heart. For centuries, it has been the focus of much of the social and religious activity of the city. The British established the pagoda as the center of the urban area when they structured their grid-street system around it in the mid-19th Century, and today, the 48-meter (157-foot) pagoda remains the tallest building in the downtown area.

The origins of the Sule Pagoda are bound up in the mythical pre-history of Burma. Perhaps the most credible tale is that of two monks, Sona and Uttara, who were sent from India as missionaries to Thaton after the Third Buddhist Synod about 230 B.C. After some hesitation, the

Preceding pages, longyi-clad balloon seller and a modern Superman; bathing in a Rangoon street, left; and the Strand Hotel dining room, right.

King of Thaton gave them permission to have a shrine erected at the foot of Singuttara Hill. In it the monks preserved a hair of the Buddha which they had carried from India.

For centuries, the pagoda was known as Kyaik Athok ("Pagoda containing the hair relic" in the Mon language) or Sura Zedi, after Maha Sura, minister to the King of Thaton who supervised construction of the pagoda. The name Sule Pagoda comes from a later period and can be linked with the Sule Nat, guardian spirit of Singuttara Hill.

The octagonal structure of the Sule Pagoda, which is consistent up to the bell and inverted bowl, clearly indicates its Brahman-Buddhist heritage. During the first centuries of the Christian era, when the influence of Indian merchants and settlers was especially strong, astrology blended with *nat* worship and Buddhist doctrine to create the unique Burmese brand of Buddhism. Even today, the Sule Pagoda, whose name and shape document this development, is a center for astrologers and fortune-tellers.

Around the outside of the Sule Pagoda, which in the daytime acts as a tranquil traffic island in the middle of the city's busiest streets, are a variety of small shops and businesses. Inside the pagoda are the usual shrines and Buddha images, including four colorful Buddhas with neon halos behind their heads! Temple festivals and feasts are frequent evening events, and visitors might be lucky enough to catch one after dark. If a special procession is expected, the gates of the Sule Pagoda are kept open past the usual 10 p.m. closing time.

As with all pagodas, visitors should saunter around in a clockwise direction. The Sule Pagoda's eight sides, like those of the Shwedagon, are dedicated respectively to the days, planets and animals of the eight cardinal points. Its gold coat has worn off, so generous donations are now being collected to finance a new gilding.

Colonial Remnants And Museum Relics

On the northeast corner of Sule Pagoda Road and Maha Bandoola Street, facing the pagoda, is the **Rangoon City Hall**. Built by the British (of course), it is a massive stone structure worth a glance for its colonial architecture with a Burmese touch. Especially, note the tradi-

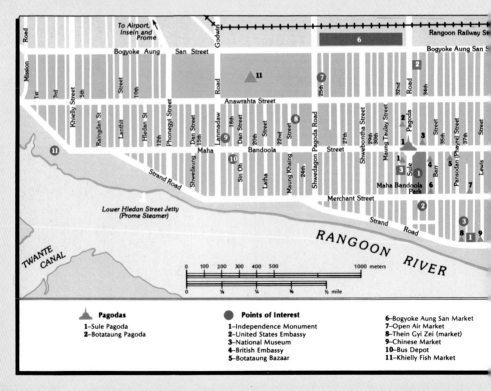

Pagodas
1–Sule Pagoda
2–Botataung Pagoda

Points of Interest
1–Independence Monument
2–United States Embassy
3–National Museum
4–British Embassy
5–Botataung Bazaar

6–Bogyoke Aung San Market
7–Open Air Market
8–Thein Gyi Zei (market)
9–Chinese Market
10–Bus Depot
11–Khielly Fish Market

tional Burmese peacock seal high over the entrance. On the southeast corner of the intersection is **Maha Bandoola Park,** named after a Burmese general of the First Anglo-Burmese War. In the center of the park is the **Independence Monument,** a 46-meter (150-foot) obelisk surrounded by five smaller nine-meter (30-foot) pillars. The monument represents Burma's five former semi-autonomous states—Shan, Kachin, Karen, Kayah and Chin—in harmonious union with their larger Burmese brother. Facing the square on the east side is the British-built **Supreme Court and High Court Building.**

If you travel east a block on Merchant Street, south of the park, then turn south on Pansodan (Phayre) Street, you'll find the **National Museum.** The showpiece of the museum is the Lion's Throne, on which King Thibaw once sat in his hall of audience at Mandalay Palace. Taken from Mandalay in 1886 after the Third Anglo-Burmese War, the throne and 52 other royal regalia were carried off by the English. Some items were left in the Indian Museum in Calcutta; others were kept in the Victoria and Albert Museum in London. They were returned to Burma

as a gesture of good will in 1964 after Ne Win's state visit to England.

The throne, made of wood, is 8.1 meters (27 feet) high and is inlaid with gold and lacquer work. It is a particularly striking example of the Burmese art of wood carving. Among the other Mandalay Regalia, as they are known, are gem-studded arms, swords, jewelry and serving dishes. In the archaeological section of the museum are artifacts from Burma's early history in Beikthano, Sri Kṣetra and Pagan. There is a 18th Century bronze cannon, a crocodile harp and many other items. The museum is open from 10 a.m. to 3 p.m. Sunday through Thursday and from 1 to 3 p.m. Saturday. It is closed Friday and public holidays.

Living in the Past

Just around the corner from the National Museum, on Strand Road, is the famous **Strand Hotel.** By stopping for a night or just for a meal, a visitor can get nostalgic for the British colonial era. Most of the mosquito-infested rooms are still cooled by electric "paddle fans;" Indian waiters hover over every table in the high-ceilinged restaurant; and while the

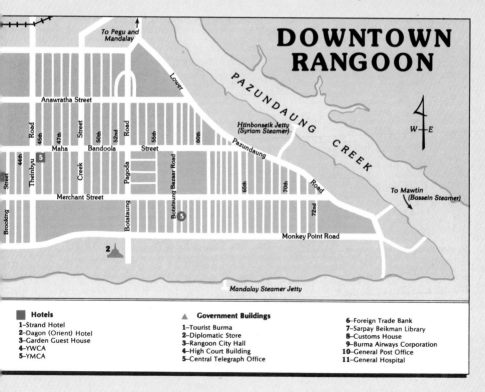

Hotels
1–Strand Hotel
2–Dagon (Orient) Hotel
3–Garden Guest House
4–YWCA
5–YMCA

Government Buildings
1–Tourist Burma
2–Diplomatic Store
3–Rangoon City Hall
4–High Court Building
5–Central Telegraph Office

6–Foreign Trade Bank
7–Sarpay Beikman Library
8–Customs House
9–Burma Airways Corporation
10–General Post Office
11–General Hospital

hotel facade may be crumbling and the paint peeling, it's worth stepping into the teak-furnished lounge for a Mandalay Beer from the People's Brewery. With the bar open nightly until 9, the Strand is one of the few places in Rangoon to offer any semblance of "night life."

Across the street from the Strand, on the other side of a small park, you can see the muddy **Rangoon (Hlaing) River.** Several wharves jut into the river from one end of Rangoon to the other, handling the country's maritime trade. Further downstream are jetties for steamers plying the route between Rangoon and Mandalay.

Beholding the Botataung

Heading east on Strand Road for several blocks, you'll come to the **Botataung Pagoda.** When eight Indian monks carried some relics of the Buddha here more than 2,000 years ago, 1,000 military officers *(bo tataung)* formed a guard of honor at the place where the rebuilt pagoda stands today.

The original Botataung was destroyed on Nov. 8, 1943, when an Allied bomb scored a direct hit. During the clean-up

work, a golden casket in the shape of a stupa was found—and it contained a hair and two other relics of the Buddha. In addition, about 700 gold, silver and bronze statues were uncovered, as well as a number of terra-cotta tablets. One of these tablets was of special interest; it was inscribed both in Pali and in the south Indian Brahmi script, from which modern Burmese developed.

Part of the find is displayed in the pagoda today. However, the relics and more valuable objects have been locked away once again. Among them is the tooth of the Buddha, which Alaungsithu, one of the kings of Pagan, tried unsuccessfully to acquire from Nan-ch'ao (now China's Yunnan province) in 1115. It was presented to the Burmese people by the People's Republic of China in 1960.

The 40-meter (131-foot) stupa is unusual in that it is hollow, and visitors are able to walk around inside of it. A glass mosaic covers the interior of the room enclosed within the bell-shaped form of the stupa. There are many small alcoves for private meditation. Outside the pagoda is a small lake with thousands of turtles; nearby stalls sell food for the tur-

Victorian High Court building.

tles, enabling the generous to acquire merit for a future existence.

At the end of Botataung Pagoda Road is the Syriam Jetty. Persons intent on making the 45-minute ferry trip across the river to Syriam should be warned, however, that the Syriam ferry leaves not from this jetty, but from the Htinbonseik Jetty on Pazundaung Creek, some distance east on Monkey Point Road (the eastern extension of Strand Road), then north. On the way, you'll pass near the lively **Botataung Bazaar** on the left and a teak mill on the right.

Cigarettes, Spices, and Black-Market Stereos

West and north of the Sule Pagoda is Rangoon's market district. Before the Second World War, a large majority of the inhabitants of Rangoon were Indian or Chinese. The influence of their particular lifestyles is still reflected in Burmese markets today. The flavor of an Oriental bazaar—the supermarket of pre-industrial times—pervades despite the inevitable adaptation to modern needs.

Largest of Rangoon's markets is the **Bogyoke Aung San Market** (formerly the Scott Market). At the corner of Sule Pagoda Road and Bogyoke Aung San Street, across from the red-brick **Railway Administration Building** with its Moorish arches, you can find under one roof all the consumer goods a Burmese family could possibly need or want. From spices to bicycles, local artifacts to Japanese stereo systems (smuggled into the country), everything is here. One can quite easily find the Western whisky and cigarettes sold to black marketeers earlier the same day by Western travelers, who purchased the goods in duty-free shops in Bangkok or Calcutta airports!

The days when it was difficult to buy so much as an electric light bulb in Rangoon seem to be over, however. Today, nearly everyone can get hold of the most important items for everyday use. Those with special demands go to the "gray importers" and pay a deposit on the particular item they want; this is then procured, sooner or later, from Thailand. Larger items are landed by ship somewhere on the Tenasserim coast, where effective customs control is impossible. Smaller items are carried directly over the mountains on the Thailand-Burma border by smugglers. Prices of goods ac-

Travelers' choice, the Strand Hotel.

quired in this manner are correspondingly high, but once the smuggled goods reach the market stalls, authorities seem to turn a blind eye to them. Small street vendors are subjected to sporadic raids, but the richer merchants seem to have few problems.

Apart from consumer goods, visitors to Burma will find a wide variety of textiles and craft items in the Bogyoke Market. Woodcarvers, metalworkers, artists and weavers all have their stalls; lacquerware, dolls, musical instruments, printed *longyis,* Shan bags and wickerware are all attractive. And the fruit is delicious—just be sure to wash and peel it before eating!

The Fabled '1,000 Scents of the Orient'

To the south of the Bogyoke Market, off Shwedagon Pagoda Road, are the **Open Air Market**—especially noted for the delicious Chinese soup sold at many of its stalls—and, on the other side of an interesting **Hindu Temple** on Anawrahta Street, the **Thein Gyi Zei** (Indian market). The oft-described "1,000 scents of the Orient" dominate this wholesale fruit and vegetable market. Mounds of red chilies and fragrant cinnamon bark, boxes of tropical fruits like mangosteen and durian, dried fish and seafoods, medicinal herbs and bottled concoctions, indigenous snack treats to tempt the palate . . . it's hard to turn away.

Mushrooms and Songbirds

But there's an equally fascinating destination when you leave the Indian market. Turn west on Maha Bandoola Street and follow it to Rangoon's Chinatown. Here, at the corner of Lan Ma Daw Road, is the **Chinese Market.** Here amidst the flowers, live crabs and dried mushrooms, you'll find caged songbirds, tropical fish for aquariums, and handmade rice paper. As with the Indian market, the earlier you arrive in the morning, the better the selection. Adjoining the Chinese market is an iron bazaar, and on the next block south are a row of night food stalls and a colorful **Chinese Temple.**

Those who aren't yet tired of walking can continue several blocks further west of Maha Bandoola Street to the **Khielly Fish Market.** But most will be satisfied to

Outdoor cafe on Sule Pagoda Road.

spend hours browsing through the streets between the Chinese Market and the Sule Pagoda, and north to the Bogyoke Market. For this quadrant is the scene of an almost picture-book-like hustle and bustle, especially in the early evening hours. The racial diversity and air of industry for which Rangoon was famous in the British colonial era can still be found here today.

A half-block north of the Sule Pagoda, on the west side of Sule Pagoda Road, is the **Diplomatic Store**. Tourists are encouraged to shop here, especially for precious stones, on which the Burmese government has a monopoly. In fact, it is safer to make jewelry purchases here, as quality is guaranteed. There is a wide selection of other goods as well—but all payment must be made in foreign currency, and diplomats who shop here pay only about a third of what tourists must pay for the same items. One thing the tourist may find of interest, however, is the domestic cigarette Duya, of which he is allowed to buy five cartons daily. As Burmese are not allowed to shop in the Diplomatic Store, they are frequently found just outside its door, hoping to bargain for the Duyas.

The harbor, where old meets new.

North of the Market, Where the Music Always Plays

Traveling north on Shwedagon Pagoda Road, just past the Bogyoke Market, is the **State School of Music and Drama**. Associated with the State School of Fine Art, Music and Dancing in Mandalay, this is where the traditional Burmese art forms, once promoted by the Royal Family, are taught and demonstrated. Performances of dancing, music, drama and puppet theatre take place during the rainy season at 2 p.m. every Saturday and Sunday, in the great Jubilee Hall. Weekdays from November to June, traditional music and dance lessons can be observed.

Beyond the Shwedagon, on a hill on Transport Road just to the north, is the **Martyrs Mausoleum**. This patriotic monument contains the tombs of Aung San, the father of the Burmese independence movement, and seven of his ministers who were assassinated during a cabinet meeting on July 17, 1947. Aung San was only 31 at the time. The prewar prime minister, U Saw, was later found to be the instigator of the plot, and was executed in May 1948 along with the hired assassins.

From the mausoleum, go north to the intersection of Shwegondine Road, then turn east. You'll pass the Burma Kitchen, an exclusive restaurant noted for its fine native cuisine, and soon reach the **Kyauk Htat Gyi Pagoda**. Not really a pagoda in the traditional sense, the Kyauk Htat Gyi is actually a *tazaung* (pavilion) housing a 70-meter (230-foot) long reclining Buddha. The Buddha figure is little more than a decade old, and required a total donation in excess of 500,000 kyats (US $68,000) to produce. Prior to that an older Buddha figure dating from the turn of the 20th Century was housed under the pagoda's roof. The newer sculpture is larger than the reclining Buddha of Pegu, but is not as well known or venerated. Elsewhere in the pagoda enclosure is a center for the study of sacred Buddhist manuscripts. About 600 monks live in the monastery annex and spend their days meditating and studying the old Pali texts.

Traveling south from here, you'll pass the **Nga Htat Gyi** on Campbell Road. Here, a huge sitting Buddha, sometimes called the "five-story Buddha" because of its size, is housed in the **Ashay Tawya Kyaung** monastery.

Picnics and Playgrounds
Beneath the Martyr's Gaze

On the north shore of the **Royal Lakes** is **Bogyoke Aung San Park**, featuring a statue of Burma's most famous martyr. The park stretches beyond the statue into the lake like fingers on a hand. Plants and trees have been labeled for easy identification as in a botanical garden. The children's playgrounds and picnic areas have become favorite attractions for Rangoon's citizens, and families can be seen idling away leisure hours beside the lake. Tourists seeking a break from the rigors of sightseeing can find it here beside the lake, famous for its shimmering reflection of the Shwedagon Pagoda.

Another memorable view is from the **Karaweik Restaurant** on the lake's eastern shore. This luxurious dining spot, constructed in the early 1970s, was designed after the distinctive *pyi-gyi-mun* barge of Burmese royalty. With its double bow depicting the mythological *karaweik*, a water bird from Indian pre-history, and a many-tiered pagoda carried on top, the Karaweik represents a fine work of traditional Burmese architecture. Although the restaurant was constructed of brick

The Karaweik Restaurant on the Royal Lakes.

and concrete (wood was ruled out because of its relatively short lifespan) and anchored to the lake bottom, the interior contains some marvelous lacquer work embellished with mosaic in glass, marble, and mother-of-pearl. You have to pay a small admission charge just to take a look, but once inside, the food is good—and the view of the Shwedagon is stunning. Classical dance performances are held here on a nightly basis.

From Orchids to Apes

On the southern shore of the Royal Lakes are several attractions. The Natural History Museum no longer exists—it has been remodeled into the new Kandawgyi Royal Lake Hotel—but the flora can be examined in more detail at the **Horticultural Gardens** off Lu Oh Yone Street, while the **Zoological Gardens** on King Edward Avenue have a good collection of birds, reptiles, apes and the like. The main attraction used to be a white elephant, the very possession of which was enough to begin wars during the course of Burma's rocky history (see below). But the animal died in 1979. The zoo is open from 6 a.m. to 6 p.m. daily, and at 4 o'clock every afternoon, visitors are permitted to ride the elephants and camels.

The next station northwest of Rangoon on the circle line is Kemendine where, a short walk away from the station, is the **Koe Htat Gyi Pagoda** on Bargayar Road. There is a 20-meter (65-foot) high sitting Buddha inside the pagoda, and a small casket inside the statue is said to contain relics of the Buddha and some of his disciples. In the area of the pagoda are a great many *kyaungs* (monasteries), so this is a good place to watch the *pongyis* (monks) as they pour onto the streets early in the morning with their begging bowls. If you happen to come to Kemendine in the evening, the **Night Market (Nya Zei)** is lively.

Continuing northeast through the winding residential streets north of the Shwedagon, past the "Rangoon modern" stucco houses built for westerners during the colonial era, you'll reach the huge man-made Inya Lake. On the southern shore are the **Rangoon Arts and Sciences University**, with over 10,000 students and some of the most modern architecture in the city, and the **Burma Sailing Club**, which sponsors regular races on the lake. There are a variety of

---

Its Exalted Majesty The White Elephant

At the center of the Brahman cosmology to which Burma's kings turned for ritual was the *chakravarti,* or universal monarch. There were seven "gems" or visible signs by which he could be recognized, all of them necessary for him to rule over the four main islands and 2,000 smaller islands in the cosmos of Buddhism. The "gems" were the golden wheel of the law (the Dharma), the heavenly guardians of the treasury, the divine horse, the bejeweled maiden, the miracle-working gem, the invincible general, and the white elephant.

Of these seven, perhaps the white elephant was the most widely sought, Gautama Buddha, in his last but one incarnation, was (according to legend) a white elephant. And even the Irrawaddy River was named after the white elephant (Erawon) on which the god Indra rides.

The last two Burmese kings, Mindon and Thibaw, both were in possession of a white elephant. The animal had its own palace, was guarded by 100 soldiers and taken care of by 30 servants, one of them a minister. As a sinecure it was granted a province whose revenue it could "eat up." Every day it was bathed in water scented with sandalwood, while dancers and singers entertained it. Indeed, the elephant was accorded second place to the king in the ritual hierarchy. White umbrellas, nine of which were mounted over the king, were the exclusive symbols of regal majesty; only the white elephant was allowed to possess two white umbrellas in addition to its four golden ones.

It was not necessary that an elephant be pure white to qualify for these luxuries. But it had to have several other distinguishing features, as well as meet these three conditions: (1) It must have four toenails instead of five. (2) Its skin must turn red, not black, when sprayed with water. (3) Its eyes must have a yellow iris enclosed by a red ring.

When King Thibaw was forced into exile, Its Majesty the White Elephant was exiled as well. But its normal expenses proved to be too much for the British, who brought it to the Rangoon Zoo in 1886. It died soon thereafter—and some say the cause of death was a broken heart.

artisans shops in the area of the lake, including weavers (No. 113 Windermere Road is a noted location), woodcarvers (especially near the corner of University Avenue and Kaba Aye Pagoda Road) and glassblowers (just off Yogi Kyaung Street). But perhaps the best known structure on the lake is the **Inya Lake Hotel**, built by the Soviet Union in the early 1960s. Unfortunately for Burma, as *New York Times* correspondent Robert Trumbull once noted, "the Soviet architects drew plans for a building more suited to the Russian climate than the steamy heat and humidity of tropical Rangoon."

U Nu and the Legend
Of the Kaba Aye Pagoda

Just a little north of Inya Lake is the **Kaba Aye Pagoda**. U Nu, the first prime minister of independent Burma, had this structure built between 1950 and 1952. Although it is a contemporary building, there is already a legend surrounding its origin. An old man dressed in white appeared before the monk Saya Htay while the latter was meditating near the town of Pakokku on the Irrawaddy, and handed the monk a bamboo pole covered with writing. He requested that Saya Htay pass the pole on to U Nu, with the demand that the prime minister do more for Buddhism. U Nu, as well versed in religious affairs as in politics, received the bamboo pole—and complied with this miraculous demand. He built the Kaba Aye Pagoda 12 kilometers (7½ miles) north of downtown Rangoon in preparation for the Sixth Buddhist Synod of 1954 to 1956, and dedicated the pagoda to the cause of world peace.

While lacking some of the aesthetic appeal of other Rangoon pagodas, the Kaba Aye is interesting nonetheless. Circular in shape, its height and diameter are an identical 34 meters (112 feet), and it contains relics of the two most important disciples of the Buddha. These were discovered in 1851 by the English general Cunningham in India, and given to Burma after many years in the British Museum. Five 2.4-meter (7-foot, 10-inch) high Buddha statues stand opposite each of the five pagoda entrances, and a platform holds another 28 small gold-plated statues, representing the 28 previous Buddhas. In the inner temple is a Buddha figure cast with 500 kilograms (1,102 pounds) of silver.

Kyauk Htat Gyi Pagoda.

A 'Great Cave' Built By Volunteer Labor

On the grounds of the Kaba Aye is the Maha Pasana Guha, or "great cave." U Nu had this artificial cave specially built for the Sixth Buddhist Synod. It is supposed to resemble India's Satta Panni Cave, where the First Buddhist Synod took place shortly after the Buddha's death. Devout Buddhists worked voluntarily, without pay, on the construction of the cave, which measures 139 by 113 meters (456 by 371 feet) and has an assembly hall which can contain up to 10,000 people. The cave was completed after 14 months' work on May 14, 1954, just three days before the start of the synod.

Upon conclusion of the Sixth Buddhist Synod, an **Institute for Advanced Buddhistic Studies** was founded with headquarters in the Kaba Aye Pagoda compound. Ford Foundation funds helped with construction of its handsome building, a blend of modern architecture and traditional symbolism.

Further north, near the Rangoon Airport in the suburb of Okkalapa, is the **Mai La Mu Pagoda**. It is named after the mother of King Okkalapa, founder of Dagon. Legend maintains that Mai La Mu had this pagoda built to alleviate the suffering she felt upon the death of her young grandson. Her statue can be seen on the southwestern flank of the Shwedagon Pagoda. This pagoda is of particular interest because it contains illustrations and figures from the *Jataka* tales—depicting the Buddha in earlier lives—fashioned in a curiously Burmese style. There is also a reclining Buddha.

West of the airport, in Insein township, is the **Ah Lain Nga Sint Pagoda**. This pagoda serves as a center of worship for the branch of Burmese Buddhism laying greatest emphasis on the belief in occult and supernatural phenomena. The grounds contain a five-story tower, a hall with statues of all kinds of occult figures, and a *kyaung* where monks and believers in the occult live.

It is fitting that this pagoda is outside Rangoon city itself. Generally speaking, Rangoon residents are not as inclined to worship supernatural deities as are their rural counterparts. But even though few houses in Rangoon today have coconuts hung in their corners in tribute to the house *nat*, few urbanites would totally deny the existence of such spirits.

The Six Buddhist Synods

Theravada and Mahayana Buddhists are not in complete agreement about the dates of the Buddha's life. While Mahayana reckons his birth at 556 B.C. and his death at 476 B.C., Theravada chronicles specify the years 623 B.C. to 544 B.C. The latter date is the starting point for the Buddhist calendar valid in Southeast Asia.

Whichever calendar may be correct, the First Synod took place three months after Gautama Buddha's death and entry into nirvana. It was held in the Satta Panni Cave in Rajagriha in the present-day Indian state of Bihar. The Second Synod was convened in Vesali in northern Bihar not long after. King Ashoka convened the Third Synod—the last joint meeting between the divided sects—in 235 B.C. in Pataliputra. Then the two schools of thought went their separate ways.

The Fourth Synod, summoned by King Kanishka, took place in 78 A.D. in northern India. Theravadins later denied the validity of this synod, maintaining that the Fourth Synod took place in Lanka (Ceylon) between 29 and 13 B.C.

The Fifth Synod, at which the entire text of the *Tripitaka* (Buddhist scripture) was committed to stone tablets for the first time, was held in Mandalay in 1871–72 (see Mandalay chapter).

Modern legend has it that Prime Minister U Nu, who in the early 1950s took a pilgrimage to Buddhism's most important religious sites, had a vision while sitting under the Bodhi tree in Bodhgaya, India. He saw that on the 2,500th anniversary of Gautama's death—a date that would also represent the halfway point of the Buddha's 5,000-year world regency—faithful Buddhists from all over the world would meet in Burma to hear the message of peace and light in a world of hate and war.

Upon his return to Burma, U Nu ordered that work be started immediately on the Maha Pasana Guha artificial cave. It was completed in 1954 three days before the official opening of the Sixth Synod on May 17, the day on which Theravada Buddhists celebrate the birth, enlightenment and death of the Buddha. The synod—which recited, interpreted and emended the *Tripitaka*—lasted for two years, until the next but one full moon day in May, the 2,500th anniversary of Buddha's death.

PEGU, SYRIAM AND THE SOUTH OF BURMA

Near the small town of Hlegu, high-wheeled ox-carts piled high with golden rice trundle down the road, driven by beaming country youths delivering their just-harvested bounty to state purchase stalls.

In ancient Pegu, multitudes of reverent Buddhist worshippers offer incense and flowers to the Shwethalyaung Buddha, a 55-meter (180-foot) long reclining Buddha with a smile to make the Mona Lisa envious.

In Syriam, Moulmein, Bassein and other cities whose names ring like temple bells from Burma's past, citizens carry on their daily activities as they have for centuries, little affected by the modern Western influence that has so dramatically altered lifestyles in other parts of Southeast Asia.

Indeed, once the visitor gets out of Rangoon, he will find a different Burma waiting to be explored and savored. One of the best ways to begin is by making the 80-kilometer (50-mile) day trip to Pegu.

The many monuments of Pegu today stand in solemn witness to the glory that once belonged to this provincial capital. Formerly Burma's greatest seaport—many medieval European travelers commented on its magnificence—the city of 50,000 lies northeast of Rangoon on the Pegu River. The massive Shwemawdaw Pagoda, the famous reclining Buddha and many other reminders of bygone empire are worthy of a visit.

Down the Salween To a 'Golden Land'

To appreciate a trip to Pegu, one must first understand the history of the Talaing (Mon) people in Burma. Like the Pyus (predecessors of the Burmese), they arrived from the north—but the Talaings came a little earlier, and ventured down the Salween River instead of the Irrawaddy. Their "Golden Land of Suvannabhumi" stretched from present-day Malaysia to the Bay of Bengal, with its capital of Thaton situated on the east side of the Sittang River.

According to legend, Pegu at the time was a tiny island off the coast in the Gulf of Martaban. It was so small that there

Preceding pages, the Kyaikpun Pagoda at Pegu; and left, the renowned "Golden Rock."

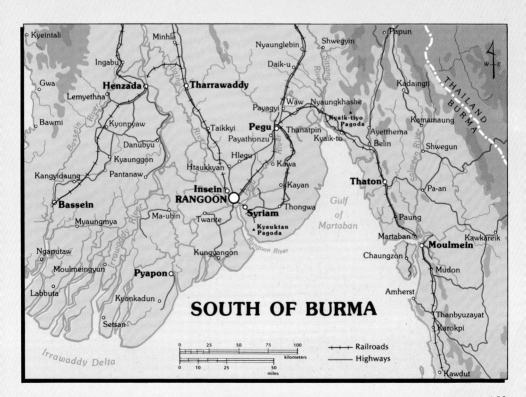

SOUTH OF BURMA

was only room enough on the island for one *hamsa (hintha)*, a mythological duck. Indeed, the duck's mate had to perch upon his back—and even today, the women of Pegu are teased about their "*hamsa*-like" attachment to their men. The legend gave the town the name by which it was known during the years of its greatest power: Hamsawaddy.

From Ducks' Nest
To Talaing Seaport

Over the years, the mythological nesting place was joined to the Burma coastline by the accretion of silt deposited by the rivers. A seaport was founded there, allegedly in 825 A.D. by two brothers from Thaton, who like other inhabitants of this coastal stretch were descendants of Talaing and Indian settlers. (Many historians believe the name "Talaing," which until recently referred to the Mon people along the Gulf of Martaban coast, can be traced to immigrants from Telingana near Madras, India. Others maintain the word is derived from the Burmese for "trampled under foot.")

In 1057, Anawrahta of Pagan conquered Thaton, the Mon capital, and the whole of southern Burma fell under Burmese sovereignty for the next 250 years. Thaton never recovered from the conquest. When Wareru established his own Talaing Empire in 1287 after the downfall of the First Burmese Empire at the hands of Kublai Khan, he chose Martaban, near Moulmein, as his capital. His successor, Byinnya-U, transferred the capital to Pegu (Hamsawaddy) in 1365, beginning a golden era for Pegu that lasted until 1635, when the capital was transferred by King Thalun's Second Burmese Empire to Ava, near Mandalay. By that time, the harbor at Pegu had become so shallow, as a result of silt deposits, that trading vessels could no longer dock there.

Shinsawbu and Dhammazedi

During its 270-year "golden era," however, Pegu's Hamsawaddy Dynasty produced rulers who are still loved by the people of Burma today, and who left behind many sacred monuments. They included King Razadarit (1385–1425), Queen Shinsawbu (1453–1472) and King Dhammazedi (1472–1492).

Born in 1394, Shinsawbu was the daughter of King Razadarit. Twice widowed, she was married to the King of Ava when, in her 30s, she began to study ancient Buddhist texts. Two Mon *pongyis* living in Ava, Dhammazedi and Dhammapala, helped her in her studies. In 1430, unhappy with her life at the Ava court, she decided to flee to her homeland, assisted by the two monks. Both men were familiar with the science of runes, a branch of alchemy, and every day they changed the color of the boat in which they were fleeing down the Irrawaddy to escape their pursuers.

When Shinsawbu became Queen of Hamsawaddy 23 years later, she sought to find a successor to the throne during her own lifetime and concluded that it must be one of the two monks. One morning she placed a robe, a model of a white (royal) umbrella, a yak's tail, a crown, a sword, and some sandals in one of the begging bowls used by the monks, and hoped the more worthy of the two would take up the bowl. Dhammazedi made the choice. Dhammapala felt he had been unfairly pushed into the background and challenged Dhammazedi in a battle of runes, but the weakness of his symbols led to Dhammapala's death.

She Died With Her Eyes
Fixed on the Shwedagon

Shinsawbu devoted her final years to enlarging the Shwedagon Pagoda, and actually settled in the village of Dagon. She lived to be 78 years old, and legend says she cast a final glance at the famous golden stupa as she died.

Dhammazedi ruled for 20 years after Shinsawbu's death, but was followed by weaker rulers. In 1541, Tabinshweti, king of the Toungoo Dynasty and founder of the Second Burmese Empire, peacefully annexed Pegu and made it the capital of his empire. His successor, Bayinnaung, extended the empire's boundaries but drained the treasury with his campaigns. He twice conquered Ayutthia, capital of Siam, but was never in a position to leave a stable government in the subjugated region. Although Pegu may have been the most splendid city in Asia at the time, the country itself was reduced to poverty. In 1599, the finishing touches were applied when Anaukhpetlun, ruler of Toungoo, conquered Lower Burma and razed Pegu as well as Syriam. Thus Bayinnaung's magnificent Hamsawaddy, which had in no small measure been built up from the proceeds of his

Paddy work is a family matter.

campaign booty, was reduced to ashes within 33 years of his ascendancy.

In 1740, Pegu became the capital of a short-lived Mon Empire. After only 17 years, however, the city again had to suffer the agony of total destruction. Alaungpaya, founder of the Konbaung dynasty, was ruthless in suppressing the upstart empire. Pegu's Mon inhabitants either fled to Thailand or interbred with the victorious Burmans. King Bodawpaya (1782–1819) attempted to rebuild the city, but with the changing of course of the Pegu River, it never again approached its former greatness. Today, only Pegu's many monuments serve as reminders of a glorious past.

Day Trip to Pegu
By Train, Bus or Taxi

A day trip to Pegu is to be highly recommended. As in all Burmese towns, there is a circuit house, but tourists are offered a night's lodging only in exceptional circumstances. No matter. Trains depart hourly from Rangoon, and overcrowded buses leave every half-hour from 18th Street. A taxi, costing about 200 kyats (US$27), is probably the best way to travel, especially if the cost can be split among several people.

An extra bonus in traveling by taxi is the vista across the countryside between the Pegu Yoma and the Sittang River, one of the most intensive rice-cultivating regions of Burma. During the harvest months of January and February, it is especially rewarding to stop about halfway through the journey in **Hlegu,** where the government operates stalls to accept delivery of the bounty from newly-harvested rice paddies. Watching the cheerfulness of the country people, the visitor gets a clear sense of the easy-going spirit which, together with Buddhism, has determined the pattern of village life here for centuries.

Before reaching Hlegu, though, the traveler from Rangoon comes to a fork in the highway at **Htaukkyan.** The western road heads into Upper Burma via Prome and the Irrawaddy Valley. The eastern road follows the Sittang Valley and leads to Mandalay via Pegu and Toungoo. Taking the eastern fork, you'll discover the **British War Cemetery** shortly after leaving Htaukkyan on the right. Some 27,000 Allied soldiers who fell during the Second World War campaign in Bur-

A *naga* on the road to Pegu.

ma are buried there. The Imperial War Graves Commission maintains the grounds.

Buddha and the Cobra:
The Naga Cult

A little further along the road, at a military checkpoint, you'll see to your left a long wall built in Mandalay style. Behind this is a *kyaung* and a huge **Naga-Yone Enclosure**: a Buddha figure sits entwined by a cobra, whose head is bent over the Buddha. The enclosure is surrounded by a moat, and houses the eight astrological guardian animals at its eight cardinal points. An expression of typical Burmese religion, this combination of Buddhism, Brahman astrology and the *naga* cult is nonetheless fascinating.

The origin of the *naga* cult is unknown. It left traces of its pure form in China and India, and was worshipped in pre-Buddhist times in Tagaung. But when Buddhist kings assumed power in those areas where the *naga* cult had been dominant, the cult was assimilated in folk Buddhism.

According to legend, during the fifth of the seven weeks he spent meditating after achieving enlightenment, the Buddha's life was threatened by a storm which blew up over Lake Mucalinda. A *naga*, or serpent, living nearby observed the peril. The animal coiled its body protectively around the Buddha, covering the Enlightened One's head with its own hooded head, thereby shielding the Buddha from the storm.

This story symbolizes the assimilation of the *naga* cult with Buddhist doctrine, and forms the basis of all *naga-yone* enclosures in Burma. The *naga* itself, half snake and half dragon, is no longer worshipped. But it is still present in the customs of Upper Burma. A man who has been a monk, for instance, will never, if he can avoid it, travel in the opposite direction to that in which the head of the *naga* is pointing. Every three months, the *naga* is said to change the direction of its gaze, and a journey "into the jaws of the *naga*" can only bring disaster, it is said.

Shwemawdaw Pagoda:
The Pride of Pegu

Just as Rangoon's glory is reflected in the stupa of the Shwedagon, Pegu has its own golden landmark. This is the **Shwemawdaw Pagoda** ("Great Golden God Pagoda"), visible from about 10 kilometers (6 miles) outside the city. At the eastern end of Pegu, it has many similarities to the Shwedagon—and is in fact even taller than its more fabled cousin, standing 114 meters (374 feet) in height.

Legend has it that two merchant brothers, Mahasala and Kullasala, returned from India with two hairs personally given to them by Gautama Buddha. They built a small stupa over the relics, a shrine which was enlarged several times over the years, once by the historical founders of Pegu, Thamala and Wimala. Sacred teeth were added to the relic collection in 982 and 1385. King Dhammazedi had a bell cast and inscribed it with runes that are still indecipherable today from their post on the pagoda's main platform. In the 16th Century, King Bayinnaung gave the jewels from his crown to make a *hti* for the pagoda, and in 1796 King Bodawpaya donated a new umbrella and raised the height of the pagoda to 90 meters (295 feet).

The Shwemawdaw has been hit by three serious earthquakes this century, and was almost completely destroyed by the last one in 1930. After the Second World War, however, it was rebuilt larger

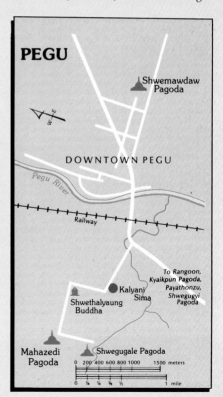

than ever with voluntary donations and unpaid labor. In 1954, it got a new diamond-studded *hti.*

Climbing to the Terrace

Like Rangoon's Shwedagon, the Shwemawdaw's main terrace is approached from four directions by covered stairways. There are not as many brightly colored *tazaungs* or *zayats* as at the Shwedagon, but there is a small museum containing some ancient wood and bronze Buddha figures salvaged from the ruins of the 1930 quake. The terrace also contains the eight planetary prayer posts, of course, as well as a number of statues honoring certain *nats.* The latter are especially revered by the people of Pegu, as the *nats* are heroes of Pegu's history.

The stairways leading to the pagoda are guarded by huge white *chinthes,* each containing a sitting Buddha in its mouth. The stairways themselves are like bazaars, with everything from medicinal herbs to monastic offerings for sale. Faded murals along the main entrance steps recall the destruction of the pagoda by the 1930 earthquake and its later reconstruction.

Behind the Shwemawdaw is **Hinthagone Hill.** The ruins of an ancient pagoda stand on top of the hill; in front of it is a statue of a pair of *hamsa (hintha),* one on top of the other, as in the legend of Pegu. Indeed, geologists suspect that this hill was at one time an island in the Gulf of Martaban. A high-roofed platform atop the hill provides a good view of the region surrounding Pegu.

As the Shwemawdaw is at the opposite end of Pegu from other buildings of tourist interest, the visitor should retrace his steps in the direction of Rangoon, crossing the Pegu River bridge (behind which lies the interesting market) and the railroad tracks. About 1½ kilometers (one mile) west of the station, a short distance to the north of the main road, are a number of sacred structures.

Ceylon Saved the Day
For Burmese Buddhism

The first one you'll encounter is the **Kalyani Sima,** or hall of ordination. King Dhammazedi built this *sima* in 1476 for the rejuvenation of the Burmese Sangha. When the unity of Buddhism in Burma was threatened by schisms in the wake of

Pegu's Shwemawdaw Pagoda.

the downfall of the First Burmese Empire, Dhammazedi sent 22 monks to Ceylon, then regarded as the stronghold of Theravada Buddhism. The monks were ordained at the island's Mahavihara Monastery, founded in 251 B.C. on the banks of the Kalyani River. Upon their return to Burma after surviving a shipwreck, Dhammazedi had this building constructed and named it after the Ceylonese river. The Mahavihara *pongyis* performed a unified ordination of Burmese monks early in the 16th Century, thus assuring the continuity of Burmese Buddhism. To this day, novices are ordained into the Sangha in this hall.

To the west of the Kalyani Sima are 10 large tablets containing detailed information on the history of Buddhism in Burma, and on the country's 15th Century trade with Ceylon and south India. Three stones are inscribed in Pali, the other seven in Mon. Although some of the tables are shattered and illegible in places, the complete text has been preserved on palm-leaf copies.

The Kalyani Sima, model for 397 other *simas* built by Dhammazedi, did not escape the ravages of the Mons' warlike history. The Portuguese adventur-er de Brito destroyed it first in 1599. Alaungpaya razed the reconstructed hall when he sacked Pegu in 1757, and the *sima* suffered the same fate as the Shwemawdaw during the earthquake of 1930. It was rebuilt in 1954 and dedicated to its original purpose at a ceremony attended by U Nu. Around the *sima* are lodgings for monks, and the park-like grounds radiate a feeling of peacefulness readily associated with Buddhist *kyaungs*.

The Shwethalyaung Buddha: Gautama Enters Nirvana

Just to the northeast is the **Shwethalyaung Buddha,** revered throughout the country as the most beautiful reclining Buddha. It is said to depict Gautama on the eve of his entering nirvana. Some 55 meters (180 feet) long and 16 meters (52 feet) high, it is not as large as Rangoon's Kyauk Htat Gyi Buddha built in the 1960s, but is much better known and loved—a result of its artistry and long history. Pegu's reclining Buddha was built in 994 by King Migadippa I, well before the Mons had been overpowered by the Burmans. But it was left to decay for nearly 500 years until it was restored

The great reclining Shwethalyaung Buddha.

during Dhammazedi's reign. In the centuries that followed, Pegu was twice destroyed, and again the Shwethalyaung Buddha was covered by tropical vegetation. It was not until 1881, when the British were building a railway nearby, that a contractor discovered this lucrative "source of brick and stone" hidden in an earthen mound in the jungle.

In 1906, after the undergrowth had been cleared away, an iron *tazaung* was erected over the Buddha. Although the appearance of the *tazaung* detracts from the statue inside, the pavilion does a sufficient job of protecting the Buddha from tropical downpours. The statue was re-renovated in 1948, regilded and given a new coat of paint.

Under Reconstruction: The Mahazedi Pagoda

The road leading from the Shwethalyaung turns north, and the tourist—after passing a wall on the left of the road—will come upon the **Mahazedi Pagoda,** currently being completely rebuilt. *Maha zedi* means "great stupa," and the appropriateness of this name will be evident once reconstruction is complete.

Original plans are being followed in their entirety. Unlike most other large stupas in Lower Burma, the Mahazedi has steep stairways winding two-thirds of the way up its exterior. It is reminiscent of some of the most beautiful buildings of Pagan.

Legend of King Bayinnaung: The Stupa and the Tooth

The Mahazedi was built in 1560 by King Bayinnaung to house a tooth of the Buddha. Bayinnaung, whose 11 white elephants (including seven taken from the King of Siam during the conquest of Ayutthia) confirmed his divine reign, was intent on obtaining a tooth to assure his place in history as the greatest king of all time. After all, he reasoned, Anawrahta and Alaungsithu had sought the tooth of the Buddha in vain. If only . . .

As luck would have it, 1560 was the height of Portugal's power in India. Don Constantino de Braganca attacked the Buddhist kingdom of Jaffna in Ceylon and made off with a large booty that included a tooth, inlaid with gold and adorned with precious stones. He thought it was the Tooth of Kandy, the most revered of all Buddhist relics, which

Bustling market in Pegu.

had been taken to Jaffna for a religious festival shortly before the Portuguese raid.

The greedy Bayinnaung, upon hearing the news, offered the Portuguese a huge sum of money for the tooth. The governor of Portuguese Goa was willing to deal—but the threat of the Inquisition led him to think twice. He ordered the tooth to be publicly pulverized in a mortar, then strewn into the open sea. Thus the Portuguese felt they had gotten rid of one more heathen symbol.

'The Heavens Have Looked Upon Me With Favor'

But, no! The indestructible tooth reappeared soon thereafter in the court of the King of Colombo. Bayinnaung dispatched a delegation to Ceylon to negotiate for the tooth and the king's daughter. (One of Bayinnaung's four wives had recently died, so he was able to take another wife.) The delegation returned to Burma in 1576, their journey a success. Bayinnaung greeted them at Bassein. Medieval documents tell of an enormous welcoming party: It was Bayinnaung's greatest day. "The heavens have looked upon me with favor," said the king. "Anawrahta could only get a replica of the tooth from Ceylon, Alaungsithu went in vain to China, but this tooth has been granted to me because of my piety and wisdom."

Not long thereafter, Bayinnaung was informed that the Tooth of Kandy had never left Ceylon, and was still to be found there. He apparently chose not to give credence to the report, and locked the tooth away in the Mahazedi Pagoda with a begging bowl said to have supernatural powers.

But the tooth of the Buddha remained in the Mahazedi for only 34 years. In 1599, Anaukhpetlun conquered Pegu, and he insisted the pagoda's cherished relics be transferred to his capital of Toungoo. This was done in 1610. A short time later, King Thalun transferred the Burmese capital to Ava and built the Kaunghmudaw Pagoda in nearby Sagaing for the relics. The tooth and begging bowl are still to be found there today.

The Mahazedi Pagoda was destroyed during Alaungpaya's time, and was leveled again by the 1930 earthquake. Upon completion of the current reconstruction work, the uppermost walkway around

Mandarin oranges at a street stall.

the stupa will afford a marvelous view of the surrounding plain, bejeweled with ancient monuments.

64 Buddhas in a Circle

A short distance west of the Mahazedi stands the **Shwegugale Pagoda**, in which 64 Buddha figures sit in a circle in a gloomy vault around the central stupa.

Four kilometers to the south of Pegu, about 100 meters off the road to Rangoon, sits the **Kyaikpun Pagoda.** Built by Dhammazedi in 1476, it consists of four Buddha figures, each 30 meters (98 feet) high, seated back to back against a square pillar facing the four cardinal directions. The figures represent Gautama Buddha (he faces north) and his three Buddha predecessors, Konagamana (south), Kakusandha (east), and Kassapa (west). The latter was largely destroyed by the 1930 earthquake. An old legend holds that four sisters took part in the building of the monument, and it was prophesied that if any of them were to marry, one of the statues would collapse. Believers feel the collapse of the Kassapa Buddha statue points a finger at one of the sisters.

Another kilometer or so toward Rangoon lies **Payathonzu,** where there are a number of buildings dating to the time of Dhammazedi. The most important of these is the **Shwegugyi Pagoda,** modeled on India's Bodhagaya Temple. In a circle around the temple are earlier buildings and figures, representing the seven stages through which the Buddha passed during the seven-week period of meditation which followed his enlightenment. Unfortunately, there is not much left of these structures.

Syriam: Oil, Beer, And a Rich Hindu Culture

The Syriam of the 1980s belies the Syriam of the 17th and early 18th centuries. Once the center of foreign trade for all of Lower Burma, Syriam remains an important industrial town today, well worth a day trip from Rangoon. But its glory, like so many other Burmese cities, lies in the past.

At various times prior to Syriam's destruction at the hands of King Alaungpaya in 1756, it was home to trading posts of Portuguese, Dutch, French and British merchants. Its greatest impor-

The Ye Le Paya (Kyauktan) Pagoda near Syriam.

tance was in the early 1600s when the Portuguese adventurer de Brito established his own private kingdom here; the ruined walls of Lusitanian baroque-style buildings can still be seen.

Many of Syriam's 20,000 people today are employed by Burma's largest oil refinery or by the "People's Brewery." Others are involved in the rice trade, as Syriam is a center for Burma's "East Delta" rice-cultivating region.

When the British opened up the Irrawaddy Delta for rice growing, they imported Indian labor to work the fields. During the height of the British colonial period, an estimated 1 million Indians lived in Burma, the majority of them in the delta region. The largest of the holdover Indian communities—of those that survived both the Second World War and Ne Win's 1960s nationalization movement—remains in the Syriam region.

Even though Syriam's Indians have Burmese citizenship, their customs and way of life are still very much determined by the Hindu religion. Every February, for example, after the rice harvest has been gathered, the community observes the ritual of penitence known as Thaipusam. Devotees repenting past sins or asking future favors walk trancelike through the streets, carrying heavy weights which dangle from sharp hooks thrust through their flesh, or stroll barefoot across a bed of burning coals.

It's a 45-minute ferry trip from Rangoon to Syriam across the Pegu River. Boats leave the capital hourly from the Htinbonseik Jetty on Pazundaung Creek. As there are neither seats nor cabins on these ferries, you'd be well advised to carry a blanket on which you can sit or lie on the deck of the boat.

Upon arriving in Syriam, there are three modes of transport from which to choose: horse-drawn cabs, buses and Jeeps. The latter tend to charge exorbitant rates, but Syriam's buses are always crowded and don't leave the dock until the last seat is taken.

Portuguese Ruins
And a Hilltop Pagoda

If you're not planning to go far from Syriam, find an English-speaking horse-drawn cab driver to take you to the Portuguese ruins and the **Kyaik Khauk Pagoda.** Like the Shwedagon and the Shwemawdaw, this pagoda is situated at

A Syriam peasant takes his geese to market.

the top of a hill, and its golden stupa is visible for miles across the delta silt. In fact, the Kyaik Khauk matches its two more famous cousins in architecture and atmosphere as well as hilltop location. In front of the pagoda are the graves of two venerated writers, Natshinnaung and Padethayaza.

Isle of Giant Catfish

A more unusual monument is the **Kyauktan Pagoda,** about 20 kilometers (13 miles) south of Syriam on a tributary of the Rangoon River. The journey by Jeep or bus takes about 45 minutes from Syriam. Also called the Ye Le Paya ("situated in the middle of the river") Pagoda, the Kyauktan is indeed on an island in the middle of the river. The island, which is completely covered by buildings, can be reached by rowboat from the riverbank. Within the pagoda complex are paintings of all the most important pagodas in Burma, and some in other Theravada countries.

At the boat landing, pilgrims can buy food for the huge catfish (some over 100 centimeters, or three feet, in length) whose dorsal fins can be seen piercing the waters on all sides of the island. Feeding these harmless fish is a favorite pastime for Kyauktan visitors. Stretching along the riverbank opposite the colorful pagoda buildings is an interesting market.

Those who make the day trip to Syriam and Kyauktan should leave plenty of time to be back at the Syriam jetty by 6 p.m. That's when the last ferry of the day returns to Rangoon, and there is no suitable accommodation in Syriam for Western travelers.

The Land of the Mons

East of Rangoon—across the Gulf of Martaban—in the fertile area between the Sittang and Salween rivers lies Suvannabhumi, the "golden land" of the Mon people. This was Lower Burma's original cradle of civilization, and it was from here that Buddhism spread to the rest of the country. It is now generally off-limits to Western tourists.

It was probably **Thaton** to which the great Indian King Ashoka sent two missionaries (Sona and Uttara) to spread the gospel of Theravada Buddhism in the 3rd Century B.C. In any case, it was Thaton that served as the first great capital of the

Mahout and elephant in Mon State.

164

Mon Empire, and Thaton which posed the greatest threat to Upper Burma. It was only after King Anawrahta of Pagan was victorious over Thaton's King Manuha in 1057 that Anawrahta established the First Burmese Empire.

Although Thaton's influence waned from that point on, visitors to the ancient capital can still see some remains of the medieval fortifications—although modern Thaton was built on top of the old town. Local legend maintains that the **Shwezayan Pagoda**, believed to contain four of the Buddha's teeth, dates to the 5th Century B.C. The **Thagyapaya Pagoda**, situated nearby, has three terraces, the uppermost terrace containing four large recesses with standing Buddha figures. Various terracotta glazed tiles, dating from the 11th and 12th centuries, illustrate the *Jataka* tales. Scenes from the 10 best known *Jataka* stories also decorate the **Kalyani Sima**, hall of ordination. Also worth seeing is the **Pitakat Taik**, or library.

'By the Old Moulmein Pagoda'

Some 70 kilometers (44 miles) south of Thaton is **Moulmein**, the third largest city in Burma with a population of 200,000. It was British Burma's administrative center between 1827 and 1852, but is best known today from Kipling's verse: "By the old Moulmein Pagoda, looking lazy at the sea ..." The English writer probably was referring to the **Kyaikthanlan Pagoda**, whose hilltop location offers splendid views over the city and its harbor, a center for the export of rice and wood (especially teak). Just up the Salween River—navigable for a short distance from Moulmein and its sister town, **Martaban**, across the river—there is a sawmill where the words of Rudyard Kipling again come to life: "Elephants a-pilin' teak ..."

Moulmein boasts many beautiful pagodas. Among them is the **Uzina Pagoda**, with four life-sized statues representing the four images—an old man, a sick man, a dead man and a religious ascetic—which convinced young Siddhartha Gautama to devote his life to finding a means to ending people's suffering. Also in the vicinity of Moulmein are two large caves. The **Cave of Payon** contains many Buddha figures among its stalagmites and stalactites. The **Cave of Kawgaun**, also known as the Cave of the

Moulmein Pagoda at the turn of the century.

Ten Thousand Buddhas, holds an enormous number of Buddha figures of all shapes and sizes.

A POW Cemetery
And a Colonial Resort

About 65 kilometers (40 miles) south of Moulmein, near the town of **Thanbyuzayat**, is a large and well-kept war cemetery. Buried here are Allied prisoners-of-war who died constructing the World War II railway to Thailand for the Japanese.

The Burmese government currently is planning a hotel near **Amherst**, a coastal resort some 45 kilometers (28 miles) south of Moulmein. During the British colonial period, there was a bustling holiday center here, the beach at **Setse** being particularly well known. The opening of this area to Western tourists depends, however, on the success of government troops in reducing rebel activity in southern Burma.

North of Thaton 45 kilometers (28 miles) is the village of **Ayetthema**, near which lies the ruin of an old city wall. This is believed to be the wall of the fort of Taikkala at the original Mon settlement of Suvannabhumi. Also in the area is the **Kyaiktalan Pagoda** with inscriptions dating to the time of King Kyanzittha in the 11th Century. To the south, standing on an octagonal base, is the conical **Tizaung Pagoda**. Another 1½ kilometers (one mile) south of this pagoda are the remains of another wall, this one two meters (6½ feet) high, with beautiful animal scenes chiseled into the rock.

Pilgrimage to Kyaik-tiyo,
The Famed 'Golden Rock'

About halfway between Thaton and Pegu lies the town of **Kyaik-to**, famous for its pagoda situated east of the town at the end of a 10-kilometer (6-mile) long footpath. This is the **Kyaik-tiyo Pagoda**—the "Golden Rock." The small (5.5 meters, or 18 feet high) shrine is built on a gold-plated boulder atop a cliff, and it gives the viewer the sensation that it is about to crash into the valley at any moment. Local Burmese will tell you that could never happen; the fine balance is maintained by a hair of the Buddha preserved inside the pagoda.

According to legend, King Tissa, who lived in the 11th Century, was the son of a

Harvesting rice.

166

zawgyi and a *naga* princess. He was given the Buddha's hair by an old hermit who had preserved it in his own hairknot from centuries earlier when the Buddha had personally visited his cave. In giving King Tissa the hair, however, the hermit set one condition: The king must find a rock which exactly resembled the hermit's head, and on this rock he must build a pagoda to enshrine the hair relic.

With the help of Thagyamin, king of the nats, Tissa located the perfect rock on the bottom of the sea. It was transported to the mountaintop by a ship—which subsequently turned to stone. Today it can be found a few hundred meters (about 1,000 feet) away from the Kyaik-tiyo, and is known as the **Kyaukthanban,** the "stone boat pagoda."

Queen Shwe-nan-kyin
And the Man-eating Tiger

During the time King Tissa was building the remarkable pagoda, he fell in love with the beautiful Shwe-nan-kyin, daughter of a highland chief. He made her his queen, and brought her to his palace. Some time later, during pregnancy, she became sick, and concluded that only by making offerings to her family *nat* would she recover. Her family had not rejected their traditional beliefs even while absorbing Buddhism, so with King Tissa's permission, her father and brother arrived to escort her home. About halfway from the palace to the pagoda, a tiger—presumedly sent by the offended family *nat*—sprang from the jungle. Father and brother instantly fled, and poor Shwe-nan-kyin, terrified, watched death approach. Then her eyes fell upon the golden Kyaik-tiyo shrine on the distant cliff-top. With her eyes fixed on the pagoda, she surrendered herself to whatever fate was to be hers. The tiger walked away.

Shwe-nan-kyin continued her journey to the platform of the pagoda. Here she laid down and died, the truth of the Buddhist Dharma lodged in her mind. She is now the guardian *nat* of the Kyaiktiyo Pagoda, a *nat* radiating compassion.

An Arduous Climb
From Base Camp to Pagoda

Only a few non-Burmese have ever made the pilgrimage to the Kyaik-tiyo Pagoda. Not only is it remote from other

Hilltop Buddha near Kyaik-tiyo.

spots of tourist interest; it is situated in a government "brown area," a region in which rebellion has been quelled but which is not yet open for foreigners unless special permission can be obtained. On top of that, it's a fairly arduous walk—about five hours from the **Kinpun** base camp near sea level to the pagoda at 1,200 meters (almost 4,000 feet) elevation. Most pilgrims carry a bedroll and spend the night at the *kyaung* near the pagoda.

A Way to Gain Merit
And Cleanse One's Soul

For Burmese, the climb to Kyaik-tiyo is a kind of soul-cleansing experience. It is a means of gaining merit, of worshipping the *nats* of the region and of being reminded again and again of the Buddhist Dharma.

The millennium-old path leads through otherwise impenetrable bamboo jungle and along a seemingly interminable mountain ridge. There is an oasis halfway up the second hill, where a thoughtful businessman has built several bamboo sheds over a clear spring; here journeyers can cool off in the refreshing water before continuing the trek. At various stages along the way, images have been erected describing the chapters of the temple legend, integral to the pilgrims' appreciation of the trip. Once on the ridge, the going gets a little easier—the Golden Rock can be seen in the distance, and this seems to relax the walker's limbs and reinvigorate his soul.

As tiresome as the climb may be, even the sick and the old are not kept from reaching the golden boulder. Neither, for that matter, are the rich or idle. Baggage will be carried from Kin-pun to the temple for a small charge (which varies depending on the weight of the baggage), and there are palanquins to carry persons unable—or unwilling—to manage the trek on their own two feet. It is quite a sight to see a pair of 15-year-old boys marching up the steep mountain slopes, toting an overweight merchant who mutters, *"Ahmya,"* which means, "Share with me the merit I gain by doing good things."

Finally, there is the Kyaik-tiyo Pagoda itself at the highest point of the mountain ridge. Seemingly perched at the top of the world, one cannot help but be awed by this wonder of the world balancing on a

Meandering route to the "Golden Rock."

ကျိုက်ထီးရိုးဘုရားလမ်းစဉ်

168

projecting boulder that even a few young boys can rock and move.

How to Reach the 'Rock'

Adventurous foreigners who arrange to make the trip to the "Golden Rock" have time to do so even on a seven-day tourist visa, provided careful planning is done. One suggestion is to wander down to Rangoon's Strand Road and find a vintage taxi, one with a driver willing to accompany you on a two- or three-day trip. The price should be in the vicinity of 400 kyats, about US$55 at the official rate.

Arrange for the driver to pick you up at your hotel about 6 o'clock the following morning. It will take at least six hours of solid driving along the Moulmein Road—passing through Hlegu, Pegu, Payagyi and Waw in the fertile rice country east of Rangoon—until you reach Nyaungkhashe, where you cross a bridge over the Sittang River into Mon State. Another 30 kilometers (19 miles) due south is the town of Kyaik-to, from which a 15-kilometer (9½-mile) side road leads to the base camp of Kin-pun.

If you intend to arrive at the pagoda before sunset, you should set out as soon after noon as possible. There is something truly spectacular about watching the sun's last rays of the day play on the golden boulder—and even more so, to watch the first joyful sparkle gleaming off the pagoda the following morning.

The descent to Kin-pun is as exhausting as the ascent. If possible, an extra day on the mountaintop is recommended.

The Charming Isles Of the Mergui Archipelago

One of the most scenic and charming island groups in Southeast Asia is the **Mergui Archipelago.** Comprising more than 800 islands off the south Tenasserim coast, it is home to the Salons, sea gypsies who until recently were notorious for their piracy. Like the Bajaos of the Sulu Sea, they live on their small boats; the countless bays of the archipelago offer shelter from storms and a bountiful supply of food.

The Japanese currently are engaged in the lucrative business of pearl fishing in the Mergui Archipelago. Other unusual products of this island group include sea cucumbers *(bêches-de-mer)* and edible birds' nests, popular in soups. These

The town square in Bassein.

swifts' nests are found in cathedral-like limestone caves, many of them accessible only at low tide.

Onshore capital of the district is the town of **Mergui,** a short distance from the mouth of the Tenasserim River. A small offshore island helps to enclose Mergui's sheltered harbor. This harbor—plus the short overland route to the Gulf of Siam—made Mergui an important trade settlement for both the Indians and the Arabs long before the Europeans visited this part of the world. In the 19th Century, the British considered Mergui as a possible location for the capital of their East Indian empire.

Unfortunately, Mergui is almost inaccessible to outsiders today. It is a major center of the illegal Burma-Thailand smuggling trade, and the Rangoon government has been forced to take extreme security measures in the area.

The Irrawaddy Delta
Port of Bassein

With a population of 140,000, **Bassein** is the biggest town in the Irrawaddy Delta. Situated 112 kilometers (70 miles) from the Bay of Bengal, it is a port of

export for rice and jute (fiber), and is well known for its colorful umbrellas.

Bassein can be reached from Rangoon by train in a roundabout fashion, but an inland-waterway ship voyage is probably the best way for visitors to get to know the countryside and people of the delta region. It's an 18-hour journey through the pottery town of **Twante,** but well worth it. The flight from Rangoon is only 30 minutes, if Bassein is presently open for Western visitors.

The British, with the consent of the court of Ava, had attempted as early as 1753 to establish a settlement where the Irrawaddy empties into the sea at Cape Negrais. After the conquest of Syriam soon thereafter, though, King Alaungpaya had the young settlement burned to the ground. It was not until the annexation of Lower Burma in 1852 that the British were able to install a garrison in Bassein. At the same time, they endeavored to open up large areas of land for rice cultivation.

The name "Bassein" was a European pronunciation of *Pathein,* said to derive from the Burmese word for Moslems: *Pathi.* This was a sizeable settlement centuries ago for Indian merchants, many of them Moslems. Today, the inhabitants of Bassein include many Karens and Arakanese, some of whom are Christian.

The town spreads out around the **Shwemokhtaw Pagoda,** which during the full moon in May becomes the goal of pilgrimage for the population of the entire surrounding delta region. According to legend, a Moslem princess was responsible for the pagoda having been built in ancient times. The princess, Onmadandi, had three lovers—all of whom, presumably, were Buddhists—and she told each one of them to build a pagoda. One man constructed the Shwemokhtaw, another the **Tazaung Pagoda** at the southern end of Bassein, and the third built the **Thayaunggyaung Pagoda.**

About 70 kilometers (45 miles) northeast of Bassein, near the village of Kyonpyaw, is beautiful horseshoe-shaped **Inye Lake,** seven miles in circumference and with a large island in the center. It is important as a fresh-water fishery.

Off the mouth of the Bassein (Ngawun) River, in the Andaman Sea a good 110 kilometers (70 miles) from Bassein city, is tiny wooded **Diamond Island.** This islet is important commercially for the hundreds of thousands of turtle eggs laid on its banks each year.

Glimpses of Bassein: Shwemokhtaw Pagoda (left) and Delta pottery.

MANDALAY, THE 'GOLDEN CITY'

"For the wind is in the palm-trees,
an' the temple-bells they say:
"'Come you back, you British soldier; come you back to Mandalay!'"

—*Rudyard Kipling,*
The Road to Mandalay *(1887)*

Mandalay, the capital of Upper Burma, is a young city, barely more than a century old. But its lyrical name ignites images as ancient as the languid Irrawaddy flowing past the city. Nostalgia for Burma's last royal capital, enchantment with the myriad pagodas dotting all corners of the region's landscape, and the warmth and vitality of the native people weave a spell around the visitor that is difficult to escape.

Sprawling across the dry plains of the upper Irrawaddy rice-growing district, Mandalay—with a population approaching 600,000—is dusty and often quite hot, lacking the tree-lined neatness and colonial character of Rangoon.

Trishaws and pony carts are more numerous than motorized vehicles, which more often than not are World War Two-vintage Jeeps. To the Burmese people, however, it is Mandalay, not Rangoon, which is truly representative of Burma's past and present. And it is Mandalay which is regarded as the center of Burmese culture and Buddhist learning.

Here in Mandalay, scenic beauty and historical tragedy are inextricably meshed. There is the indestructible Mandalay Hill with its kilometer-long covered stairways and remarkable pagodas; and below it, the totally destroyed Royal Palace, King Mindon's "Golden City" of ancient prophecy. In the city center is the fascinating Zegyo Market, center of trade for all the people of Upper Burma, who can be seen every evening in their colorful national costumes dispensing a variety of smuggled goods. There are the skilled artisans and craftsmen, working their age-old wonders with gold and silver, marble and chisel, thread and loom. And there is the sluggish Irrawaddy with its bustling wharves and flotilla of rice-laden boats. Mandalay, 620 kilometers (400 miles) north of Rangoon, is only 80 meters (262 feet) above sea level.

The Konbaung Dynasty

The last Burmese dynasty—those rulers ensconced in central Burma during the early period of British colonialism—took its name from the region that was the original home of its founder, Alaungpaya (1752–1760). Celebrated today as a national hero, he drove the Mons from Ava and eventually put all of Burma under his control.

Before his death, Alaungpaya—seeking to assure the future of the dynasty—decreed that his five surviving sons were to succeed him in order of their ages. First Naungdawgyi (1760–1763), who moved the capital briefly to Sagaing, then Hsinbyushin (1763–1776), who took the throne. But the latter broke from his father's will and appointed his son, Singu, as heir—even though two brothers were still alive.

Singu (1776–1781) had the elder of the two surviving brothers executed. But the youngest, Bodawpaya, remained in seclusion in Sagaing and waited for the ensuing turmoil to run its course. When Singu was visiting Shwebo, Naungdawgyi's son Maung Maung (1781) usurped the throne

and had the king killed upon his return to Ava. But only seven days later, Maung Maung himself was executed as Bodawpaya—the rightful heir to the throne—stepped in and assumed power.

Bodawpaya (1781–1819) is regarded as one of the most powerful rulers in Burma's history. He built the royal city of Amarapura and moved the capital in 1782, and there it remained throughout his reign. When his son and heir died in 1808, he appointed his grandson, Bagyidaw, as his successor.

Bagyidaw (1819–1838) was on the throne at Ava during the First Anglo-Burmese War, which resulted in Burma's loss of Arakan and Tenasserim to the British. He was dethroned by his brother Tharrawaddy (1838–1846), who in turn was succeeded by his eldest son, Pagan (1846–1853). The Second Anglo-Burmese War led to a bloodless coup by Pagan's brother, Mindon (1853–1878).

It was King Mindon who constructed the great city of Mandalay and moved his court there in 1861. His son Thibaw (1878–1885) took the throne upon his father's death for a brief but merciless reign. He was exiled in 1885 at the conclusion of the Third Anglo-Burmese War.

Preceding pages, the Sandamuni Pagoda; left, the Buddha points from Mandalay Hill.

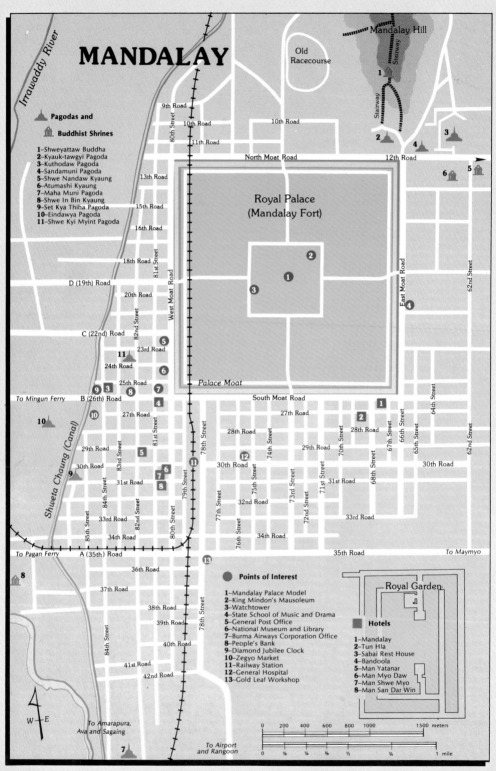

MANDALAY

Irrawaddy River

Mandalay Hill

Stairway

Old Racecourse

Stairway

Stairway

🔺 **Pagodas and**

🏛 **Buddhist Shrines**

1–Shweyattaw Buddha
2–Kyauk-tawgyi Pagoda
3–Kuthodaw Pagoda
4–Sandamuni Pagoda
5–Shwe Nandaw Kyaung
6–Atumashi Kyaung
7–Maha Muni Pagoda
8–Shwe In Bin Kyaung
9–Set Kya Thiha Pagoda
10–Eindawya Pagoda
11–Shwe Kyi Myint Pagoda

9th Road

10th Road   10th Road

80th Street

11th Road

North Moat Road   12th Road

13th Road

Royal Palace
(Mandalay Fort)

15th Road

16th Road

18th Road

81st Street

D (19th) Road

20th Road

82nd Street

C (22nd) Road

West Moat Road

East Moat Road

23rd Road

11 24th Road

25th Road

To Mingun Ferry   B (26th) Road

27th Road

Palace Moat

South Moat Road

27th Road

28th Road   28th Road

Shweta Chaung (Canal)

29th Road   29th Road

83rd Street   30th Road   30th Road

81st Street   31st Road

84th Street   82nd Street   32nd Road

85th Street   33rd Road   33rd Road

34th Road   34th Road

To Pagan Ferry   A (35th) Road   35th Road   To Maymyo

36th Road

37th Road

38th Road

84th Street   39th Road

78th Street   40th Road

41st Road

42nd Road

64th Street
67th Street
66th Street
65th Street
62nd Street
68th Street
70th Street
71st Street
72nd Street
73rd Street
74th Street
75th Street
76th Street
77th Street
79th Street

W ← → E

To Amarapura,
Ava and Sagaing

To Airport
and Rangoon

⬤ **Points of Interest**

1–Mandalay Palace Model
2–King Mindon's Mausoleum
3–Watchtower
4–State School of Music and Drama
5–General Post Office
6–National Museum and Library
7–Burma Airways Corporation Office
8–People's Bank
9–Diamond Jubilee Clock
10–Zegyo Market
11–Railway Station
12–General Hospital
13–Gold Leaf Workshop

Royal Garden

🟦 **Hotels**

1–Mandalay
2–Tun Hla
3–Sabai Rest House
4–Bandoola
5–Man Yatanar
6–Man Myo Daw
7–Man Shwe Myo
8–Man San Dar Win

0 200 400 600 800 1000   1500 meters

0   ⅛   ¼   ⅜   ½   ¾   1 mile

Mandalay was founded in 1857 by King Mindon to coincide with an ancient Buddhist prophecy. Tradition has it that Gautama Buddha visited the sacred mount of Mandalay Hill with his disciple Ananda, and proclaimed that on the 2,400th anniversary of his death, a metropolis of Buddhist teaching would be founded at the foot of the hill. Mindon, a deeply religious man, believed he had achieved Buddhist enlightenment; but he also felt that the injustices wrought during his reign could only be set straight by building temple grounds of great magnificence. The "Golden City" was formally completed in 1859. Mindon shifted his government and an estimated 150,000 population from nearby Amarapura in 1861, dismantling most of the previous palace and taking it with him to help create the new capital.

But the dream of Mandalay was short-lived. On Nov. 29, 1885, King Thibaw handed the town over to British General Prendergast and went into exile with his queen. Mandalay became just another outpost of British colonialism, albeit one crowned by the richly furnished palace buildings, which by now had been renamed Fort Dufferin.

The palace structures were almost universally built of teak, and this was their demise. On March 20, 1945, British troops shelled the stronghold, then defended by a handful of Japanese and Burmese soldiers. By the time the siege had ended, the interior of the "Golden City" was in ashes. All that remains intact today are the walls and moat.

'The Center of the World'

Mindon had built his **Royal Palace** on the model of Brahmin-Buddhist cosmology to represent the center of the world, the fabled Mount Meru. The palace formed a perfect square, with the outer walls facing the four cardinal directions and the 12 gates—three on each side—marked with the signs of the zodiac. In the exact center of the palace was the throne room, called the "Lion's Room." Above it rose a gold-plated, seven-story, 78-meter (256-foot) high *pyathat* (tower). Through this tower, it was believed, the wisdom of the universe funneled directly upon the king's throne to assist in his decision-making.

Anthropologist Charles Keyes, in his 1977 study, *The Golden Peninsula: Cul-*

Mandalay Palace walls.

ture and Adaptation in Mainland Southeast Asia, reported:

"The walls were a mile and one-eighth (almost two kilometers) long and were, in turn, surrounded by a moat. The homes of the common people and of 'aliens,' the markets, the workshops of the craftsmen and the shops, were located beyond the walls of the capital city. In contrast to Chinese and medieval European cities, the walls of a traditional Theravadin city were built not so much to serve as barriers against potential invaders as to demarcate a sacred space . . ."

Today, "Mandalay Fort" serves as the headquarters of the Burmese Army. To enter the grounds, therefore, a permit and escort must be obtained at the south gate. Where the king's chambers once stood, all that remains is an empty raised platform. A little to the west, however, is a scale model of the ancient palace created by archaeologists. The model indicates the location of all main and secondary buildings within the old palace walls, and gives a good idea of the "center of the world" concept. Also on the palace grounds is King Mindon's mausoleum.

Mandalay Hill

You should perhaps start your visit to Mandalay by climbing famous **Mandalay Hill,** which rises 236 meters (774 feet) above the surrounding countryside. British and Indian troops suffered heavy casualties here in March 1945, storming the Japanese stronghold which controlled the plains around Mandalay. Today, there is only the regimental insignia remaining near the hill's summit.

The slopes of Mandalay Hill are clothed in covered stairways, which contain small temples at regular intervals. Many of the temples are the work of the late monk U Khanti. Two main stairways ascend from the south, beginning under the glare of the ever-present *chinthes* demanding the removal of shoes before entering sacred ground. There are 1,729 steps to the top, but the walk is not particularly difficult. The roof which shades the stairways keeps the stone steps cool, protects the visitor from the sun and still allows fresh air to circulate through. Along the way, astrologers and souvenir peddlers ply their trades while monks and nuns, children and women smoking huge cheroots scale the steps.

Reading palms on Mandalay Hill.

178

About halfway up the hill, you'll encounter the first large temple, which contains three bones of the Buddha. These relics were sent to Burmese Buddhists as a present from the viceroy of India at the beginning of this century. (See below.)

About two-thirds of the way to the top stands a gold-plated statue of the **Shweyattaw Buddha**. His outstretched hand points to the place where the Royal Palace was built. This stance is unique: in all other Buddha images anywhere in the world, Gautama is in a *mudra* position. The statue was erected before King Mindon laid the first stone of his "Golden City," and symbolizes Gautama Buddha's prophecy.

Also on the way up the steps, there is a statue of a woman kneeling in front of the Buddha, offering to him her two severed breasts. According to legend, **Sanda Moke Khit** was an ogress—but she was so impressed by the Buddha's teachings that she decided to devote the rest of her life to following the Enlightened One. As a sign of humility, she cut off her breasts. The Buddha smiled as he accepted the gift, and the ogress' brother asked why he did so. He replied that Sanda Moke Khit had collected so many merits that in a future life, she would be reborn as Min Done (Mindon), king of Mandalay.

The view from the summit of Mandalay Hill is phenomenal. To the west lies the Irrawaddy and beyond that the Sagaing and Mingun hills, themselves encrusted with pagodas and temples. To the north, the Irrawaddy rice country extends into the distance. The purple Shan Plateau can be seen in the east; and to the south, in the midst of this vast plain, the city of Mandalay lies with its huge palace fortress. In all directions, the Irrawaddy plain—from which the hill juts like a huge boulder—is studded with pagodas, erected over the centuries by devout Buddhists seeking merit for future lives.

'The World's Largest Book'

At the base of Mandalay Hill's southeast stairway, surrounded by a high wall, is Mindon's **Kuthodaw Pagoda**. Its central structure, the 30-meter (98-foot) high **Maha Lawka Marazein Pagoda**, was erected in 1857, modeled on the Shwezigon Pagoda in Nyaung U, near Pagan. Around it are 729 *"pitaka* pagodas," built in 1872 during the Fifth Buddhist Synod to individually house the

The Peshawar Relics

Gautama Buddha died at the age of 80 in Kusinara, India, the apparent victim of tainted meat unknowingly brought to him by a smith named Chundra. The smith was consoled by the fact that his gift had started the Buddha on his transition to nirvana, and this would be to the advantage of his karma.

As Gautama did not leave instructions regarding disposal of his body, the Buddha's followers elected to cremate it. When only his bones remained, a violent downpour extinguished the flames. The Mallas of Kusinara took possession of the remains, and refused to share them with neighboring kings until the threat of war arose. Only then did they divide the bones equally among eight monarchs to be enshrined in stupas across the country.

When King Ashoka extended his powerful reign over India some three centuries later, he ordered the relic chambers of the eight stupas opened, and their contents distributed among the 80,000 stupas of South and Southeast Asia. He did so primarily to create more places of worship for Buddhist devotees who were spread throughout the subcontinent.

King Kanishka, the second great Buddhist king of the Kushan dynasty, had some of the Buddha relics brought to Peshawar, and built a 168-meter (551-foot) high stupa for them. The Chinese traveler Hiuen Tsang provided a marvelous description of the stupa in 630 A.D., but it was apparently destroyed by Moslem conquerors following the Battle of Hund in the 11th Century. It remained for the curator of the Peshawar Museum, conducting excavations at the Ganji Gate in 1908, to unearth the fabled Kanishka relic casket. Inside the casket he found a crystal vessel containing three bones of the Buddha. As these relics were of little importance to the Islamic peoples of northwest India, the British government presented them to the Burmese Buddhist Society.

The Burmese built a temple for the relics halfway up Mandalay Hill. It is surprising that, although the verity of the relics is confirmed by the inscription on the Kanishka casket, these relics are accorded relatively little esteem in Burma. Others, including the seemingly countless teeth of the Buddha enshrined in many stupas, are highly venerated.

marble tablets on which, for the first time, the entire *Tripitaka* (Buddhist canon) was recorded in Pali script. Sometimes called "the world's largest book," it was created by a team of 2,400 monks who required almost six months to recite the text. The canons were recorded on the marble slabs by devoted Buddhist scholars. Originally, the letters were veneered with gold leaf. When they had to be retraced a sixth time, however, a blue color was used instead, and the original metal protective coverings were replaced by stone arches.

Close to the Kuthodaw are several other important pagodas and monasteries. The **Sandamuni Pagoda** was built on the site where King Mindon had his provisional palace during construction of the Mandalay Palace. It was erected over the burial place of Mindon's younger brother, Crown Prince Kanaung, who was assassinated in an unsuccessful palace revolution in 1866. Commentaries on the *Tripitaka* have been chiseled onto 1,774 stone tablets housed in the pagoda, a work credited to U Khanti.

Not far from the south staircase is the **Kyauk-tawgyi Pagoda.** Begun in 1853, the original plan was to model this after the Ananda Temple at Pagan, but the 1866 revolt hampered this and other projects. The building was completed in 1878. The main point of interest is a huge Buddha figure, carved from a single block of marble from the Sagyin quarry. This undertaking was of ancient Egyptian proportions: 10,000 men required 13 days to transport the rock from the Irrawaddy to the pagoda site. It was dedicated in 1865. There are 20 figures on each side of the image, representing the Buddha's 80 disciples. A painting of King Mindon is contained within the pagoda.

There are two monasteries located south of the Kuthodaw Pagoda, not far to the east of the palace moat. The **Shwe Nandaw Kyaung,** at one time part of the royal palace, is the only building from Mindon's "Golden City" which has survived the ravages of the last century. It was in this building, then within the palace walls, that Mindon died. Thibaw dismantled it after his father's death and had it re-erected on its present site, where it was able to escape the World War Two destruction that burned the teak-built royal palace to the ground. Thibaw used the building for a time as a private meditation center, but then gave it to the

"World's largest book," the Kuthodaw Pagoda.

monks as a monastery. In 1979, the monastery celebrated its 100th anniversary. The abbot (he has been the *kyaung* superior for more than 40 years) enjoys talking with foreign tourists, a younger monk acting as interpreter.

Today the Shwe Nandaw is most famous for its intricate woodcarvings. At one time, Mindon's entire "Golden City" must have looked like this: every available space is covered with figures or ornamental flowers. Although the *kyaung* was once plated with gold and adorned with glass mosaic both inside and out, today the only gold is layered on the imposing ceiling. Thibaw's couch and a replica of the royal throne are contained within.

Beside the Shwe Nandaw lie the remains of the **Atumashi Kyaung.** The name means "Incomparable Monastery;" before it burned down in 1890, taking with it four sets of *Tripitaka* in teak boxes, this was a building of extraordinary splendor. Today, only the foundation walls, embellished with stucco work, and an impressive stairway are left standing. A famous Buddha image, clothed in silk, coated with lacquer, and with an enormous diamond set in its

forehead, was once the pride of the *kyaung,* but it was stolen during the British takeover of Mandalay in 1885. The *kyaung* was described by European visitors as one of the most beautiful buildings in all of Mandalay.

On the East Moat Road, close by the Royal Palace, is the **State School of Fine Art, Music and Drama.** Like its counterpart in Rangoon, this is a center of Burmese classical arts. Visitors can watch students practicing or giving recitals of Burmese music, or see the training of male and female dancers who later will travel through the country in small troupes to perform the traditional *zat pwe* for the peasant population.

The Fabled Maha Muni

The most important religious structure in Mandalay is the **Maha Muni** ("great sage") **Pagoda.** It is also called the "Arakan Pagoda" or "Payagyi Pagoda." Located a little over three kilometers (two miles) south of the city center on the road to Amarapura, this pagoda was originally built in 1784 by King Bodawpaya and was reconstructed after a fire a century later.

A bamboo raft on the Irrawaddy.

182

The Maha Muni Buddha image within the shrine, taken as booty by Bodawpaya's troops during an Arakan campaign, is an object of intense devotion to pilgrims from throughout the world. A legend helps to explain why.

It is said that Gautama Buddha himself went to teach for a week among the people of Dhannavati (now northern Arakan), stressing the five precepts and the Eight-fold Path, and showing the way to salvation. King Candrasuriya asked Gautama to "leave us the shape of yourself," and the Buddha agreed. He spent an additional week meditating under a Bodhi tree while Sakka, king of the gods, produced a likeness of the Buddha that was so lifelike, it could only have been created by a heavenly being. The Buddha was pleased. He breathed upon the image and said: "I shall pass into nirvana in my eightieth year, but this, with my essence, will live the 5,000 years I have prescribed for the duration of the religion." Gautama then departed, but the Maha Muni took its place upon a diamond-studded throne atop Arakan's Sirigutta Hill. It was one of only five likenesses of the Buddha said to have been made during his lifetime; according to tradition, two are in India, two are in Paradise.

This is the legend. In fact, archaeologists claim the city of Dhannavati was built in the 1st Century A.D., about 600 years after the Buddha lived. The Maha Muni Buddha probably was cast during the reign of Chandra Surya (Candrasuriya), but he did not ascend the throne until 146 A.D. It was during his reign that Buddhism spread to Arakan.

King Anawrahta of Pagan conquered the northern part of Arakan late in the 11th Century. All non-Buddhist buildings and statues were destroyed. He was unable, however, to carry the Maha Muni to Pagan. Anawrahta's grandson, Alaungsithu, again raided Arakan in 1118; his soldiers destroyed all temples, removed the gold from the Maha Muni, and took one of its legs as booty. But the ship transporting the treasure home sank in the Bay of Bengal. By the late 12th Century, when another foray from Pagan was made to Arakan, jungle had enveloped Sirigutta Hill and the legendary Maha Muni could not be found. The people of Arakan later succeeded in restoring the Buddha image, only to have it carried off by Bodawpaya's forces in 1784. The king sent his crown prince with a force of 30,000 men to take Arakan; the troops

returned with the Maha Muni in three separate pieces. It was reassembled at Amarapura, and Bodawpaya had an unusually beautiful seven-story pagoda built eight kilometers (five miles) north of Amarapura to house it. The original pagoda was destroyed by fire in 1884, and the current structure is a copy of the first one, although its terraced roof of gilded stucco is unmistakably late 19th Century.

Watching the Gold Grow

The Maha Muni Buddha figure is 3.8 meters (12 feet, 7 inches) high and is coated with layers of gold leaf several centimeters (one to two inches) thick. Except during the rainy season, when the Buddha's body is cloaked with robes, one can watch the Buddhist faithful pasting on the very thin gold leaf. The statue was originally cast of metal, but the gold leaf has had an unusual effect—the Maha Muni now has an irregular outline.

Carried back from Arakan with the Maha Muni were six bronze Khmer sculptures. Their story provides a vivid glimpse of Southeast Asia's speckled history. The statues originally stood as

The fabled Maha Muni, left, and a bronze *dvarapala*, right.

guardians of Cambodia's Angkor Wat. They were among 30 statues taken during a Thai raid in 1431. In 1564, the Mon King Bayinnaung looted Ayutthia and removed the statues to Pegu. Another 36 years later, in 1600, King Razagyi of Arakan razed Pegu and carried the statues to his capital of Mrauk-U (Myohaung). Bodawpaya's forces took them in 1784.

Only six of the Khmer bronzes have survived the centuries—two *dvarapalas* (warriors or temple guardians), three lions and a three-headed elephant. They are kept in a small building in the Maha Muni Pagoda courtyard. The warriors are a special attraction for pilgrims: it is said they have the power to heal any disease if one touches the corresponding place on their bodies. The gleaming, smooth indentations in the warriors' stomach areas is indicative of the kind of suffering most widespread in Burma.

Near the bronzes is a shed containing a five-ton gong. Also in the courtyard are hundreds of stone slabs with religious inscriptions which Bodawpaya collected during his many campaigns. A statue of Bodawpaya can be found on the southwestern side of the pagoda, in front of a curio museum. The museum displays life-

sized statues of King Mindon, King Thibaw and Thibaw's queen, Supyalat—all behind glass.

Streets with covered stalls lead up to the Maha Muni Pagoda from all directions, providing the bazaar atmosphere for which Burma was once famous. Along with simple artifacts, one can find precious stones and antiques—whose export, by the way, is strictly forbidden. On one side of the pagoda is located a small pond containing holy fish and turtles; feeding them improves one's merit.

The Charms of Mandalay

There are four other Buddhist buildings in the vicinity of downtown Mandalay which are definitely worth visiting. The city's grid street plan makes them easy to find. Heading north from the Maha Muni Pagoda, one first encounters the **Shwe In Bin Kyaung.** This monastery, situated to the south of 35th Road, contains very fine 13th Century woodcarvings. At 31st Road and 85th Street stands the **Set Kya Thiha Pagoda**, rebuilt after being badly damaged in the Second World War. The pagoda contains a five-meter (16-foot) high bronze Buddha, cast

Marble polishers at an image maker's workshop.

at Ava by King Bagyidaw in 1823. A Bodhi tree in front of the entrance was planted by U Nu, the deeply religious first prime minister of Burma.

Continuing north, the **Eindawya Pagoda** at 27th Road and 89th Street contains a Buddha figure made of chalcedony, carried to Burma in 1839 from Bodhgaya, the place in India where Gautama achieved Buddhahood. The pagoda was built in 1847 by King Pagan Min. Today it is covered with gold leaf.

The oldest pagoda in the city is the **Shwe Kyi Myint Pagoda** on 24th Road between 82nd and 83rd streets. Erected in 1167 by Prince Minshinsaw, the exiled son of King Alaungsithu of Pagan, it houses a Buddha image consecrated by the prince himself. It also contains a collection of Buddha figures made of gold and silver and adorned with precious stones, removed from the Royal Palace during the British occupation and previously worshipped by Burmese kings. They are brought out for public veneration on important religious occasions.

A couple of blocks from the Shwe Kyi Myint, at 24th Road and West Moat Road, are the **National Museum and Library**. The museum collection extends across many eras of Burmese history; one of its most interesting pictures shows King Thibaw and Queen Supyalat on the eve of their exile. The library is widely noted for its assemblage of important Buddhist documents.

Market Center of the North

The city of Mandalay is not only the religious and cultural center of Upper Burma; it is also the economic center. For the Chins of the west, the Kachins of the north, and the Shans of the east, Mandalay is the primary market for goods. And the **Zegyo Market**—located on the west side of the city center, on 84th Street between 26th and 28th roads, is Mandalay's most important bazaar.

The Italian Count Caldrari, first secretary of the Mandalay municipal government, had the Zegyo Market laid out around the **Diamond Jubilee Clock**, which had been erected in honor of Queen Victoria's 60-year reign. Today, the market offers visitors, who ordinarily cannot travel far from the beaten track, a fine opportunity to see Burma's ethnic minorities in their national costumes, and at the same time gives an idea of the

The Zegyo Market.

types of goods in daily use in Burmese homes.

The market becomes especially active in the evening hours. Then, the so-called "night market" is set up along 84th Street, with goods illegally smuggled across the border from Thailand being offered for sale under the carbide lamps of makeshift stalls. For a few hours, the streets are filled with shoppers as the flavor of an Eastern bazaar is combined with the "gray market" availability of Western consumer goods.

Part of Mandalay's enchantment comes from its location beside the **Irrawaddy River.** At the western end of A Road, which follows the railroad tracks north of the Shwe In Bin Kyaung, one finds the jetties where the ships that ply the "Road to Mandalay" are docked. The hustle and bustle of the wharves is fascinating. But perhaps even more enthralling is the marvelous view across the river to the Sagaing and Mingun hills on the Irrawaddy's west bank, studded with pagodas and *kyaungs.* The "Prome Ferry" to Pagan leaves from the piers here; the boat to Mingun departs from a location just a short distance upriver, at the end of B Road.

Early in the morning of May 12, 1981, a tragic fire—fueled by a horded black-market gasoline cache—ignited at a bus depot in northwest Mandalay and quickly raced up and down the banks of the Irrawaddy. By the time it had been extinguished, 6,150 houses had burned and more than 35,000 people were left homeless. Over a dozen monasteries, eight schools, four rice mills and many public buildings were victims of the blaze. It is not believed that any national treasures were destroyed, but the scars of the conflagration are certain to be felt for some time in Mandalay.

The Craftsmen's Quarters

In the southern part of Mandalay, especially in the precincts of the Maha Muni Pagoda, one finds the artists' and craftsmen's quarters.

Buddha figures are hewn from alabaster and marble by stonemasons on a street very near the pagoda. One can watch as Burmese men, using the same skills and methods as their forefathers, pursue their trade in religious sculpture—Buddha images in all positions, Buddha footprints, lotus-blossom pedestals, even an occasional Virgin Mary (a reminder of missionary days).

West of the Maha Muni are the makers of pagoda crafts, a booming trade given the Burmese propensity to seek merit through the building and renovating of pagodas. Not far away are the woodcarvers, who create more Buddhas, as well as altars for worship in home and pagoda. Foundry workers cast replicas of ancient Buddha images, plus musical instruments and opium weights.

The makers of oiled bamboo paper live on 37th Road, between 80th and 81st streets. This kind of paper, which is placed between layers of gold leaf, is produced by means of a remarkable three-year process of soaking, beating flat and drying.

Gold leaf is produced in many houses in the southeast section of Mandalay. This craft is extremely old, and the manufacturing process is carried out according to time-honored tradition.

In the area around Mandalay, visitors should make it a point to see other artisans—the silk and cotton weavers of Amarapura; the silversmiths from the village of Ywataung near Sagaing; and the bronze and brass workers from Kyi Thun Kyat, near Amarapura.

The *chinthes* of Mandalay Hill, left; and the abbot of Shwe Nandaw Kyaung.

GREATER MANDALAY
AND NORTH BURMA

One of the basic tenets of Buddhism is that nothing is permanent, that everything is in a constant state of change. As one departs Mandalay and roams the surrounding countryside, one can begin to understand how this idea permeates Burmese history. Three ancient capitals—Amarapura, Ava and Sagaing—as well as the medieval town of Mingun lie within a stone's throw of Mandalay. Here, amongst the ruins of palaces, pagodas and *kyaungs,* one can find abundant reminders of the political and religious power that was Upper Burma's in the 14th through 19th centuries, between the fall of Pagan and British occupation.

Sagaing was the capital of a Shan-dominated Upper Burma for a brief period beginning in 1315. The seat of government was shifted to Ava in 1364, and there it remained almost 400 years. Shwebo (Moksobo) became the royal capital from 1760 to 1764, but the government returned to Ava, and 19 years later King Bodawpaya moved the capital

to his newly built Amarapura. Kings often moved their headquarters at this time; Ava was again the capital of Upper Burma from 1823 to 1841, then Amarapura regained the distinction for 20 more years until King Mindon moved his court to Mandalay.

East of Mandalay, in the foothills of the vast Shan Plateau, is a town that is far from deserted, but does recall an earlier time. This is Maymyo, a former British hill station. Beyond here is the wild Shan State and the Kachin country of the north, off-bounds to tourists because of persistent rebel activity and perpetual smuggling and opium trading.

'Immortal' Amarapura

Once known as the "city of immortality," Amarapura is now called Taungmyo, "the southern city," by those in Mandalay. It is only 12 kilometers (7½ miles) south of Burma's second city, and as the metropolitan area burgeons, the two are slowly joining. Centuries ago, Bodawpaya had a colonnade-flanked road built from his Palace of Amarapura to the Maha Muni Pagoda near present-day Mandalay.

Preceding pages, a coach from bygone times in Maymyo. Left, the earthquake-damaged Mingun Pagoda.

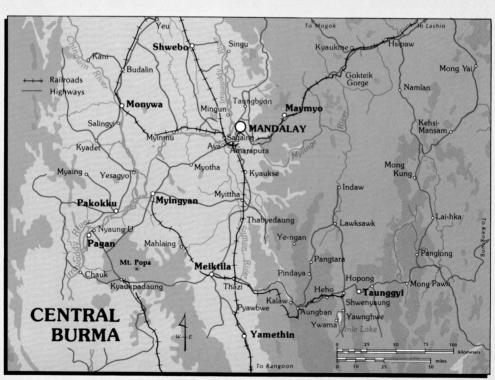

The youngest of the royal cities near Mandalay, Amarapura was built by King Bodawpaya in 1782. It was moved there from Ava on the advice of court astrologers, the Manipurian Brahmans, who were concerned about the circumstances surrounding Bodawpaya's ascendancy to the throne. The power struggle had begun with a massacre and was followed by the horrifying destruction of Paungga village near Sagaing, where the entire population was ordered burned. The Brahmans felt the only way to prevent further mishaps was to transfer the capital; so in May 1783, all of the inhabitants of Ava, together with the court, packed their belongings and moved to land allocated to them around the new Amarapura palace.

The Barnabite priest Sangermano witnessed the mass migration, and described in some detail the new city of 200,000 people. Foreigners had their own quarters—Chinese, Indians, Moslems and Manipuris alike—and the smattering of Christians (primarily Portuguese and Armenians) lived in the Chinese quarter. At the center of the city was Bodawpaya's palace, surrounded by a wall 1.6 kilometers (one mile) in circumference, with a pagoda standing at each of its four corners. Within the wall were the secular buildings made of wood; 75 years later, they were partly torn down and rebuilt in Mandalay by the Konbaung King Mindon.

Bodawpaya was finished with Ava. He had the final remains of the city pulled down, the ancient trees felled and the river diverted to flood the city. His actions did not, however, prevent his successor, King Bagyidaw, from rebuilding the city of Ava and moving the capital back there in 1823. But in 1841, King Tharrawaddy resettled in Amarapura, and the capital remained there until Mindon moved the seat of the Konbaung dynasty to Mandalay.

Weavers and Bronze Casters

Today, Amarapura is a city of 10,000 inhabitants whose main livelihood is weaving cotton and silk into Burma's loveliest festive clothing. The *acheithtameins* (ceremonial *longyis*), which can be knotted over the breasts or worn as a train on all special occasions, are the most famous product of this city in which every second house is said to have a loom. New generations of weavers are

Deserted Amarapura monastery.

trained at Saunders Weaving Institute, founded here in 1914. Many of the Amarapura weavers' products, as well as materials, can be seen at the state purchasing center and cooperative on the town's main street.

A second noted industry of Amarapura is bronze casting. Cymbals, gongs and Buddha images are made here out of a special alloy of bronze and lead. The famous statue of Bogyoke Aung San at the entrance to Aung San Park in Rangoon was cast here.

Nothing remains to be seen of the **Royal Palace.** Some of the wooden buildings were reconstructed in Mandalay by Mindon, and the walls that remained standing were taken by the British as a cheap source of materials for roads and railways. The four pagodas which once marked the corners of the city wall, however, can still be seen. So can two stone buildings—the treasury and the old watchtower. The graves of Bodawpaya and Bagyidaw are also here.

In the southern part of the city sits the well preserved **Patodawgyi Pagoda,** built by King Bagyidaw in 1820. A bell-shaped stupa, it stands on five terraces which are covered with *Jataka* reliefs. There is an inscription stone nearby which tells the story of the construction of the pagoda.

One of the largest monasteries in Burma is on the outskirts of Amarapura. The presence of 700 monks in the **Bagaya Kyaung** contributes a great deal to the religious atmosphere of the city.

To the south of Amarapura is **Lake Taungthaman,** an intermittent body of water which dries up in the winter and leaves fertile, arable land in its stead. It is spanned by the 1.2-kilometer (¾-mile) long **U Bein Bridge,** constructed from the teak planks of Ava by King Bodawpaya's mayor (U Bein) following the move to Amarapura. This rickety teak bridge stands today just as sturdily as it did two centuries ago. It takes about 15 minutes to cross, and during the hot season one is thankful for the rest houses which line it, providing shelter from the sun.

In the middle of a widely scattered village on the east side of the bridge is the **Kyauktawgyi Pagoda,** built by King Pagan in 1847. Like the Kyauk Tawgyi in Mandalay, this pagoda was intended to be a replica of the Ananda Temple in Pagan. The exterior is a successful imitation, but the interior arches do not do justice to the original. Instead of the four standing

A farmer goads his animals through the ruins of Amarapura.

Buddhas found in the Ananda Temple, this pagoda contains an enormous Buddha made of Sagyin marble. The color resembles that of jade; its height reaches the ceiling of the inner cella.

Within the shrine are 88 statues of the Buddha's disciples, as well as 12 *manusihas*, mythical half-man half-beast beings. The temple's east and west entrances are decorated with murals depicting the daily life of the Burmese at the time of the pagoda's construction. Under careful scrutiny, European faces can be seen among the Burmese in the paintings. A repeated theme of the murals is the good will of King Pagan toward his people; this is ironic because Pagan was one of the cruelest kings of Burma's Konbaung dynasty. It is said that as many as 3,000 death sentences were carried out in a single year during his reign.

The area surrounding the Kyauktawgyi Pagoda is full of smaller pagodas in various stages of decay. These temples have been systematically plundered ever since the prices of ancient Burmese artifacts reached astronomical levels in the antique shops of Bangkok.

On Amarapura's Irrawaddy bank, two white pagodas—the Shwekyetyet Pagoda and the Shwekyetkya Pagoda—remain from the Era of the Temple Builders. They were built by a 12th Century king of Pagan, and can be found about 30 minutes' walk from Amarapura's main street.

A short distance downriver lies the Thabyedan Fort, which King Mindon had French and Italian advisors erect in European style. The fort was intended to stop any hostile armies from striking with warships from the Irrawaddy. Yet when the British invaded Mandalay in 1886 in exactly such a fashion, not a shot was fired: the Burmese, lacking strong armed forces, had already given up.

Ancient Ava: 'The City of Gems'

The No. 8 bus from Mandalay travels right down the main street of Amarapura and continues to Ava. Near the famed Ava Bridge over the Irrawaddy, a dusty, pot-holed road leads to the Myitnge River ferry; on the river's opposite bank, horse-drawn carriages wait to take travelers on to the ancient capital. During the rainy season, this entire region is flooded, and Ava can be reached only by boat.

The U Bein Bridge, left; and Ava's Maha Aungmye Bonzan Monastery.

194

Indeed, the city's name means "entrance to the lake," a variant of the Shan phrase *in-va*. It is appropriate, as the entire rice trade of the Kyaukse Plain was once controlled from this capital at the junction of the Irrawaddy and Myitnge rivers. Such economic control was a necessity for the foundation of a sound state and strong dynasty, and it was in this region, around the 11 hamlets of the Kyaukse district, that the nucleus of a new Burmese empire took shape after the fall of Pagan in 1287 to the Mongol army of Kublai Khan.

The city of Ava was founded in 1364 by King Thadominbya, who built it in the northeast corner of an artificial island created by the Myittha Chaung, a channel dug from the Myitnge to the Irrawaddy. It remained standing through various conquests as capital of Upper Burma until 1634, and as capital of all Burma for another century and a half after that. Even during the 19th Century, the entire Burmese Empire was generally known as "Ava;" and when the seat of government moved to Amarapura and later to Mandalay, the government was still referred to as the "Court of Ava." The classical name by which Ava is

known in Burma, however, is Ratnapura—"the city of gems."

Unlike most other royal cities of Burma, Ava's city wall is not square, but is shaped like a sitting lion, such as those found in front of large pagodas. Only a part of the wall still stands; the most complete section is at the north gate, known as **Gaung Say Daga**, the gate of the hair-washing ceremony. Every April during the Thingyan Festival, this ritual hair-washing takes place as a purification rite to welcome the king of the nats. Today it exists only in private homes, but in imperial times, the king was required to wash his hair at this gate.

Near the north gate are the ruins of the **Nanmyin Watchtower**, the so-called "leaning tower of Ava." All that remains of Bagyidaw's palace, this erstwhile 27-meter (89-foot) lookout was damaged so heavily by an 1838 earthquake that its upper portion collapsed and it began leaning because the earth was sinking beneath it. The same earthquake, which caused widespread damage throughout the area, hastened the final abandonment of Ava.

Not far from the "leaning tower" is the best preserved of all buildings in Ava, the

The Ava Bridge.

Maha Aungmye Bonzan monastery. Also known as the Ok Kyaung, the brick structure was built in 1818 by Nanmadaw Me Nu, wife of King Bagyidaw, for the abbot Sayadaw Nyaunggan, who was rumored to have been her lover. A tall, stucco-decorated building, it was built in the same style as that of more common teak *kyaungs;* yet its masonry guaranteed it would survive longer than its wooden cousins.

In the middle of the monastery is a statue of the Buddha, placed on a pedestal trimmed with glass mosaic. Beside the archway leading into the building is an old marble plaque which tells, in English, the story of an American missionary's Burmese wife who was a staunch convert to Christianity until her death during the First Anglo-Burmese War.

Next door to the *kyaung* is a seven-tiered prayer hall. This building suffered heavy damage in the 1838 earthquake, but was repaired in 1873 by Hsin-byumashin, daughter of Nanmadaw Me Nu.

In the vicinity of the monastery is the **Adoniram Judson Memorial.** Judson, an American missionary who compiled the first Anglo-Burmese dictionary, was jailed during the First Anglo-Burmese War and endured severe torture during his imprisonment. He had mistakenly assumed that the Burmese would distinguish between the British colonialists and the American missionaries. The white stone memorial is on the site of the notorious Let Ma Yoon prison.

There are many pagodas in the Ava region. Among them is the **Htilainshin Pagoda,** built by King Kyanzittha during the Pagan era. Other important shrines include the four-story **Leitutgyi Pagoda** and the **Lawkatharaphu Pagoda,** both in the southern part of the city. Some 1½ kilometers (one mile) south of the city stands **Ava Fort,** which was considered part of the "unconquerable triangle" including Thabyedan and Sagaing forts.

South of the existing city of Ava is an old brick causeway leading across the canal to the village of **Tada-u.** Within the old city walls are several other small villages with thriving paddy fields where once the center of the Burmese Empire stood.

North of Ava is the famous **Ava Bridge,** built by the British in 1934 and still the only bridge across the Irrawaddy River. It connects Ava with Sagaing (the cross-

The hills of Sagaing.

ing can also be made by ferry) some 20 kilometers (12½ miles) south of Mandalay. There are military posts at each end of the bridge, and a small toll is collected there. Because of its strategic importance, the British blew the bridge up in the face of the Japanese advance in 1942, and not until 1954 was it reopened.

Sagaing: Living
Center of the Faith

Whereas Amarapura and Ava are ancient capitals left largely at the mercy of the elements, Sagaing remains very much alive. In fact, some consider Sagaing to be the living center of the Buddhist faith in Burma today.

The city reverberates with the echoes of cymbals, gongs and pagoda bells. Refugees from the hectic pace of urban life retreat here—for a day or a lifetime—to meditate. Devout families bring their young sons to undergo the *shin-pyu* ceremony and thereby join the community of the faithful.

In the hills and in the many-fingered valleys of the west bank of the Irrawaddy are some 600 monasteries, as well as numerous temples, stupas and caves dedi-

cated to the memory of the Gautama Buddha. About 5,000 monks live in this arcadian landscape laced with endless stairways and colonnades. From Sagaing north to Mingun, the slopes are covered with frangipani, bougainvillea, tamarind and mango trees, in whose shadows earthen water bowls await thirsty pilgrims. The monasteries and private houses are hidden in the hills and valleys, but the big temples and pagodas ride the crests of the verdant heights and glitter across the land.

Sagaing is different each hour of the day—in the morning, when the *pongyis* and their students stream out of the *kyaungs* with their begging bowls; in the midday heat, when the ringing of the stupa bells and the droning of the monks' prayers rise over all other sounds; in the evening, when the lights of Mandalay light up the far bank of the Irrawaddy. Burmese view Sagaing as a "foothill" of mystical Mount Meru: it is easy to rise above everyday banalities here.

If you've come here on a booked tour, there will be no time for contemplation. The Jeep stops briefly at the **Sun U Ponya Shin Pagoda**, the snapshot enthusiast's favorite viewpoint, then rushes on to

The U Min Kyaukse Pagoda.

other sights which can be crammed into a single day's sightseeing. The independent traveler can better savor the inimitable atmosphere of Sagaing by staying overnight in one of the many monasteries, whose abbots are very generous.

From Mandalay, Sagaing is most quickly reached by collector bus from the corner of 29th Road and 83rd Street. Horse carriages will take the visitor to the monastery-studded hills behind the town, but hiring a Jeep is recommended for travels further afield.

Ancient Shan Capital

Sagaing was the capital of an independent Shan kingdom beginning about 1315, after the fall of Pagan. The capital was moved to Ava in 1364. Most of the buildings in the vicinity were constructed during the Ava period.

Probably the most famous temple in Sagaing is the **Kaunghmudaw Pagoda.** It actually lies 10 kilometers (six miles) behind the city on the far side of the Sagaing Hills. Built by King Thalun in 1636 to house relics formerly kept in the Mahazedi Pagoda in Pegu, it is said to contain the Buddha's "Tooth of Kandy" and King Dhammapala's miracle-working begging bowl.

Built in Ceylonese style, this pagoda's rounded shape—a perfect hemisphere—is according to legend a copy of the perfect breasts of Thalun's favorite wife. The huge egg-shaped dome, 46 meters (151 feet) high and 274 meters (900 feet) in circumference, rises above three rounded terraces. The lowest terrace is decorated with 120 *nats* and *devas,* each of which can be found in a separate niche. A ring of 812 molded stone pillars, each 1½ meters (five feet) high, surround the dome; each of these posts has a hollowed-out head in which an oil lamp is placed during the Thadingyut Light Festival on the occasion of the October full moon. Burmese Buddhists come to the Kaunghmudaw Pagoda from far and wide to celebrate the end of Buddhist lent at this annual festival. The history of the pagoda, which is also called the Rajamanicula, is written in Burmese script on a white marble pillar 2½ meters (8½ feet) high in a corner of the pagoda grounds.

Two lakes lie behind the Kaunghmudaw Pagoda. One of them was formed when bricks used in construction of the pagoda were stacked; it is now used for

A *sayadaw* leads a procession of monks.

198

breeding fish. The other lake, called **Lake Myitta Kan,** is legendary: it is said that no leaf from surrounding trees has ever touched the lake's surface.

There are two interesting attractions on the road between the Kaunghmudaw Pagoda and Sagaing. One is the village of **Ywataung,** home of silversmiths who still work the precious mineral in much the same way as their ancestors did. The other is the **Hsinmyashin Pagoda,** also called the Pagoda of Many Elephants. Built in 1429 by King Monhyin, it was destroyed in 1482 by an earthquake. It was restored, but a 1955 quake nearly leveled it, and it is currently being rebuilt. Two colorful large elephants have been reconstructed at the long entrance to the pagoda.

The Unfinished Pagoda

The **Htupayon Pagoda** in Sagaing town, built by King Narapati in 1444, is also unfinished. It was destroyed by the 1838 earthquake, and King Pagan—who wanted to have it rebuilt—was dethroned before repairs were completed. The 30-meter (98-foot) high base is standing, however, and it represents a rare style of temple architecture in Burma. In a nearby hut are a collection of stone engravings which include the history of the Shan Prince Thonganbwa. The prince wanted to re-establish the ancient Nan-chao Empire in present-day Yunnan (China), but he was pursued by a Chinese army and took refuge in Ava. King Narapati provided him sanctuary and defeated the Chinese in a battle on the prince's behalf in 1445. A year later, however, the Chinese returned with a stronger army—and rather than allow himself to be handed over to the Chinese, Prince Thonganbwa committed suicide. His body was surrendered, and Ava was committed to paying allegiance to the Chinese.

Like the Htupayon, the **Ngadatgyi Pagoda** rests on the western side of Sagaing. There is an enormous seated Buddha image in this temple. The Ngadatgyi was erected in 1657 by King Pindale, the ill-fated successor to King Thalun. Pindale was dethroned by his brother in 1661, and a few weeks later was drowned together with his entire family. (This was a common means of putting royalty to death because there was no blood spilled on the soil.)

Htis for Sagaing's pagodas.

The **Aungmyelawka Pagoda,** built by King Bodawpaya in 1783 on the Irrawaddy riverfront near the Htupayon Pagoda, is a cylindrical sandstone replica of the Shwezigon Pagoda in Nyaung U. Bodawpaya had it built on the site of the house where he spent the years prior to his coronation. According to the will of Bodawpaya's father, King Alaungpaya, he should have become king upon the death of his brother, Hsinbyushin. But when the latter proclaimed his son Singu to be his successor, Bodawpaya had to stand aside until a short-lived coup by another aspiring ruler gave him the opening he needed in 1782 to claim the throne that was rightfully his. In the interim, Bodawpaya lived in Sagaing. Construction of the Aungmyelawka Pagoda was intended to balance the "necessary cruelties" of his reign and improve his merit for future incarnations. This pagoda is also known as the Eindawya Pagoda.

The **Datpaungzu Pagoda** is of rather recent vintage, having been built only upon the completion of the Myitkyina Railway. It is a repository for the relics of a number of stupas which had to be demolished or relocated in clearing the way for the railway to cross the Ava Bridge.

The relics are much venerated by the people of the region.

On the most easterly point of the two ridges rising above Sagaing stands the **U Min Kyaukse Pagoda,** the architectural style of which is immediately reminiscent of a mosque. Its roof affords a fine view over Mandalay and the Irrawaddy. The **Shwe Ume Kyaung,** a monastery attached to this pagoda, is a popular *shinpyu* site because of its location.

On the western hill stands the **Sun U Ponya Shin Pagoda,** easily reached by car from the Sagaing market. Further back in the western hill chain lies the **U Min Thonze Pagoda,** where 45 Buddha images bask in a soft light, posed in a semicircle. Mural paintings hundreds of years old can be found in the **Tilawkaguru Cave** and the **Myipaukgyi Pagoda.**

The **Pa Ba Kyaung** is one of the best known monasteries of all Burma. Situated in the floor of the valley between the two ridges, it is enveloped in silence and ideal for the quiet meditation demanded by *pongyis.*

A road passes the monastery and leads to the Irrawaddy, from where a rowboat will carry visitors to the Sagaing market for one kyat.

Mystic mood of a monk at twilight.

Mingun: A Big Bell
And a Mound of Bricks

At the northern end of the chain of hills flanking Sagaing, resting on the banks of the Irrawaddy, is the village of Mingun, home of the largest intact bell in the world—as well as an unfinished pagoda sometimes described as the biggest pile of bricks on earth. Sharp eyes can see it from Mandalay Hill, although it lies more than 10 kilometers (6½ miles) to the northwest.

Mingun is accessible only by river. Boats leave Mandalay daily at 7:30 and 8:30 a.m. bound for the little village; it takes about an hour to make the trip from the end of B Road. Visitors who do not intend to take the Irrawaddy steamer from Mandalay to Pagan should not miss this short trip, as there is no better way to observe life on Burma's throbbing artery. Ferries, teak and bamboo rafts, paddle steamers, and numerous small boats which always appear to be on the brink of sinking ply the Irrawaddy between Myitkyina in the far north and Bassein in the delta. Women can often be seen traveling north from Mandalay, walking down the river bank and towing their boats behind them, as their husbands sit at the tillers to make sure the boats don't strike any obstacles. Parallel rows of well trodden paths are evidence of the widely varying water levels of the Irrawaddy: the banks can sometimes be 12 meters (39 feet) above the river during the dry season.

Mingun is a favorite destination for Mandalay residents on day outings. To cater to their tastes, a series of tea shops line the road from the jetty. Where the row of tea shops ends, there is a convalescent home for homeless Burmese behind the embankment.

Behind and to the left of the home is the famous **Mingun Bell.** It weighs 87 tons, stands 3.7 meters (more than 12 feet) high, and is five meters (16½ feet) wide at its mouth. And it still works. It is said the world's only larger bell is in the Kremlin in Moscow, but that one is cracked and can no longer be used. King Bodawpaya had this bell cast in 1790 to be dedicated to his huge Mingun Pagoda, which was intended to be the world's largest. If you can imagine how painstaking the molding and casting procedures must have been in the 18th Century, you can begin to appreciate what a fine work of

The Mingun Bell, left; and bottled Buddhas.

art this bell is. Bodawpaya recognized this fact, so to prevent the feat from being repeated, he had the artist executed.

During the 1838 earthquake, the Mingun Bell and its original *tazaung* collapsed. Fortunately, there was no damage. Today the bell is held up by heavy iron rods beneath a shelter. Small Burmese boys who frequent the site are only too willing to show visitors where to strike the bell with a wooden mallet to produce the best sound.

Bodawpaya's Pet Project

The **Mingun (Mantara Gyi) Pagoda** stands some 100 meters (328 feet) south of the bell. From a distance, its appearance is that of a large mound, nothing more. Yet it played a very important role in Burmese history in the last century.

The pagoda was built between 1790 and 1797 by Bodawpaya, fourth son of Alaungpaya, founder of the Konbaung dynasty. Bodawpaya was lord of Tenasserim, the Mon lands, and Arakan, as well as central Burma. He had underscored his invincibility by carrying the Maha Muni from Arakan to Amarapura, and he had just become the proud owner of a white elephant. He was at the peak of his power and wanted the world to see.

In 1790, a Chinese delegation visited Bodawpaya's court, carrying as gifts a tooth of the Buddha and three of the Chinese emperor's daughters as wives. Bodawpaya had the pagoda built to house the tooth—the same one that both Anawrahta and Alaungpaya had coveted but had failed to obtain. Bodawpaya moved his residence to an island in the Irrawaddy for the next seven years while he supervised the construction work. Bodawpaya intended to make his Mantara Gyi a full 152 meters (499 feet) in height. He imported thousands of slaves from his newly conquered territories to the south, and set them to work on the pagoda.

Too Many Rods
In the King's Fire

The pagoda, however, was not Bodawpaya's only project. At the same time that pagoda construction was commencing, the king had renewed work on the enormous Mektila Dam project, for which he also had "recruited" thousands of workers. In addition, large armies were deployed to help keep his empire under

Hsinbyume Pagoda, left, is modeled on Mount Meru with its seven ranges of hills, right.

his control. Under great oppression, 50,000 Arakanese fled to neighboring Bengal, which was then under British rule, and began a guerrilla war against the Burmese. This conflict later exploded into the First Anglo-Burmese War.

The lack of available labor in central Burma was irritating to Bodawpaya. Worried rumors which had circulated 500 years earlier during construction of the Minglazedi Pagoda had resurfaced, and concerned voices were saying, "When the pagoda is finished, the great country will be ruined." But Bodawpaya, convinced of his destiny as a future Buddha, was not to be dissuaded. He had the pagoda's shrine rooms lined with lead and filled with 1,500 gold figurines, 2,534 silver images, and nearly 37,000 of various other materials. He even included a soda-water machine, just invented in England, according to Hiram Cox, British envoy to Bodawpaya's court. The rooms were then sealed.

The economic ruin which raged at the turn of the 19th Century persuaded Bodawpaya to halt construction work on the pagoda. The king died in 1813, aged 75, having ruled for 38 years. He left 122 children and 208 grandchildren—but none of them continued his work on the great pagoda.

Even though it was never completed, the ruins of the Mingun Pagoda are most impressive. The upper sections of the pagoda collapsed into the hollow shrine rooms during the great 1838 earthquake, but the base of the structure still towers nearly 50 meters (162 feet) over the Irrawaddy. An enormous pair of griffins, also damaged in the quake, guard the riverfront view. The lowest terrace of the pagoda measures 137 meters (450 feet) square in size, and arches project from each of its four sides.

Miniature Monstrosity

In the immediate vicinity is the smaller **Pondawpaya Pagoda,** a small replica of the original Mantarà Gyi. Compare it to its large neighbor, and you'll see that King Bodawpaya's monstrosity on the Irrawaddy reached only one-third of its planned height. After making the comparison, take off your shoes and climb to the platform on the north side of the Mingun Pagoda for the view.

A short distance downstream is the **Settawya Pagoda.** This building is en-

tirely white, and has a stairway leading to its hollow vault from the water's edge. Built by Bodawpaya in 1811, it holds a marble footprint of the Buddha.

At the north end of Mingun, beyond the village, one of the prettiest pagodas in Burma is found. This is the **Hsinbyume** or **Myatheindan Pagoda,** built by Bodawpaya's grandson Bagyidaw in 1816, three years before he ascended the throne, as a memorial to his favorite wife, Princess Hsinbyume. The temple's architecture is founded in Buddhist cosmology, according to which the Sulamani Pagoda stands atop Mount Meru in the center of the universe. The king of the gods (known variously as Indra, Sakka, or Thagyamin) lives here on top of the mountain, surrounded by seven additional mountain chains. The Myatheindan Pagoda is based on this model: seven concentric terraces with wave-like railings lead to the central stupa, which is guarded by five kinds of mythical monsters placed in niches around the terraces. (Temple robbers have unfortunately decapitated most of the monsters.) In the highest part of the stupa, reachable only by a steep stairway, is the cella containing a single Buddha figure. This pagoda suffered severe damage in the 1838 earthquake, but was rebuilt by King Mindon in 1874.

Most visitors to Mingun remain only a half-day, thereby depriving themselves of the magical scenery at the foot of the Mingun hills. As in Sagaing, the mountainside is covered with *kyaungs* and small pagodas woven together by a network of shadowy paths. Those who wish to explore the enchanting hinterland of Mingun must plan on spending the night in one of the monasteries, as the return boat to Mandalay leaves Mingun at 3 p.m.

Maymyo: Where British Escaped the Heat

Those who have a weak spot for the atmosphere of British colonial times, and others just seeking to escape the dusty misery of Mandalay's hot season, must visit Maymyo, in the foothills of the Shan Plateau. A 2½-hour drive by Jeep collective from Mandalay takes the traveler to 1,070 meters (3,510 feet) elevation, from where there are breathtaking views across the Mandalay plain.

Maymyo is named after Colonel May, a British officer in the Bengal Infantry

who was stationed at this hill station in 1887 in order to suppress a rebellion which flared after the annexation of Upper Burma to India. The city, called Pyinulwin by natives, lies at a strategically important point on the road from Mandalay to Hsipaw, one of two major Shan principalities in the north of Burma.

Pleasant temperatures predominate in Maymyo even during the hot season, and in the cold season there is no frost. It's no wonder the British felt at home here. All varieties of European vegetables are grown, and there are coffee and banana plantations as well as pineapples and strawberries. Chrysanthemums, which decorate pagodas throughout Burma, are grown here in the highlands.

General Ne Win has a summer house in Maymyo, and the Burmese army maintains a large garrison. A number of Indian and Nepali gurkhas whose forebears (and in some cases, who themselves) entered the country with the Indian army have settled here, retaining many of the old colonial traditions in their work as hoteliers, carriage drivers and gardeners.

Maymyo's central attraction is the **Candacraig.** This hotel, once a relaxation center for the Bombay Burma Trading Company, was built in 1905 in the style of an English country home. It still offers many of the niceties which once made the lives of the company's clerks so pleasurable—English food, early-morning tea, and a big fireplace. The hotel is set in the hills, surrounded by pines, poplars, oaks, eucalyptus, chestnut trees and rhododendron bushes, and quickly makes one forget the oppressive heat of the lowlands.

Maymyo also has a 175-hectare (432-acre) **Botanical Garden,** an 18-hole golf course, and three waterfalls in the vicinity for swimming and picnics. Horse-drawn carriages are the chief mode of transportation; these closed vehicles with their high doors appear to have been left behind by the 19th Century.

Burma's Isolated Northern Frontier

Beyond Maymyo, Burma's northern and eastern frontiers are accessible to Westerners only with a special government pass, obtainable only in Rangoon and then only in the rarest of circumstances. The rail line which passes through Maymyo (it's a five-hour train trip from Mandalay) continues as far as the northern Shan administrative center of Lashio. But the continuing conflict between government troops and rebellious tribesmen and opium traders makes strict security necessary.

Paul Theroux's *The Great Railway Bazaar* contains a couple of classic chapters about the joys and hazards of this unusual rail passage. Theroux's tales of vendors carrying fried locusts and skewered sparrows on rice, government soldiers in dented helmets reddening the earth with betel-nut spittle, and cavernous tunnels "smelling of bat shit and sodden plants" are essential advance reading for the would-be back-country Burma traveler.

It is unlikely you will be able to get a pass, but if you do, you can travel by train across the famous **Gokteik Viaduct,** which traverses a 300-meter (984-foot) deep gorge in the Shan mountains. When it was built in 1903, the viaduct was considered a masterpiece, even by Western standards, because of the technical difficulties and transportation problems that had to be overcome. Theroux, in his 1973 travels, called the viaduct "a monster of silver geometry in all the ragged

rock and jungle . . . Its presence there was bizarre, this manmade thing in so remote a place, competing with the grandeur of the enormous gorge and yet seeming more grand than its surroundings, which were hardly negligible—the water rushing through the girder legs and falling on the tops of trees, the flights of birds through the swirling clouds and the blackness of the tunnels beyond the viaduct."

Beyond the viaduct is the town of **Kyaukme,** where every March the Shan Festival is held. Thousands of Shan tribesmen, representing the second largest ethnic group in Burma, flock to this town from all over the Shan Highlands to participate.

'Chinese Jade' From The Mines of Mogok

A road from Kyaukme leads 80 kilometers (50 miles) to the northwest to the town of **Mogok.** Famous for its jade and ruby mines, Mogok for centuries sold Chinese artists the shiny jade known elsewhere as "Chinese jade." Most visitors to Burma are secretly offered jade and rubies from these mines, but only those persons with a real knowledge of stones, and who are willing to risk their illegal export, should consider buying any of them.

Continuing from Kyaukme on the main rail line toward Lashio, one passes near **Sakhtana,** where the palace of the *sawbwa* (prince) of the Hsipaw district stands. Finally, the train arrives in **Lashio.** The city is situated in a very pretty area, at its best during the winter months when trees and other plants are in blossom. The market is an important gathering spot for northern Shans, who come here from remote valleys to do their trading.

From Lashio, the **Burma Road**—built by the British prior to World War II— leads into the rugged Chinese province of Yunnan. Shortly before reaching the international border, it intersects with the **Ledo Road,** which crosses Burma from India. Built by American engineers during the war, it weaves through river valleys and around mountain ridges to Myitkyina, capital of the Kachin State, then on to India's Brahmaputra Valley.

In **Bhamo,** which lies on the road to Myitkyina, there is another colorful market where a real mixture of tribes is found. The Kachins (also called

A "shaman" of north Burma, left; and the distant Shan hills.

Jinghpaws) can be identified by their black turbans. The Shans are dressed in brown, the Palaungs in multi-colored robes and the Lishus in their blue-and-red-striped national dress. Thirty kilometers (19 miles) east of here, very near the Chinese border, is the ancient city of **Sampanago.** A former trading town mentioned in many early books and travel documents, its functions were moved to Bhamo in the 17th Century.

Bhamo sits on the Irrawaddy's east bank, and is the departure point for what is potentially the most impressive river trip in Burma. The Irrawaddy steamer from Bhamo to Mandalay goes through dense jungle and across three rapids, and Tourist Burma has already prepared plans to make this trip accessible to tourists. The final okay, however, must come from the upper echelons of the Burmese government; given the army's continuing problems with insurgents, it may be a long time in coming.

Ancient Cities

Should the trip be approved, travelers will have an opportunity to visit some of Burma's most ancient cities. **Tagaung,** a thriving city before the Buddha was born some 2,500 years ago, lies on the Irrawaddy's east bank about 200 kilometers (125 miles) downstream from Bhamo, and about the same distance due north of Mandalay. The city is said to have been founded by a Sakya king from India, although its name derives from the Shan *takwang,* "drum ferry." But the modern city was built upon the ruins of the old, so there is nothing to be seen of it except the old fortification.

In a nearby archaeological dig called **Old Pagan,** however, the remains of the original Shwezigon Pagoda can be seen. It was repaired in 1902, only to collapse again shortly thereafter. Not one Buddha image has been unearthed here, convincing evidence of the settlement's age: Buddha images were not produced until the 1st Century A.D. During the First Burmese Kingdom, both Old Pagan and Tagaung apparently conducted a lively commercial and cultural exchange with Pagan itself: votive tablets found in Tagaung, dating from that time, are an indication of this.

Myitkyina, Burma's northernmost sizeable town, lies in the foothills of the great Himalaya Range. Beyond here are the

nearly inaccessible climes of the remote Kachin State. A number of smaller tribes live by hunting in this wilderness which harbors tigers, leopards, bears, elephants, even an occasional rhinoceros.

The three-day-long Manao Festival takes place in Myitkyina every January. It is a stimulating "feast of merit," a get-together for the spirit-worshipping mountain folk of the surrounding wilderness, traditionally involving the sacrifice of a buffalo to the *nats* and the non-stop recitation by priests of *nat* sagas for days on end. Were tourists permitted to visit, this festival would be a unique opportunity to observe the customs and rituals of isolated tribespeople who are otherwise totally cut off from the world.

Alaungpaya's Capital

The northern rail line from Mandalay has its terminus in Myitkyina. On the return trip to Mandalay, the traveler passes through **Shwebo**, about 100 kilometers (60 miles) north of Upper Burma's metropolis. Shwebo was an 18th Century capital for Alaungpaya, and it was from here that the reconquest of Burma began after the Mons had seized Ava in 1752.

Alaungpaya's grave is in Shwebo, and his headstone displays an inscription in very fractured English. Otherwise, all trappings of royalty have disappeared.

Eighteen kilometers (11 miles) southeast of Shwebo are the ruins of the old Pyu city of **Halin** (**Halingyi**). Legend takes its origins back into pre-history—an Indian dynasty is said to have produced a continuous line of 799 kings until the city one day disappeared under a cloud of ash. Archaeologists, however, place the city's establishment between the 2nd and 6th centuries A.D., based upon radiocarbon analyses of the burnt remains of the city wall. Remnants of 12 gates in the 3-by-1½-kilometer wall can still be seen today. In all likelihood, Halin was the northern Pyu capital overrun by the Nan-chao kingdom of the Tai in 832.

Near Shwebo are the small villages of **Monhla** and **Chantha** where European *Bayingyis*, exiled by Burmese kings, once settled. Missionary priests served here as early as 1702. But no *Bayingyis* (the word means "foreigner") have been exiled in Burma for some 200 years now, and the only reminder of the villages' European history is an occasional blond head on an otherwise Burmese body.

Taungbyon Spirit Festival

For eight days before the last full moon every August, the village of Taungbyon, 20 kilometers (13 miles) north of Mandalay, becomes the focus of the Taungbyon Spirit Festival. Tens of thousands of Burmese attend this annual celebration, held in honor of the Taungbyon Brother Lords. The rites for these two brothers, honored as *nats*, originated during Anawrahta's 11th Century reign. Wooden figures, representing the brothers, are ceremonially washed and paraded through the crowds as everyone present strains to touch each of the figures at least once.

The brothers are in fact historical figures. They were sons of Byatta, a Moslem warrior from India who used supernatural means to recover the Mons' Buddhist scriptures during Anawrahta's conquest of Thaton. According to legend, Byatta was appointed Anawrahta's flower officer, but he fell in love with Me Wunna, an ogress who lived on the wooded slopes of Mount Popa. She bore him two sons, Shwepyingyi and Shwepyinnge. Byatta was so fond of his family that he often dallied at Mount Popa, and when he failed for a third time to

fulfill his duty of providing the king with daily flowers, he was executed.

Anawrahta coerced Byatta's two sons to his palace, plied them with gifts of "inferior gold" (gold mixed with copper), and took the brothers with him on a campaign in Yunnan. Upon their return, the king's forces paused at the present site of Taungbyon village, where Anawrahta ordered construction of a pagoda. The two brothers, preferring marbles to hard work, shirked their assignment of laying a brick in this new Taungbyon Pagoda and were condemned to death. The Burmese people mourned the death of the two young men. These two new spirits quickly became so powerful that Anawrahta proclaimed them *nats*, had a shrine built for them in Taungbyon, and ordered an annual festival be held in their honor.

Perhaps nowhere else is there such an open display of Burmese Buddhism's animistic essence as at the brothers' festival in this small village. There are ritual offerings, ceremonial dances, dozens of *pwes*, consultations with shamans, an enormous bazaar, and lots of eating, gambling and general carousing. In the words of anthropologist Melford Spiro, it is "a combination, Burmese-style, of an American state fair and a medieval miracle play."

Celebrant at the Taungbyon Festival.

THE PAGODA-STUDDED PLAIN OF PAGAN

Pagan (is) in many respects the most remarkable religious city in the world. Jerusalem, Rome, Kieff [Kiev], Benares, none of these can boast the multitude of temples, and the lavishness of design and ornament that make marvellous the deserted capital on the Irrawaddy. ... the whole space is thickly studded with pagodas of all sizes and shapes, and the very ground is so thickly covered with crumbling remnants of vanished shrines, that according to the popular saying you cannot move foot or hand without touching a sacred thing.

—*Shway Yoe (Sir James Scott)*, The Burman: His Life and Notions (1882)

The Pagan of the 1980s is not the Pagan that Scott knew in the 1880s. There were no tourist hotels then, no camera-carrying travelers and no airport. Horse-drawn wagons were the only means of transportation, not a mere alternative.

But in many respects, Pagan has changed very little in the past century. It is still as Scott saw it—Burma's "deserted capital on the Irrawaddy," "thickly studded with pagodas of all sizes and shapes," a veritable elephants' graveyard of medieval Burmese culture. There is nowhere, perhaps, a sight so striking as the view across the plain of Pagan—one red-brick pagoda after another, with an occasional white spire reaching heavenward, encasing a large area on the dusty eastern shore of Burma's greatest river.

Era of the Temple Builders

Between the time of Anawrahta's conquest of Thaton in 1057, until Pagan was overrun by Kublai Khan's forces in 1287, some 13,000 temples, pagodas, *kyaungs* and other religious structures were built on this vast plain. Seven centuries later, only 2,217 of these remain standing. Many of the others persist as piles of rubble, although the Irrawaddy has washed away about one-third of the original city. The legacy of Burma's Era of the Temple Builders is here for all to see, however. If Pagan were situated on a main Asian tourist route rather than on a hot dusty plain in central Burma, every child in the West would know Pagan as well as Kyoto's temples or the Taj Mahal.

There has been a settlement in the region of Pagan since early in the 2nd Century A.D., when Thamuddarit, a Pyu king, led his followers here. The walls of the city were erected by King Pyinbia in 849, but it was left to King Anawrahta, 42nd ruler of the Pagan dynasty, to usher in the city's age of glory, and to his successor, King Kyanzittha, to perpetuate that glory.

Anawrahta ascended to the Pagan throne in 1044 after killing his predecessor, Sokkate, in a duel. His victory over the Mons through the conquest of their capital of Thaton in 1057 marked the turning point in Pagan's history.

Theravada Buddhism had not yet permeated Upper Burma at the time of Anawrahta's ascent. Instead, a mix of animistic beliefs blended with Shaivism, Mahayana Buddhism and Tantrism. But a young monk from Thaton, a Brahman priest's son named Shin Arahan, was so successful in converting Anawrahta to the Theravada school that the king became consumed with spreading the doctrine among his people.

There are several stories about how this came to occur. The most generally accepted is that Shin Arahan, as a young man of about 20, traveled north from his home in Thaton to live as a hermit in the woods near Pagan. Anawrahta heard of his presence there and sent for him, curious about what this saffron-clad monk might have to offer. Upon arriving at the king's palace, Shin Arahan promptly sat himself down on the king's throne—an act normally punishable by death—to illustrate his belief that the only truth was that of the Buddha.

An Intrepid Ally

Rather than punishing this dauntless monk, Anawrahta took him as an ally. At the time of his meeting with Shin Arahan, the king was engaged in a cultural and religious campaign against *nat* worship and the Tantric debauchery of the Ari monks of Upper Burma. In Shin Arahan's teachings, he found a belief based upon rationalism rather than mysticism.

Now committed to exposing his empire to Theravada doctrines, Anawrahta sent to King Manuha of Thaton requesting copies of the *Tripitaka* (scriptures).

But Manuha hesitated, repulsed by the thought of sharing sacred writings with "barbarians," and that was his demise. Anawrahta wasted no time in responding to this affront: he massed his armies and invaded Lower Burma, sacking Thaton and bringing back to Pagan everything his elephants and men could carry—30 sets of the *Tripitaka*, architects, Buddhist monks, even King Manuha himself and the royal family.

Almost immediately upon returning to his capital, Anawrahta embarked on his program of embellishing the countryside with Buddhist monuments. The Shwesandaw Pagoda was the first of these, and many others followed.

As king, Anawrahta was entitled to several wives. He had been given glowing reports of an Indian princess named Panchakalyani, and sent an envoy to woo her to his court. The princess' father consented to the match. But on the return journey, the envoy had an affair with the princess. In order to keep this a secret and avoid the king's wrath, he ordered Panchakalyani's escorts back to her father's court, then informed Anawrahta that he doubted the princess' claim to royal descent because she did not have escorts.

European artist's impression of Pagan in 1825.

Anawrahta could not return Panchakalyani to her home because he was by law already married to her. So he banished her to Payeinma on the Chindwin River, and it was here that her son Kyanzittha, later to become Pagan's greatest king, was born. The boy was by law the king's son, but was probably the envoy's.

Like Father, Like Son

Like his biological father, perhaps, young Kyanzittha was easily enthralled by a pretty face. Some time after the conquest of Thaton, he was ordered to accompany the daughter of the king of Pegu to the court of Pagan, where she was to become Anawrahta's wife. But Kyanzittha fell in love with her, and when Anawrahta caught wind of the affair, he ordered Kyanzittha bound. Anawrahta planned to kill the youth himself. But according to legend, on this one occasion Anawrahta's mythical spear "Areindama" failed him; instead of piercing Kyanzittha's flesh, the blade cut his bonds, and the youth fled and hid near Sagaing with a sympathetic monk.

Anawrahta was killed in 1077 by a wild buffalo. His son Sawlu, who succeeded to the throne, was faced with quelling major rebellions among the Mons to the south, and asked Kyanzittha—a master warrior—for assistance.

Still, there was no love lost between the half-brothers. In one important battle in 1084, Sawlu ignored Kyanzittha's tactical advice and attacked the Mon forces. His army was soon defeated, and Sawlu taken prisoner. Kyanzittha stole into the enemy camp one night to attempt to free his king, but Sawlu thought Kyanzittha had come to kill him, and called on his own enemies to save him. Kyanzittha escaped, but Sawlu was killed in order to prevent further rescue attempts.

That put the popular Kyanzittha on the Pagan throne. Shin Arahan, who had been Buddhist primate since Anawrahta's time, crowned him, and Hkin U, the Pegu princess whose love had almost cost Kyanzittha's life, became his wife. Under Kyanzittha, Pagan became known as "city of the four million pagodas." Thousands of monuments were erected during his 28-year reign. A deeply religious man, Kyanzittha established the Mon Buddhist culture as paramount. It was not difficult to do so; the 30,000 Mon captives who had been brought

The Kings of Pagan

According to *The Glass Palace Chronicle of the Kings of Burma,* compiled during King Bagyidaw's rule beginning in 1829, there were 41 kings of Pagan prior to Anawrahta's crowning in 1044. Little is known of the first 41 apart from their names, the length of their reigns and their relationships to one another. The most significant events in the early years of the Pagan dynasty were the founding of the settlement by Thamuddarit in 108 A.D.; the establishment of a new Burmese calendar under King Popa Sawrahan in 638; the building of the Pagan city wall under King Pyinbya in 849.

Many scholars question the accuracy of the *Chronicle,* but a more complete source of early Burmese historical data does not exist. The following list of Pagan kings during the city's "Golden Era" came from that document, with the dates later verified by temple inscriptions.

NAME	OTHER NAMES	RELATIONSHIP	DATES OF RULE
1—Anawrahta	Aniruddha, Anorahta	—	1044–1077
2—Sawlu	Man Lulan, Tsaulu	Son of 1st	1077–1084
3—Kyanzittha	Thiluin Man	Son of 1st	1084–1112
4—Alaungsithu	Cansu I, Rhuykudayaka	Grandson of 3rd	1112–1167
5—Narathu	Imtaw Syan	Son of 4th	1167–1170
6—Naratheinhka	Min Yin Naratheinkha	Son of 5th	1170–1173
7—Narapatisithu	Cansu II	Brother of 6th	1173–1210
8—Nantaungmya	Htilominlo	Son of 7th	1210–1234
9—Kyaswa	Klacwa, Caw Kri	Son of 8th	1234–1250
10—Uzana	Uccana	Son of 9th	1250–1254
11—Narathihapate	Tarokpyemin	Son of 10th	1254–1287

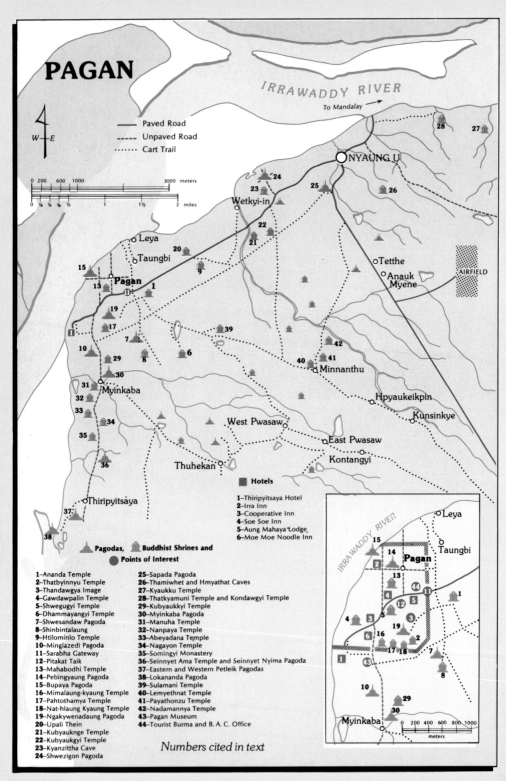

PAGAN

IRRAWADDY RIVER

To Mandalay →

W—E

Paved Road
Unpaved Road
Cart Trail

0 200   600 1000   3000 meters
0   ⅛ ¼ ½   1   1½   2 miles

○ NYAUNG U

○ Leya
Taungbi

15
13   ○ Pagan   1
19
17
10   29
30
31   ○ Myinkaba
32
33   34
35
36
37
38   ○ Thiripyitsaya

Wetkyi-in

○ Tetthe
○ Anauk
Myene

AIRFIELD

○ Minnanthu

○ Hpyaukeikpin
○ Kunsinkye

West Pwasaw
○ East Pwasaw
○ Kontangyi
Thuhekan

■ Hotels

1–Thiripyitsaya Hotel
2–Irra Inn
3–Cooperative Inn
4–Soe Soe Inn
5–Aung Mahaya Lodge
6–Moe Moe Noodle Inn

▲ Pagodas, ☖ Buddhist Shrines and
● Points of Interest

1–Ananda Temple
2–Thatbyinnyu Temple
3–Thandawgya Image
4–Gawdawpalin Temple
5–Shwegugyi Temple
6–Dhammayangyi Temple
7–Shwesandaw Pagoda
8–Shinbintalaung
9–Htilominlo Temple
10–Minglazedi Pagoda
11–Sarabha Gateway
12–Pitakat Taik
13–Mahabodhi Temple
14–Pebingyaung Pagoda
15–Bupaya Pagoda
16–Mimalaung-kyaung Temple
17–Pahtothamya Temple
18–Nat-hlaung Kyaung Temple
19–Ngakywenadaung Pagoda
20–Upali Thein
21–Kubyauknge Temple
22–Kubyaukgyi Temple
23–Kyanzittha Cave
24–Shwezigon Pagoda

25–Sapada Pagoda
26–Thamiwhet and Hmyathat Caves
27–Kyaukku Temple
28–Thatkyamuni Temple and Kondawgyi Temple
29–Kubyaukkyi Temple
30–Myinkaba Pagoda
31–Manuha Temple
32–Nanpaya Temple
33–Abeyadana Temple
34–Nagayon Temple
35–Somingyi Monastery
36–Seinnyet Ama Temple and Seinnyet Nyima Pagoda
37–Eastern and Western Petleik Pagodas
38–Lokananda Pagoda
39–Sulamani Temple
40–Lemyethnat Temple
41–Payathonzu Temple
42–Nadamannya Temple
43–Pagan Museum
44–Tourist Burma and B. A. C. Office

Numbers cited in text

IRRAWADDY RIVER

○ Leya
Taungbi
Pagan
○ Myinkaba

0 200 400 600 800 1000
meters

216

north after the conquest of Thaton already had altered the lifestyles of the Pyus and Burmans.

Kyanzittha's grandson Alaungsithu succeeded him as ruler of Pagan, and held the throne for another 45 years after Kyanzittha's death in 1112. A highly developed system of irrigation canals supported the production of rice by 17 surrounding communities and provided the economic backbone of the empire. But the empire began to weaken in the 13th Century under the threat of growing Shan power and the menacing Mongol army of Kublai Khan, which already had overwhelmed China. When King Narathihapate refused to pay a tribute to the khan, his armies were annihilated on the battlefield, and the Mongols took Pagan.

Pagan was not, as some say, laid waste by the Mongols. Kublai Khan was a Buddhist himself, and never would have permitted his armies to intentionally damage Buddhist shrines. Many of the temples were probably torn down by the Burmese themselves in a last-ditch attempt to build fortifications to slow the Mongol advance. Others became victims of the ages, of the neglect which followed the transfer of power. Only religious monuments were built of brick; royal buildings and other structures were of wood, and they could not have stood unmaintained in Upper Burma for more than 100 years.

The Pagan Plain Today

Today there are still a number of wooden structures on the Pagan plain—but they're of much more recent vintage. These are the riverside homes where the poor farming families of the district carry out their day-to-day existences, as well as the small guest houses and shops catering to the tourist trade.

The economic center of the Pagan plain today is at Nyaung U, about five kilometers (three miles) to the north of the walled village of Pagan. There are a few important monuments in the immediate vicinity of Nyaung U, notably the Shwezigon Pagoda, and there are others a few kilometers to the south of Pagan village near Myinkaba. But Pagan village itself is the tourist center, and it is here most visitors will begin their exploration of the ruins.

A massive earthquake jolted the plain of Pagan on July 8, 1975, raising fears throughout the nation and world that the ancient bricks had crumbled and the city left flattened. Thankfully, that was not so. There was, indeed, serious damage to many of the most important temples; but Burma's Directorate of Archaeology, led by U Bokay, immediately began repair work. The reconstruction was completed during 1981.

Many of Pagan's temples—especially those containing wall paintings or glazed *Jataka* panels—are closed to protect them from vandalism. All of these temples have wardens, however, who are pleased to admit visitors for a small fee.

The best way to get around the ancient city is by horse-drawn cab. Drivers waiting outside the Tourist Burma office in Pagan usually speak passable English and are more than happy to work as a guide as well as driver for a small retainer fee. Many of the most interesting monuments are not far from Pagan's ruined city walls.

Among ancient Pagan's greatest monuments—those which have withstood earthquake damage and temple vandals to survive, with renovation and maintenance, to this day—are 10 within easy traveling distance from Pagan village. They are the most frequently visited of all the plain's structures.

Decapitated Gawdawpalin Temple during repairs.

217

Ten Great Pagan Monuments

Many visitors begin their exploration of the ancient ruins at the **Ananda Temple (1)**, just to the east of the old city wall. This impressive whitewashed edifice dominates the view as one enters the village from the north. Considered the masterpiece of Mon architecture, it was completed in 1091.

According to the *Glass Palace Chronicle*, the Ananda Temple was inspired by the visit to Kyanzittha's palace of eight Indian monks, who arrived one morning begging for alms. They told the king they had once lived in the legendary Nandamula cave temple in the Himalaya Mountains. Kyanzittha, always fascinated by Buddhist tales, invited the monks to return to his palace daily during the rainy season to tell him more about this imaginary province. By virtue of their meditation, the monks were able to make the mythical landscape appear before Kyanzittha's eyes—and the king, overwhelmed, immediately opted to build a replica of this snow-covered cave on the hot, dry plain of central Burma.

When the great temple was completed, Kyanzittha is said to have been so awe-struck by its unique style that he personally executed the architect by Brahmin ritual to assure that the temple could not be duplicated, thereby sealing its permanence and importance.

The structure of the Ananda Temple is that of a simple corridor temple. Four large vestibules, each opening out symmetrically into entrance halls at the temple's axes, surround the central superstructure which itself is inlaid with four huge niches. The entire enclosure, 53 meters (174 feet) on a side, is in the shape of a perfect Greek cross.

In the niches facing the four cardinal points are four 9½-meter (31-foot) tall teak Buddha images which represent the four Buddhas of this world-cycle. Each is dimly lit from the slits in the sanctuary roof, giving one the impression that they not only are hovering, but are striving upward. Gautama, the most recent Buddha, faces west, Kakusandha faces north, Konagamana east and Kassapa south. The north- and south-facing statues are originals, but those facing east and west are later copies. The originals were destroyed by temple robbers.

The desecration of temples has been, in fact, a serious problem in Pagan. That the

A *tonga* waits for visitors at Pahtothamya Temple.

218

Ananda and other temples could have been vandalized as they have, and that the robbers have escaped without sanction, indicate that the rules of Buddhism have not always been followed with the same intensity as they were during the Era of the Temple Builders. Or perhaps it is a reflection on the long periods of neglect and anarchy into which Burma fell.

The true extent of temple desecration in Pagan is particularly evident at some of the less well known ruins on the plain, at those piles of brick not being renovated by Burma's Directorate of Archaeology. Many Buddha figures here have gaping holes in their stomach areas, and many smaller stupas have at least one side broken open—the legacy of thieves searching for valuable relics in obvious hiding places. Thohanbwa, a mid-16th Century Shan king of Ava, gave impetus to the temple robbers when he said: "Burmese pagodas have nothing to do with religion. They are simply treasure chambers." Thohanbwa, in fact, ordered many of the Pagan pagodas plundered in order to fill his own treasure chambers.

The damage at the Ananda, thankfully, has been restored or replaced. Precautions are still taken, however. Access to

The Ananda Temple.

Ananda's upper terraces, for example, is restricted. Temple authorities will provide a key to keen visitors, who will then be able to climb onto the roof via a narrow staircase.

Terra-Cotta Jataka

This roof above the central superstructure consists of five successively diminishing terraces/walkways. There are 389 terra-cotta glazed tiles here illustrating the last 10 *Jataka* tales. Together with those inside the temple and at its base, these tiles represent the largest collection of terra-cotta tiles at any Pagan temple.

The temple's beehive-like crown (*sikhara*), capped by a golden stupa which reaches 51 meters (168 feet) above the ground, rises from the tiered roof. Smaller pagodas, copies of the central spire, are at the roof's four corners, there bearing witness to a measured Buddhist harmony as well as creating the impression (to the imaginative) of a mountainous Himalayan landscape.

Proof of this temple's purpose as a place of meditation and learning can be found within Ananda's labyrinthian corridors. Each of the four main halls con-

tains the same 16 Buddha images as the other three, enabling four groups of Buddhist students to undergo their instruction simultaneously.

From these halls, facing the vestibules containing the large Buddhas, one can continue into the center corridor where 80 reliefs illustrate the life of the Bodhisattva from his birth until his enlightenment. On the west-facing porch are two Buddha footprints, each divided into 108 parts as dictated by ancient texts.

Nearby are two statues of particular interest. One represents Kyanzittha, the Ananda Temple's founding father, and the other, Shin Arahan. By the time the Buddhist primate died in 1115 at the age of 81, he had served four kings.

The most important time of year at the Ananda Temple is January, when the annual temple festival is held. This is a joyous, colorful spectacle. The corridors and vestibules of the temple, while normally lined with small stalls, are especially lively. In recent years, the Ananda Temple Festival has become even more exuberant, if that is possible: since the 1975 earthquake, renovation and repair of the Ananda Temple has been financed entirely through Buddhist generosity.

Temple of Omniscience

The center of Pagan is dominated by the **Thatbyinnyu Temple (2)**, some 500 meters to the southwest of the Ananda. Known as the "temple of omniscience," it is the tallest building in Pagan at 61 meters (201 feet). It stands just within the city walls, and is the archetype of the Burmese architectural style.

Built by Alaungsithu in the middle of the 12th Century, the Thatbyinnyu is similar in shape to the Ananda, although it does not form a symmetrical cross: the eastern vestibule projects out of the main structure of the building. The construction of this temple introduced the idea of placing a smaller "hollow" cube on top of a larger Burman-style structure, whereas the previous Mon-style temples were of one story. The center of the lower cube is solid, serving as a foundation for the upper temple, which houses an eastward-looking Buddha figure.

There are two tiers of windows in each story of the Thatbyinnyu, as well as huge arches inlaid with flamboyant pediments, making the interior bright and allowing a breeze to flow through. The first and second stories of this great temple

Thatbyinnyu Temple and Tally Pagoda.

were once the residence of monks. The third level housed images, and the fourth, a library. At the top was a stupa containing holy relics. The upper story can be reached by climbing interior stairs to the intermediate terraces, then taking an exterior staircase to the cella. From here a narrow internal stairway leads to the three uppermost terraces, which are crowned by a *sikhara* and a stupa. The view from this platform is marvelous. A half-kilometer away is the Ananda Temple, and beyond that stretches the huge plain where eight centuries ago 500,000 people are said to have lived.

Southwest of the Thatbyinnyu Temple are the remains of two stone pillars which at one time probably supported a huge bell. To the northwest is a small monument known as the Tally Pagoda. For every 10,000 bricks used in the construction of the Thatbyinnyu, one was set aside; this small pagoda was built with almost unbelievable architectural precision from the "tally-keeping" bricks.

A short distance north of the Thatbyinnyu is the **Thandawgya Image (3)**— a huge seated Buddha figure. Six meters (19½ feet) tall, it was erected by Narathihapate in 1284. The Buddha's hands are in the *bhumisparsa* mudra, signifying the moment of enlightenment. The plaster which once gave this image a rounded shape has crumbled away over the centuries, leaving only greenish sandstone blocks which give the statue an entranced, mystical appearance.

Earthquake's Epicenter

Back on the road through Pagan village, close to the bank of the Irrawaddy, is the 12th Century **Gawdawpalin Temple (4)**. It was built by King Narapatisithu in Burman style to resemble the Thatbyinnyu. One of Pagan's most impressive two-story temples, it was unfortunately at the epicenter of the 1975 earthquake and suffered more damage than any other structure. The *sikhara* and stupa, which previously reached a height of 60 meters (197 feet), collapsed during the quake, and a wide crack opened through the middle of the two-storied cube of the central structure. Because of the fine view this temple affords over the ruins of the Pagan plain, the Directorate of Archaeology is especially intent on its renovation. Until that work is completed, however, this vantage point will remain closed.

The Sulamani looms large on the plain of Pagan.

Just south of this temple, not far from the Thiripyitsaya Hotel, is a museum containing displays of Pagan's varied architecture, iconography and religious history. Along the museum verandas are stones collected from the region, bearing inscriptions in various languages—Burmese, Mon, Pyu, Pali, Tamil, Thai and Chinese. The exhibition was moved from a building near the Ananda Temple several years ago.

The oldest of the Burman-style temples, the **Shwegugyi Temple (5)**, is a short distance up the road toward Nyaung U. King Alaungsithu had it built in 1131. It took just seven months to raise, according to the temple history inscribed on two stone slabs within. Unlike most Buddhist monuments, which face east, the Shwegugyi stands on a high rectangular platform facing north, where the royal palace once stood. A brick pillar marking the site is all that remains where the palace was. The hall and inner corridor of this temple are well lit by large windows and doorways, one of the main features distinguishing Burman architectural style from the older Mon style.

Alaungsithu died in the Shwegugyi Temple at the age of 81. When the king lay on his deathbed in his palace, his son, Narathu, second in the line of succession after his older brother Minshinsaw, brought Alaungsithu to this temple and smothered him in his bedclothes. Minshinsaw at the time was gone from Pagan, so Narathu immediately proclaimed himself ruler. His short reign (1167-1170) was characterized by brutality.

Atonement for Patricide

Despite his brief tenure, however, Narathu is remembered as the founder of Pagan's largest shrine, the **Dhammayangyi Temple (6)**. Seriously concerned about his karma for future lives after having murdered his father, Narathu built the Dhammayangyi to atone for his misdeeds. It is today the best preserved temple in Pagan, with a layout similar to that of the Ananda Temple but lacking the delicate, harmonious touch of its prototype, perhaps reflecting the black cloud that hung over central Burma during Narathu's reign. The masonry, however, is without equal at Pagan—it is said that Narathu oversaw the construction himself, and he had masons executed if a needle could be pushed between the bricks they had laid.

The building, however, was never completed because Narathu himself was assassinated. Narathu had by law taken his father's wives as his own. He was displeased by the Hindu rituals of one of them—the daughter of the Indian prince of Pateikkaya—and he had her executed. Her vengeful father sent eight officers, disguised as Brahmans, to Pagan, and when Narathu received them in his throne room, they drew swords and killed him. The officers then slew one another, as agreed beforehand, to avoid further bloodshed.

The Dhammayangyi Temple is well over a kilometer to the southeast of the city walls in the direction of Minnanthu. About halfway between the temple and Pagan village are the **Shwesandaw Pagoda (7)** and the **Shinbintalyaung (8)**, which houses a reclining Buddha. One of only three religious structures Anawrahta built in Pagan, the Shwesandaw was erected in 1057 upon his victorious return from Thaton. Its stupa enshrines some hairs of the Buddha sent to Anawrahta by the king of Pegu.

The Shwesandaw is sometimes called the Ganesh (or Mahapeine) Temple after the elephant-headed Hindu god whose image once stood at the corners of its five successively diminishing rectangular terraces. The cylindrical stupa stands on an octagonal platform atop these terraces, which originally was adorned with terracotta plaques depicting *Jataka* scenes. The chief curiosities on the terraces today, however, are the "antique" objects being peddled to tourists by young local boys. The pagoda spire collapsed in the 1975 quake, and although it has been replaced, the original *hti* can still be seen lying near the pagoda.

The long flat building within the walls of the Shwesandaw enclosure contains the Shinbintalyaung Reclining Buddha, over 18 meters (60 feet) in length. Created in the 11th Century, this Buddha lies with its head facing south and therefore depicts the sleeping Buddha; only the dying Buddha faces north. The walls of the brick building are so tight around the reclining Buddha that it is impossible to photograph.

The last Burman-style temple built in Pagan—the **Htilominlo Temple (9)**—is about 1½ kilometers (less than a mile) northeast of Pagan village on the road to Nyaung U. King Nantaungmya had this building constructed in 1211 at the palace where he was chosen king. According to the *Glass Palace Chronicle*, he was the son of one of King Narapatisithu's concubines and was selected as heir when, as per custom, the white umbrella of the future ruler tilted in his direction. He and his four brothers created the Council of Ministers to determine state policy; the council called itself the *Hluttaw*, a title applied to Burma's parliament today.

The Htilominlo Temple is 46 meters (150 feet) high and 43 meters (140 feet) on a side at its base. Four Buddha figures on the ground and four more on the first floor face the cardinal points. Some of the old murals can still be discerned, as can a number of the friezes. Several old horoscopes, painted to protect the building from damage, can be found on the walls.

A short distance south of Pagan village is the **Minglazedi Pagoda (10)**, the last of the great stupas erected during the Era of the Temple Builders. Narathihapate— the last of the Pagan kings to reign over the entire Burmese empire—had it constructed in 1284. Six years in construction (see next page), it represents the pinnacle of Burman pagoda architecture.

The Minglazedi's stupa rises high above three terraces mounted on a square superstructure. Stairways lead up to the main platform from the middle of each side. Small stupas in the shape of Indian *kalasa* pots stand at the corners of each of the terraces, and at the corners of the uppermost terrace four larger stupas reinforce the heavenward-striving form of the pagoda, giving the proportions of the whole structure a harmonious quality. The terraces are adorned with large terra-cotta tiles depicting *Jataka* scenes. But because many of the Minglazedi's tiles have been broken over the years, the door leading to the pagoda grounds is kept locked. Visitors should contact pagoda warden U Ye Nyunt in Myinkaba village ahead of time if they wish to enter the enclosure.

'Mr. Handsome' And Sister 'Golden Face'

In addition to those already mentioned, there are a number of other structures within Pagan village which are worthy of note. Entering the city from Nyaung U, the road passes through the **Sarabha Gateway (11)**, the only section of King Pyinbya's 9th Century city wall still standing. Whereas overgrown hil-

Shwesandaw Pagoda.

locks strewn with rubble are all that remain where most of the wall used to be, Pagan's guardian spirits—the Mahagiri Nats—still have their prayer niches in this eastern gateway. These two *nats*, Nga Tin De, "Mr. Handsome," and his sister Shwemyethna, "Golden Face," are called "Lords of the Great Mountain" because they are believed to make their home on sacred Mount Popa. After Thagyamin, king of the *nats*, they are the most important spirit beings in Burma.

One of the few secular buildings in Pagan that has been preserved over the centuries is the **Pitakat Taik (12)**, King Anawrahta's library. Anawrahta had it built not far within the city's east gate to house the 30 elephant loads of scriptures he brought back to Pagan after his conquest of Thaton. From this structure, it is possible to get an idea of what the wooden secular buildings might have looked like during Pagan's golden age. Its original appearance, however, was altered in 1783, when King Bodawpaya during a renovation had finials—highly reminiscent of the buildings at Ava—added to the corners of the five multiple roofs. Bodawpaya also had a new collection of *pitaka* texts placed in the library.

The library is near the Shwegugyi Temple. Across the main road is the **Mahabodhi Temple (13)**, an exact replica of a structure of the same name in India's Bihar State, built in 500 A.D. at the site where the Buddha achieved enlightenment. The pyramid-like shape of the temple tower is of a kind highly favored during India's Gupta Period, and is quite different from the standard bell-shaped Burmese monuments. Constructed in Pagan during the reign of Nantaungmya (1210–1234), it followed a tradition of fascination with Indian architecture. Kyanzittha more than a century earlier had sent men and materials to India to carry out some renovation work on the Bodhgaya Temple, and Alaungsithu in the mid-12th Century made the king of Arakan do the same.

The lower section of Pagan's Mahabodhi is a quadrangular block supporting the pyramidal structure, which in turn is crowned by a small stupa. The pyramid is completely covered with niches containing seated Buddha figures. Apart from a copy which was erected on the terrace of the Shwedagon in Rangoon, the Mahabodhi is the only temple of its kind in Burma. It was

The Collapse of the Empire

The building of the Minglazedi Pagoda was an augury of sorts of the impending downfall of the First Burmese Empire.

Its creator, King Narathihapate, was a vain ruler. An inscription on a stone slab on the pagoda grounds tells visitors he was the commander-in-chief of an army of 36 million men, the consumer of 300 curry dishes daily, and the master of 3,000 concubines. And like many vain rulers, he was sensitive to criticism: When the rumor began to circulate through his empire that "when this pagoda is finished, the Kingdom of Pagan will be shattered into dust," he immediately ordered that construction be halted.

Narathihapate's Buddhist primate, however, reminded the king of the Buddha's teachings—that all life is transitory, and in any case, no empire could last forever. Work on the pagoda was begun once more.

It wasn't long, though, before Narathihapate's arrogance contributed to the fulfillment of the prophecy. Kublai Khan, whose Mongols ruled the world between the Baltic and Yellow Seas, sent a delegation to Pagan to bring the Burmese into his fold in a peaceful manner, through the payment of tribute to the khan. Narathihapate, however, refused to receive the first emissaries—and when a second group was sent to see him, that delegation was summarily beheaded.

This insult was more than Kublai Khan could take. His invasion forces turned their attention toward Burma, and in a series of battles advanced as far as present-day Bhamo. Then Narathihapate lost his nerve. It is said he pulled down 6,000 temples to fortify Pagan's city walls. When an inscription found beneath one of the temples again forecast the city's demise, he fled down the Irrawaddy toward its delta. He was branded with the title "Tarokpyemin," "the king who ran away from the Chinese."

Narathihapate died not long thereafter, poisoned by his son, the ruler of Prome. "In all the lives wherein I wander through eternity until I reach nirvana," Narathihapate said on his deathbed, "may I never have a man-child born to me again."

The Mongols had not wanted to capture Pagan. But when they learned of Narathihapate's death, they advanced on Pagan and took the city in 1287.

severely damaged by the 1975 earthquake, but renovation work has been successfully completed.

Of Warships and Monks

A short distance north of here is the **Pebingyaung Pagoda (14)**, notable for its conical Singhalese-style stupa. The stupa contains relics mounted on top of the bell-shaped main structure in a square-based relic chamber. The construction of this pagoda in the 12th Century confirms that close ties existed between Burma and Ceylon, a result of the concern shown by King Anawrahta for the propagation of Theravada Buddhism.

Although the Theravada school of thought had been introduced to Thaton by the Singhalese monk Buddhaghosa in 403 A.D., it was not until 1076, when Anawrahta was in power at Pagan, that the bond between Burma and Ceylon was strengthened. The Hindu Cholas had invaded Ceylon, and the island's ruler, Vijaya Bahu I, asked his fellow believer Anawrahta for assistance in driving them out. Pagan's king sent his ships laden with war materials, and the added support gave the Ceylonese the boost they needed to re-establish their hold on the island.

But after 50 years of occupation by "non-believers," the Buddhist infrastructure, especially the Sangha, had badly deteriorated. So Anawrahta sent a number of monks to help in the regeneration of Theravada Buddhism in Ceylon. A century later, Narapatisithu sent another group of monks—among them Sapada, who built a pagoda bearing his name in Nyaung U. Many scholars feel the *Tripitaka* texts which Anawrahta reputedly seized in his conquest of Thaton actually came from Ceylon.

A few steps from the Pebingyaung on the banks of the Irrawaddy is the **Bupaya Pagoda (15)**. According to tradition, it was raised by the third king of Pagan, Pyusawti (162–243 A.D.), who found a way to get rid of a gourd-like climbing plant *(bu)* which infested the riverbanks. He was rewarded by his predecessor, Thamuddarit, the founder of Pagan (108 A.D.), with the hand of his daughter and the inheritance of the throne. In commemoration of his good luck, Pyusawti had the Bupaya Pagoda built.

As the original Pagan pagoda, this edifice became the basic model for all pa-

Mahagiri Nats: "Golden Face" (left) and "Mr. Handsome."

godas built after it. It has a bulbous shape, similar in some ways to the Tibetan *chorte,* and is built on rows of crenelated walls overlooking the river. Because of the way it stands out on the banks, it is used as a navigation aid by boats. On the pagoda grounds, beneath a pavilion with a nine-gabled roof, is an altar to Mondaing, *nat* of storms.

Wife-Stealing at the Palace

The **Mimalaung-kyaung Temple (16),** near the old city's south gate, was erected in 1174 by Narapatisithu. The small, square temple—characterized by multiple roofs and a tall spiral pagoda— stands on a four-meter (13-foot) high plinth intended to protect it from fire and floods. The temple's creator, Narapatisithu, is noted in Pagan's history for the manner in which he acceded to the throne in 1173: his brother, King Naratheinka, had stolen his wife and made her queen while Narapatisithu was on a foreign campaign. The wronged sibling returned to Pagan with 80 of his most trusted men, murdered his brother the king, and ensconced himself on the throne. His wife, Veluvati, remained the queen.

Just to the east of this temple is the **Pahtothamya Temple (17),** which according to tradition dates from before Anawrahta's reign. King Taungthugyi (931–964), also known as Nyaung U Sawrahan, is said to have built the temple to look like those at Thaton. No temple ruins have ever been unearthed at Thaton, however, and the architectural style of this temple is that of the 11th Century.

Immediately to the east is the **Nat-hlaung Kyaung Temple (18),** a perfect example of the religious tolerance that prevailed in Pagan during the Era of the Temple Builders. It is thought to have been constructed by Taungthugyi in 931—more than a century before Theravada Buddhism was introduced from Thaton—and was dedicated to the Hindu god Vishnu. The Nat-hlaung Kyaung remained Pagan's greatest Hindu temple throughout its Golden Age, a time when Theravada and Mahayana Buddhism, *nat* and *naga* worship were followed and the Tantric practices of the Ari monks were tolerated.

The main hall and superstructure of the Nat-hlaung Kyaung are standing today, although the entrance hall and outer structures have long since disappeared.

Mahabodhi Temple.

The 10 *avatars* (past and future incarnations) of Vishnu once were housed in niches on the outer walls of the main hall. Seven can still be seen today.

Remains of the Nat-hlaung Kyaung's central relic sanctuary indicate that it once contained a large Vishnu figure, which sat on a *garuda* with spread wings. It is now in the Dahlem Museum in Berlin. At the turn of the 20th Century, the German geologist Dr. Fritz von Nöttling removed the treasures from several of Pagan's temples—and "behaved like a vandal," according to authorities at Pagan.

Just to the north of here is the **Ngaky-wenadaung Pagoda (19)** like the Pahto-thamya attributed to King Taungthugyi in the 10th Century. A bulbous-shaped structure on a circular base, it stands 13 meters (43 feet) high. Examples of the cylindrical form of this stupa are found in ancient Sri Ksetra.

To Nyaung U and Beyond

Walkway to the Shwezigon Pagoda.

About 1½ kilometers (one mile) down the road from Pagan village to the regional center of Nyaung U, and almost directly opposite the Htilominlo Temple, lies the **Upali Thein (20)**, or hall of ordination. Named after the monk Upali, it was erected in the first half of the 13th Century. Although it is of brick construction, it is said to resemble many of the wooden buildings of the Pagan Era which have long since disappeared. The span-roof has two rows of battlements, and a small pagoda at its center.

The Upali Thein was renovated during the Konbaung Dynasty period: in 1794 and 1795, its walls and ceilings were decorated with beautiful frescoes representing the 28 previous Buddhas, as well as scenes from the life of Gautama. Sadly, the plaster came off the walls during the 1975 earthquake, and most of the fresco work was irreparably destroyed.

Near the village of Wetkyi-in are the **Kubyauknge Temple (21)**, notable for the fine stucco work on its exterior walls, and the **Kubyaukgyi Temple (22)** a short distance further east. The Kubyaukgyi dates from the early 13th Century, and has a pyramidal spire very similar to that of the Mahabodhi. Inside are some of Pagan's finest frescoes of the *Jataka* tales. Unfortunately, many of these paintings were "collected" in 1899 by the German von Nöttling.

A short distance west of Nyaung U village is the **Kyanzittha Cave (23)**, a cave temple which served as a place of lodging for monks. Although its name would seem to indicate that it had been built by Kyanzittha, in all probability it dates from Anawrahta's reign. The long, dark corridors are embellished with frescoes from the 11th, 12th and 13th centuries; some of the later paintings depict the Mongols who occupied Pagan after 1287. Visitors are advised to carry their own flashlights when visiting this cave temple, as the attendant family has only dimly burning candles.

Pagan's Greatest Reliquary

The **Shwezigon Pagoda (24)**, a short walk north of the cave temple, is the prototype for all Burmese stupas built after the rule of Anawrahta. It was built as the most important reliquary shrine in Pagan, a center of prayer and reflection for the new Theravada faith Anawrahta was establishing in Pagan.

King Anawrahta, convinced that he was a "universal monarch," set about to obtain all possible relics of the Buddha. From Prome, he got the Buddha's collar-

bone and frontal bone; he also acquired a copy of the Tooth of Kandy from Ceylon and an emerald Buddha figure from Yunnan. To determine a location for the pagoda which would be built to house these relics, he set loose a white elephant—the animal which had borne the tooth from Ceylon—and where it rested, the Shwezigon Pagoda was built.

Ironically, only three terraces of the pagoda had been finished when Anawrahta was killed in 1077. King Kyanzittha supervised completion of the structure in 1089.

The bell of the Shwezigon stands upon the three terraces, reached by stairways from the cardinal directions. The pagoda spire, crowned by a *hti,* rises above the bell in a series of concentric moldings. Smaller stupas can be seen at the corners of the terraces, each one decorated with glazed plaques illustrating the *Jataka* tales. Small square temples on each side of the central stupa contain standing Buddhas of the Gupta style. To the left and right of the eastern entrance are two stone pillars, each inscribed on all four sides, recording the establishment of the pagoda under Kyanzittha.

Buddhist pilgrims from throughout Burma converge on the Shwezigon every year when the Shwezigon Pagoda Festival is held during the second week of the Burmese month of *Nadaw* (November/ December). This is one of the nation's most popular festivals, largely because *nat* worship was combined with Buddhism in the pagoda's construction. Anawrahta had the images of the traditional 37 *nats* carved in wood and erected on the lower terraces, believing that "men will not come for the sake of the new faith. Let them come for their old gods and gradually they will be won over." The *nats* are no longer on the terraces, but they are housed in a small hall to the southeast of the pagoda, where they are still worshipped today.

An example of a stricter adherence to orthodox Theravada Buddhism can be seen at the **Sapada Pagoda (25)**, situated at the southern end of Nyaung U town on the airport road. Built in the 12th Century by the monk Sapada, it is similar in form to the Pebingyaung Pagoda, but bears witness to a great schism in the Theravada school.

Sapada was one of the monks sent to Ceylon in the latter part of the 12th Century. He returned to Burma in 1190, after 10 years on Ceylon, expounding a very

Kyanzittha Cave (left); and the Shwezigon Pagoda.

orthodox version of Buddhism. It differed markedly from the Theravada Buddhism, absorbed from the Mons, which predominated in Pagan at the time. And it was distinctly different from the courtly religion of Mahayana Buddhism, as well as the Vishnu and Shiva cults of Hinduism. But Sapada's interpretation was accepted by King Narapatisithu and readily embraced by Pagan's people.

There are several cave temples to the east of Nyaung U. Just one kilometer to the southeast of the town are the **Thamiwhet and Hmyathat Caves (26)**, formed by the excavation of hillsides during the 12th and 13th centuries. Their purpose was to give monks a cool place to live, a refuge from the scorching heat of central Burma.

About three kilometers upstream from Nyaung U, standing on the ledge of a cliff overlooking the Irrawaddy, is the **Kyaukku Temple (27)**. This could be described as the ideal cave temple—the manner in which it is built into the hillside gives the impression that a small stupa stands on top of the temple, when it actually rests on a pillar. A maze of passages leads from the pillar into the caves behind: the stone-and-brick-built temple is in fact an enlargement of the natural structure. A large Buddha sits opposite the entrance, and the walls are covered with stone reliefs. The Kyaukku's ground story dates from the 11th Century; the upper two stories have been ascribed to the reign of Narapatisithu (1174–1211).

About a kilometer back down the Irrawaddy toward Nyaung U are a number of stupas and temples, among them the **Thatkyamuni Temple** and the **Kondawgyi Temple (28)**. In the former are panels of paintings which depict Ashoka, the great Buddhist king who ruled in India during the 3rd Century B.C., as well as scenes recording the introduction of Buddhism to Sri Lanka. In the Kondawgyi are wall paintings of *Jataka* scenes as well as floral patterns.

Myinkaba and Thiripyitsaya

When King Anawrahta returned to Pagan in 1057 with the Mon royalty in tow, he exiled King Manuha and his family to Myinkaba (Myinpagan), two kilometers south of the Pagan city walls. With Manuha present, Myinkaba became the site of the most splendid Mon-style archi-

tecture on the Pagan plain. Many of those monuments still stand.

In addition, the village has established a fine lacquerware industry which has become its economic backbone. There are a lacquer school and museum in Pagan which give visitors an opportunity to observe the various stages of lacquer production and to view some outstanding antique pieces of work.

Approaching Myinkaba from the north, a short distance after passing the Minglazedi Pagoda one encounters the **Kubyaukkyi Temple** (29). Of great importance for its inscriptions, it was built in 1113 by Rajakumar upon the death of his father, Kyanzittha. A very religious man, Rajakumar—whose mother was the niece of the monk with whom Kyanzittha found refuge on his flight from Anawrahta—was the rightful heir to the throne. But Kyanzittha had designated his grandson, Alaungsithu, as heir, and Rajakumar relinquished his right.

His one-story temple is built in pure Mon style. In the dark main hall (lit only by perforated stone windows) are nine rows of contemporaneous murals depicting the 547 *Jataka* tales. The east-facing vestibule contains a representation of a 10-armed Bodhisattva typical of Mahayana Buddhism—but not of Theravada.

The most notable feature of the Kubyaukkyi (be careful not to confuse this with the Kubyaukgyi near Nyaung U) is the **Myazedi Stone.** Sometimes called "Burma's Rosetta Stone," it was inscribed by Rajakumar in four languages of the time—Burman, Mon, Pali and Pyu. It was discovered in 1887, and provided the key to understanding the previously indecipherable Pyu language. The inscription also provided the final word on the dates of the reigns of Pagan's kings beginning with Anawrahta.

On the banks of the Myinkaba River in Myinkaba village is the **Myinkaba Pagoda** (30), marking the spot where Anawrahta slew his predecessor and half-brother, Sokkate, in a duel for the kingship in 1044. Sokkate and his elder brother Kyiso had wrested the Pagan throne from Anawrahta's father, Kunhsaw Kyaunghpyu, himself a usurper, in 986; but Anawrahta's victory over Sokkate with his mythical spear "Areindama" put an end to over a century of court intrigues. This shrine's bulbous form and round terraces mark it clearly as predating the establishment of Mon Buddhist influence in Pagan.

The **Manuha Temple** (31) was built by the captive king of Thaton just south of Myinkaba village in 1059. Because he feared he would be made a temple slave, Manuha sought to improve his karma for future incarnations—and so sold some of his jewels in order to have this temple built with the proceeds. One reclining and three seated Buddha images cramped uncomfortably within the narrow confines of the pagoda are said to symbolize the distressed soul of the defeated king.

In contrast to most Mon-style temples, the Manuha Temple has an upper story. This collapsed during the 1975 earthquake and buried the Buddhas beneath it, but renovation work on the temple was completed in 1981.

Burmese Friezes

A short path leads past two recent statues of King Manuha and his wife, Queen Ningaladevi, to the **Nanpaya Temple** (32). Said to have once been Manuha's residence, it later was converted into a temple.

The Nanpaya is square in plan, with a porch. Its interior design is outstanding evidence of the strong Brahman influence

At the Shwezigon (left), nuns and lay-women attend a lecture while the guardian *nat* of the arts rides atop his *hintha* (right).

affecting the Theravadin Mon kings. Four pillars are decorated with friezes and bas-reliefs. The relief of the god Brahma is particularly striking. Three faces can be discerned, and all have typically Mon facial features—leading one to assume they are representations of King Manuha. The relief is in a position of veneration, facing four Buddha images which might once have stood back-to-back in the center of the chamber—but have long since disappeared. On the outside of the temple are friezes of the mythological *hamsa* bird—which, besides being the heraldic crest of Mon royalty, was also the vehicle on which Brahma was always depicted riding.

A short distance south of here is the **Abeyadana Temple (33).** It bears the name of Kyanzittha's first wife, whom he married as a young warrior, and is situated at the place where she waited for him during his flight from Anawrahta. Abeyadana was probably a follower of Mahayana Buddhism: the frescoes on the outer walls of the corridor represent Bodhisattvas, or future Buddhas, and on the inner walls are images of Brahma, Vishnu, Shiva and Indra, the gods of Indian mythology.

The **Nagayon Temple (34),** where Kyanzittha is said to have hidden during that flight from Anawrahta, is a few steps away. Legend has it that a *naga* offered him protection here, much as the Naga Mucalinda shielded the meditating Buddha from a storm. Like all temples built by Kyanzittha, this one has a characteristic Mon style. It is very similar to temples in India's Orissa region; the main difference is that the Nagayon has a number of receding roofs which are topped by a *sikhara* and stupa, whereas the Orissa temples' *sikharas* tower directly from the central structures. In the interior of the Nagayon are stone reliefs depicting scenes from the life of the Buddha. A standing Buddha, flanked by two smaller seated Buddhas, is housed in the shrine.

A Rare Brick Monastery

Almost halfway between Myinkaba and the village of Thiripyitsaya is the **Somingyi Monastery (35),** one of the few brick-built *kyaungs* on the Pagan plain. It is an example of the myriad monasteries which once dotted this plain; most of them, then as now, were built of wood and left no trace. The *kyaung's* raised

A cramped Buddha at the Manuha Temple.

platform is surrounded by a lobby on the east, monks' cells on the north and south, and a two-story chapel, housing an image of the Buddha and crowned with a stupa, on the west.

The **Seinnyet Ama Temple** and the **Seinnyet Nyima Pagoda (36)** are a short distance down the road. Tradition attributes these sanctuaries to Queen Seinnyet, who lived during the 11th Century, although their architectural style is more typical of the 13th Century. The pagoda in particular is notable for its design, incorporating seated Buddhas in niches at each of the cardinal points on the bell-shaped dome, and lions guarding miniature stupas in the corners of the second terrace.

Five kilometers (three miles) south of Pagan village is tiny Thiripyitsaya, where King Thinlikyaung's 4th Century palace was situated. During Pagan's Golden Era, there was a mooring place here where foreign ships—plying the Irrawaddy from lands as far away as Sri Lanka—dropped anchor. Today the chief attractions are a trio of well preserved pagodas. Two of them, known as the **Eastern and Western Petleik Pagodas (37)**, were built in the 11th Century. But

they collapsed inward in 1905, and the terra-cotta plaques originally housed in the vaulted corridors now are preserved under replicas of the original roofs. The plaques, which are numbered, depict 550 *Jataka* tales; they are the only representations of three of the stories, as only 547 are officially recognized.

At the south end of Thiripyitsaya is the **Lokananda Pagoda (38)**, raised in 1059 as one of only three pagodas known to have been built by Anawrahta in the Pagan area. (The other two are the Shwesandaw and the Myinkaba.) The Lokananda has a cylindrical bell, and is very reminiscent of a Pyu stupa. It stands on three octagonal terraces, the lower two having stairways on each side.

The Minnanthu Temples

The village of Minnanthu is located about five kilometers (three miles) southeast of Pagan village. There are a large number of temple ruins in the vicinity, but few of major significance. One of the largest is the **Sulamani Temple (39)**, not actually in Minnanthu itself but about halfway between the village and Pagan. Considered one of Pagan's great two-

Manuha and his queen.

storied monuments, it resembles the Thatbyinnyu in plan, and was built by Narapatisithu in 1183. The Sulamani is named after the legendary palace of the god Indra, crowning the peak of Mount Meru high above the plane on which ordinary people live.

A paragon of the fully-developed Burman architectural style, the Sulamani Temple's upper story rests on a huge central pillar which itself fills out the middle of the ground story. The lower floor has seated Buddha images on all four sides. There are porches facing the four cardinal points on each story, with those facing east larger than the others. The remains of some 18th Century murals can be seen inside the temple.

Immediately to the north of Minnanthu village is the **Lemyethna Temple** (**40**). It was built by Ananthasuriya, Naratheinhka's minister-in-chief, bearing in mind a poem written by his predecessor and namesake, Ananthathurya. Sentenced to death by King Narapatisithu, this man scribed a poem still regarded as one of Burma's literary treasures. "If . . . I were to be released and freed from execution I would not escape Death," he wrote. "Inseparable am I

from Karma." The king was moved, but the minister had already been executed.

The **Payathonzu Temple** (**41**), a short distance north, actually consists of three buildings. Joined by narrow vaulted passages, each building is crowned with a *sikhara*. Three empty pedestals stand inside, their Buddha images having long since disappeared. This temple is of particular interest because of its Mahayanist and Tantric frescoes: as the Payathonzu was erected in the late 13th Century, it can be deduced that Mahayana Buddhism was practiced in Pagan throughout the Era of the Temple Builders.

Also known for its Mahayana Buddhist frescoes is the **Nandamannya Temple** (**42**), not far distant. The erotic murals contained within would not be dreamed of in a Theravada structure; but there they are, the daughters of Mara attempting to seduce the Buddha painted on the temple's southern wall. Originally called Ananta Panna ("endless wisdom"), the temple's name was changed to Nandamannya to avoid confusion with the Ananda Temple.

The Journey to Pagan

The easiest way to reach Pagan is by plane. Several flights daily connect both Rangoon and Mandalay with the airport, located a short distance south of Nyaung U.

Traveling to Pagan by train is not recommended, as the journey requires a full day to complete. Coming from either Rangoon or Mandalay, one must disembark in the town of Thazi and catch a bus for the remainder of the trip. There is also a "whistle-stop" line to Kyaukpadaung, branching off the main north-south route at Pyinmana, but it is even slower than traveling via bus from Thazi.

Scheduled bus service from Rangoon via Kyaukpadaung takes about 16 hours. From Mandalay, the Nyaung U Mann bus leaves at 4 a.m. daily from the corner of 29th Road and 82nd Street, and takes about 10 hours.

An alternative for the adventurous is to travel to Pagan by boat. The southbound Prome Ferry, which docks in Mandalay at the end of "A" Road, heads down the Irrawaddy at 5 o'clock every morning. It's an all-day voyage—more if the river is low and the boat gets wedged on a sandbank—but travelers not overly concerned with comfort will find it a fascinating experience.

The arts of Pagan: a wallpainting at the Kubyaukkyi Temple (left); and a lacquer worker in Myinkaba.

ANCIENT CITIES OF THE PYUS

Were you to remain on the Mandalay-Pagan river boat for another day beyond the great bend in the Irrawaddy, you would reach the city of **Prome**, built a short distance north of the site of the ancient Pyu capital of **Sri Ksetra**. There is not much remaining of Sri Ksetra, or Thayekhittaya as it was known to the Burmese; but at least eight brick pagodas and temples, some dating to the turn of the Christian era, give valid testimony to its greatness.

The Pyu capital was located near the modern-day railway station of Hmwaza, about eight kilometers (five miles) south of Prome. Its most famous structure is the **Shwesandaw Pagoda**, venerated throughout Burma. Eighty-three small stupas, their golden reflections dancing in the Irrawaddy, comprise a solid wall around the 60-meter (197-foot) high pagoda. Every November during the Tazaungdaing Festival an important pagoda celebration is held here.

Another seven kilometers (4½ miles) south is the **Shwenattaung Pagoda**, which has a history going back to the establishment of Sri Ksetra perhaps 2,000 years ago.

Cones and Cylinders

Throughout the Sri Ksetra region are many pagodas built in a style completely different from that of structures used for purposes of worship. There are a variety of conical and cylindrical stupas based on Indian archetypes. The **Bawbawgi Pagoda's** cylindrical form gives the impression that it is hollow inside; in fact, it is solid. The **Payagyi and Payama pagodas** north of the old city walls are conical in style. They were built about the same time as the **Bebe Temple**, between the 5th and 7th centuries. The Beba is a cylindrical stupa lying on a hollow pedestal, in which a statue of the Buddha flanked by two of his followers stands against a back wall. The **East Zegu and Lemyethna temples** are very similar in form, the latter having a central support pillar, atypical for a Burmese temple.

Sri Ksetra is the most popular site for archaeological research in all of Burma. With the exception of the World War Two period, scientists have been in the field here every year since 1907. Artifacts uncovered at Sri Ksetra show conclusively that Theravada Buddhism was common in central Burma before Anawrahta's time.

The historic origin of Sri Ksetra is shrouded in legend. King Duttabaung (whose name later became a reverential address for monarchs) is credited with founding the city. According to tradition, it was built by Sakka, king of the *nats*, with the assistance of Naga, Garuda and other heavenly spirits. Sakka delineated the city's boundaries by grabbing the tail of Naga, a dragon, and swinging him a full circle. Then he christened the city "as beautiful as Sakka's home on Mount Meru," and named Duttabaung king.

Protecting 'Religion'

The city endured until the 9th Century A.D., finally collapsing because of continual conflict between the many tribes who had moved there. When King Anawrahta of Pagan passed through 200 years later after his conquest of Thaton, he had Sri Ksetra's walls pulled down and all relics removed from the temples to add to his own. He wanted to assure that the "true religion" could have no other home than from Pagan, and that no city could approach his in size.

From Prome—about halfway down the Irrawaddy's course from Mandalay to the sea—there is regular rail service south to Rangoon. The devotee of ancient history might be inclined, however, to pay a further visit to **Beikthano**, about 135 kilometers (85 miles) north. The ruins of this large Pyu town, which predated Sri Ksetra by several centuries, are to be found near the modern-day town of Taungdwingyi in Magwe state.

No Buddha image is found here, indicating the city existed prior to the 1st Century A.D. Tradition says Beikthano was destroyed by King Duttabaung, who brought the reigning princess, Panthwar, to Sri Ksetra as a prisoner. There is little to see of the ruins today, as many of the bricks and stones were used in recent centuries by Indian contractors building roads and railways.

Despite Beikthano's great age, ruins of even more ancient civilizations exist in Burma. They are located north of Mandalay—at Tagaung and Halin, along the upper Irrawaddy—and are described in the preceding chapter.

Lonely pagodas on the dry plain.

MOUNT POPA, ABODE OF THE GODS

In 442 B.C., a great earthquake roared through central Burma—and from out of the barren Myingyan plains rose **Mount Popa**. Volcanic ash on the mountain's slopes gradually became fertile soil, and the peak blossomed with flowers of many colors. (*Popa* is the Sanskrit word for "flower.") For the inhabitants of the surrounding region, the "sugar-loaf" peak became regarded as the home of the gods, the Mount Olympus of Burma. Alchemists and occultists made the mountain's slopes their home, and others were convinced mythical beings lived in the woods and among the flowers. So it was a matter of course when Mount Popa became the focus of national *nat* worship and the official home of the Mahagiri Nats during the reign in Pagan of King Thinlikyaung.

Mount Popa, 1,518 meters (4,981 feet) high, is located about 50 kilometers (31 miles) southeast of Pagan. It's a 200-kyat Jeep trip from Pagan village, or a fatig-uing bus trip requiring transfers in Nyaung U and Kyaukpadaung. Overnight visitors can stay at the ancient Popa monastery at the foot of the peak, however. During the Burmese month of *Nayon* (May/June) the annual Festival of the Spirits is held here, and it is said that at that time the abbot of the Popa monastery runs the largest hotel in the whole country of Burma.

While the volcanic cone can be climbed by means of a path beginning at the monastery, it should be attempted only by the physically fit. The mountain rises about 1,000 meters (3,280 feet) above the surrounding plain, and given the hot, dry climatic conditions that prevail in central Burma, the ascent can be arduous. On clear days, however, the view from the top across the vast dry plain is the most beautiful panorama that can be seen in central Burma.

The goal of a trip to Mount Popa should be to see the shrine of the Mahagiri Nats, situated about halfway up the mountain. For seven centuries preceding the reign of Anawrahta, all kings of central Burma were required to make a pilgrimage here to consult with the two *nats* regarding their reign.

The Mahagiri Nats

There is a legend told in Burma about a young blacksmith and his beautiful sister. They lived outside the northern city of Tagaung around the middle of the 4th Century, when King Thinlikyaung of Thiripyitsaya ruled in the Pagan area. The blacksmith, whose name was Nga Tin De, was so strong that the blows of his hammer could be heard far across the land, and so energetic he ate 15 kilograms (33 pounds) of rice at every mealtime. He was very popular and very good-looking, so he earned the nickname "Mr. Handsome." With all these attributes, Nga Tin De was a potential threat to the king of Tagaung—who sent his henchmen to slay the young man. But Nga Tin De was warned in time to escape, and he fled into the woods.

Tagaung's king was enchanted by the blacksmith's sister, named Shwemyethna and known in English as "Golden Face," and married her. A few months later, he asked her to call her brother back from the forest; now that they were related through marriage, he convinced her, Nga Tin De could no longer be his rival. But when "Mr. Handsome" emerged from his exile and approached Tagaung, he was seized by the king's guards, bound to a tree and set aflame. As the fire lapped up over her brother's body, Shwemyethna broke free from her escorts and threw herself into the blaze.

Their physical bodies gone, the brother and sister became mischievous *nats* living in the *saga* tree. To stop them from causing harm, the king ordered the tree chopped down and thrown into the Irrawaddy River.

Because of the siblings' popularity, the story of their tragic deaths had spread rapidly throughout Burma. King Thinlikyaung, who wanted to unite the country in *nat* worship, discovered the *saga* tree floating downriver through his kingdom. He ordered the drifting tree fished out of the river and had two figures carved from it. The *nat* images were then carried with great pomp and ceremony to the top of Mount Popa, where they were given a shrine—and reside there to this day.

Every king who came to power in the Pagan region between the 4th and 11th centuries made a pilgrimage to visit these *nats*—"the climb to the Golden Mountain"—at the time of his coronation. At that time, Nga Tin De and Shwemyethna made themselves visible to the new ruler and counseled him in affairs of state.

Mount Popa, home of the *nats*.

THE SHAN PLATEAU AND INLE LAKE

Mystical. Magical. Outrageously picturesque. These and many other words have been used in attempts to describe the fairy-tale land of Inle Lake and the amazing Inthas who populate its shores—and its surface.

This minority tribe has adapted so perfectly to its lake environment that its homes are built over the water on stilts, its vegetable fields float on the lake's surface, and its fishermen stroll their long, narrow boats with a unique leg-rowing motion that has made them famous.

An oasis surrounded by the southern Shan Plateau, Inle Lake may be the area's main attraction for visitors, but it should not be the only one. About 550 meters (1,800 feet) and 27 kilometers (17 miles) by road uphill from the lake is Taunggyi, a former British hill station. Despite its lingering colonial air, Taunggyi is today the administrative capital of the Shan State, a center of Shan culture and a major marketplace for smuggled goods. In the vicinity are pine forests, colorful bazaars, and—some 110 kilometers (69 miles) to the northwest—the fabulous Pindaya Cave with its thousands of carved Buddha images.

The Shan State is by far Burma's largest, extending east from Taunggyi for 350 kilometers (220 miles) to Laos and the notorious Golden Triangle of opium trade; nearly as far north to the Ledo Road and the Chinese border; and south a lesser distance to the tribal states of the Kayahs and Karens. This is largely a region of high, roadless peaks, of rugged river gorges, of fiercely independent tribespeople, and of endless anti-government rebel activity. Because of its wildness, the Shan Plateau beyond Taunggyi is off-limits to tourists.

A Snarl of Silt and Water Hyacinths

The visitor to this region will probably arrive by plane at the **Heho airport.** From there, it's a 35-kilometer (22-mile) trip by collective bus or Jeep-taxi to Yaunghwe, the major town on Inle Lake, or a 40-kilometer (25-mile) trip to Taunggyi, both via the rail terminus of Shwenyaung.

At **Yaunghwe,** the elements of Intha surprise first begin to come to life. The town—the oldest of about 200 Intha set-tlements around the shallow, 158-square-kilometer (61-square-mile) lake—is built on the fringe of the five-kilometer (three-mile) wide belt of silt and tangled water hyacinths that girds the lake and conceals its true dimensions.

This snarl of silt and weed, left to its own devices, takes about 50 years to produce a meter-thick humus-like layer. The state sells 100-meter by two-meter (328-foot by 6½-foot) sections of this land, at 600 kyats (US \$71) a plot, to Intha villagers, who then tow the floating gardens across the lake to their homes.

Not everyone buys their garden. Many Inthas make their own, collecting the omnipresent, hollow-stemmed floating weeds and lashing and weaving them together to form a light, deep trough. Others do the same with dried reeds and grasses matted into strips. Whatever the method, the garden is anchored to the bed of the lake with bamboo poles, then filled with mud ladled with long-handled scoops from the lake bottom.

These gardens, called *kyunpaws,* are cultivated from boats—usually by women, who use both sides of the fertile strip to plant and harvest crops year-round. Cauliflower, tomatoes, cucum-

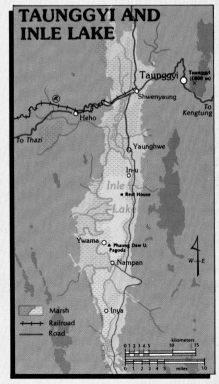

TAUNGGYI AND INLE LAKE

Taunggyi
Taunggyi (1800 m)
Shwenyaung
To Kengtung
Heho
To Thazi
Yaunghwe
In-u
Inle
Rest House
Lake
Ywama
Phaung Daw U Pagoda
Nampan
Inya

Marsh
Railroad
Road

kilometers
0 1 2 3 4 5   10   15
miles
0 1 2 3 4 5   10

Preceding pages, Inle Lake at dawn. *Left,* a leg-rowing fisherman.

bers, cabbage, peas, beans and eggplant all flourish in the moist conditions.

The Intha people like to say they live off the lake. That refers not only to their gardens, but to their remarkable fishermen, whose fame is due to their unusual technique of propelling their slender craft through the water. Perching precariously on the boat's stern with one foot, the fisherman twists his free leg around a single long oar—and thus maneuvers through the shallow lake water, keeping his eyes open to avert clumps of the tangled weeds floating just beneath the surface.

The Fishermen's Trick

Nearly as curious is the method of fishing, also unique in the world. Carrying a tall conical trap containing a gill net, the fisherman looks for indications of movement on the water's surface. Where he sees it, he thrusts the trap to the lake bottom (it is three meters, or 10 feet, at its deepest point), releasing a ring that holds the net up. As the meshwork drops, any fish within its limited range—a meter-long Inle carp, a catfish, or perhaps an eel—becomes a meal for the fisherman's family.

There are an estimated 70,000 Inthas living on the lake or near its shores. An immigrant tribe from Tavoy (Tenasserim), they left their former homeland in the 18th Century to escape the perpetual conflicts between the Burmese and Thais. They settled on Inle Lake and adopted their name, which means, "sons of the lake."

Here on the Shan Plateau, they have developed an amazing culture, as their farming and fishing skills attest. Their additional talents as metalworkers and carpenters—and, in the case of the women, as weavers—have helped to make them one of the wealthiest tribes in all Burma. The famous Shan shoulder bags and *longyis,* sold throughout the country, are manufactured here on the Inthas' looms.

While Yaunghwe provides the lake's only formal lodging at the modest Inle Inn, it is not the primary destination for Inle's visitors. That honor is reserved for the village of **Ywama,** about 12 kilometers (7½ miles) away on the lake's southwestern shore. Narrow boats outfitted with motors ply the route between the two communities, carrying 10 passengers for 10 kyats apiece.

A Shan buffalo cow, boy.

A Floating Market
and Five Balls of Gold

Ywama is the site of a daily "floating market" which, unlike its distant cousin in Bangkok, has thus far managed to retain its authentic flavor far from the madness of over-tourism. It also is the location of the **Phaung Daw U Pagoda,** which enshrines five Buddha images carried back to Burma by the widely traveled 12th Century King Alaungsithu upon his return from the Malay Peninsula. The images were deposited in a cave near the lake, and were not rediscovered until centuries later. Since their relocation to this pagoda, however, they have been covered with so much gold leaf that they look more like balls of gold or animistic fetishes than Buddha figures.

The pagoda is the focal point for the Phaung Daw U Festival, an annual celebration which takes place during two weeks of September *(Tawthalin).* The golden images are transported to Inle's 10 largest settlements aboard a recreated royal barge with a huge gilded *karaweik* bird upon its prow. The procession is a splendid reminder of the pomp that must have once marked the Buddhist courts.

The Phaung Daw U Festival draws celebrants from throughout Burma, not only for the "royal" procession, but also for the famed leg-rowing competitions, pitting crews of Inle Lake oarsmen in sprints through the lake. Anyone who has not booked a room months in advance must settle for floor space in a monastery or pagoda during the weeks of the festival.

As the Intha civilization lives by the water, it may also die by the water. Inle Lake is condemned to become a natural landfill. More and more silt is carried into the lake each year by the Balu Chaung—the canal which feeds the lake from the south—and by mountain streams; the uncontrolled growth of the water hyacinth complicates matters. Whether modern water conservation techniques can be applied in time, or whether the Inthas will again have to demonstrate their adaptability, remains to be seen.

Burmese government tourist authorities, at least, seem unconcerned. A large hotel planned for Inle Lake's western shore, near a sulphur spring, seems certain to bind the region irrevocably to the nation's tourist network.

Ywama's floating market.

The 'Big Mountain'

Inle Lake lies at an altitude of 878 meters (2,880 feet) above sea level. Overlooking the watery basin in which it lies are numerous lofty peaks—among them **Taunggyi**, or "big mountain." The wooded height offers a lovely view of Inle Lake from its summit elevation of about 1,800 meters (nearly 6,000 feet). Two paths lead to the top.

At the mountain's foot is the Shan capital which bears its name. The seat of the Shan Parliament during the British colonial period, three dozen *sawbwas*—hereditary Shan princes—met here on a regular basis to make decisions for their people.

Taunggyi was founded by Sir James George Scott, one of the most highly respected colonial officers in the history of British Burma. A devoted student of Burmese history and culture, Scott, under the pseudonym Shway Yoe, wrote the book *The Burman, His Life and Notions*—generally regarded as the 19th Century's finest work on Burma. It remains a frequently consulted source.

Today, the **Taunggyi Hotel** still radiates vestiges of colonial charm. Instead of the British, however, it houses a Burmese government tourist office, at which visitors can arrange for bus or Jeep transportation to Inle Lake, the Heho airport and other places of interest. Once called the Taunggyi Strand, the hotel is situated a short distance east of the town center in a pine and eucalyptus grove. Nearby, on the mountain's lower slopes, is a villa where the British superintendent of the Shan states once lived. Today it is reserved for state guests.

A major attraction of Taunggyi is its market. Every fifth day, markets alternately are held in Taunggyi and the towns of Yaunghwe, Shwenyaung, Heho and Kalaw. The market in Taunggyi is perhaps the best known: colorfully dressed members of the region's various hill tribes flock here in a pageantry matched only, perhaps, by native bazaars in isolated parts of Africa or South America. Taunggyi also has a noted night market at which deals are struck for goods smuggled from Thailand. Outboard motors and spare parts for motor repair are most highly prized by Inle Lake's Inthas.

In the city center, close by a monument to Bogyoke Aung San, is the **Taunggyi Museum**. It is small, but is highly recom-

mended to visitors interested in regional ethnology: indigenous costumes of the 30-plus tribes of the Shan Plateau region are displayed within, and a large map indicates their locations.

The road leading east from Taunggyi is controlled by Shan rebel troops a short distance east of the town. Were you able to continue, you would eventually reach **Kengtung**, capital of the Golden Triangle and gateway to northwestern Thailand.

On a hill three kilometers south of Taunggyi is a temple known as the **Wish Granting Pagoda**. It is a popular pilgrimage destination for Shans and other Buddhists of the region, who believe a visit to the shrine will do as the name implies— grant their wishes. The temple's architectural style is distinctly different from the Mon and Burman-style stupas of Pagan and other lowland locales. From its base there is a wonderful view available of the Shan countryside and Inle Lake.

Mission Schools
And Mandalay Rum

Perhaps because of the British influence, there are many Christians in the Taunggyi area. Until 1968, in fact, a mission school operated here; it once educated the children of the area's ruling class. Another remnant of British culture is the drinking law, which permits public taverns to exist. You won't easily find them in the lowlands, but here drinks like Mandalay Beer, Mandalay rum and Shan whisky can be purchased over the counter.

About 70 kilometers (44 miles) west of Taunggyi, well beyond the Heho airport, is the town of **Kalaw**. Perched on the western rim of the Shan Plateau, it was once a favorite hill station retreat for British administrative officials and their families during the hot season. Now a peaceful town surrounded by pine woods, it is an ideal starting point for visits to Palaung villages and the Pindaya Cave.

About 60,000 Palaungs inhabit the plateau near Kalaw. This tribe, which belongs to the Mon-Khmer language family, is easily recognized by the striking costumes worn by its women. Characteristic dress is a blue jacket with a red collar, and a skirt given a crinoline effect with bamboo. Palaung villages such as **Ta Yaw** and **Shwe Min Phone** welcome visitors; if there is insufficient time for a

Inle Lake cheroot maker, left, and one of her products being given a workout.

day's excursion, the tribespeople can be seen at the highland market held in Kalaw every fifth day.

Several kilometers east of Kalaw, a short distance before the main road passes through the village of **Aungban,** there is a turnoff to the north. This route leads to the village of **Pindaya,** 41 kilometers (26 miles) from the junction.

The road takes one through a region of such great scenic beauty that it has become known as "Burma's Switzerland." Villages of the Pa-o and Danu minorities dot the mountainsides to the left and right. In Pindaya village itself is the Taungyo tribe, a Burmese-speaking group with houses climbing the hills above a small lake.

From this lake, a covered stairway leads to the **Pindaya Cave.** No one seems to know why the countless Buddha images within the cave were stored here. Thousands of them are many hundreds of years old. But it is certain that new statues have been erected there over the years, as several different sculptural periods are represented in the work.

Near the lake is the gilded **Shwe Ohn Hmin Pagoda;** the hillside is dotted with many more white pagodas.

Near the village of **Ye-ngan,** northwest of Pindaya, are the **Padah-Lin Caves.** These caverns are Burma's most important neolithic excavation site. Countless chips created in the chipping-away of stone axes have been found here, leading archaeologists to believe the caves were a site of tool and weapon-making in prehistoric times. In one of the caves, traces of early wall paintings can still be discerned. A human hand, a bison, part of an elephant, a huge fish, and a sunset (as seen through the cave entrance) can be clearly made out.

Routes to the Plateau

As previously noted, the best way for visitors to reach the southern Shan Plateau is by plane to Heho from Rangoon or Mandalay. There are, however, other routes for the hardy or leisurely traveler. One can disembark from the main north-south railroad trunk line at Thazi and catch a time-consuming freight line to Shwenyaung, about midway between Taunggyi and Inle Lake.

Or one can travel by road. Bus services from Pagan and Mandalay follow a similar route to that of the train; both take about 12 hours and, though very tiring, offer an unusual glimpse of central Burma. The Taunggyi Mann leaves Mandalay every morning between 4 and 5 o'clock from the 27th Street terminus. The vehicle from Pagan departs at the same time from near the Burma government tourist office. In addition, buses leave hourly from Thazi.

Whereas arriving in the Shan State by rail or bus can be relatively easy for those long on patience, the departure can be a little more complicated. Visitors who hope to resume their northbound or southbound rail journey after disembarking at Thazi invariably have difficulty boarding the express train, because tickets are nearly always booked in advance from Mandalay or Rangoon. The only way around this obstacle is to buy an advance ticket for the complete Rangoon-Mandalay journey, and only use the portion from Thazi.

The bus journey to Taunggyi is especially recommended to those traveling from Pagan, as even the flight via Mandalay can take most of a day. Because of the limited amount of time available to tourists in Burma, however, it is recommended that visitors take the plane in returning to Rangoon.

An Intha weaver, left; and a Pa-o woman from Taunggyi.

ARAKAN AND ITS ANCIENT CITIES

High on a rocky plateau in western Burma rest the remains of what was once among the most spectacular royal cities of Asia. Today, jungle vines creep over its stupas, and myriad priceless Buddha images peer out from the undergrowth. Known from the 15th to 18th centuries as Mrauk-U, and now as Myohaung (or Mrohaung to the Arakanese), it is the youngest of eight ancient capitals whose bricks crumble under the dense vegetation of inland Arakan.

Rivers like the Kaladan and Lemro have carved deep indentations in the Arakan littoral. The jungle river boats that ply these waters are the only dependable means of transportation along this isolated coast. The starting point for many of these launches is Akyab (also called Sittwe), the Moslem-flavored capital of this unusual Burmese state. Further down the seaboard, 240 kilometers (150 miles) or so toward the Irrawaddy Delta, is the beach resort of Sandoway, where a beautiful stretch of tranquil sand

stretches 11 kilometers (seven miles) along a palm-fringed coastline.

Arakan. That fabled name has meant mystery and surprise to all who have stumbled upon it for millennia. Even today, it is one of Burma's best-guarded secrets. Few westerners are granted government permission to travel to Akyab and Myohaung; even Sandoway's beaches are but seldom visited.

'Wild, Uncivilized People'

Arakan is the land where the Mongol and Aryan races, the Brahmanist and Buddhist religions, had their closest encounters. Called *Argyre*, "the silver land," by Ptolemy in the 2nd Century A.D., its modern appellation came from the name given it by the early inhabitants themselves—*Rakhaingpyi*. The Indian Aryans used the term *Rakhaing* in pre-Buddhist times, referring to Mongols and Dravidians as "wild, uncivilized people."

It is generally agreed that Buddhism did not become established here until the reign of King Chandra Surya, which began in 146 A.D. It was during his time that the famous Maha Muni Buddha was cast. The Maha Muni and the Yattara Bell, with its astrological ciphers, became symbols of an independent Arakan. From their home atop Sirigutta Hill, they were the protectors—the palladia—of the small nation. When the Maha Muni was removed by King Bodawpaya in 1784 and carried away to Amarapura, Arakan's fate was sealed. Even today, the Arakanese equate the loss of their independence with that of the Maha Muni.

Until 957 A.D., when Arakan was overrun by the Pyus, the land was dominated by the Indian culture. Ten centuries of blending the Pyu and Indian races have produced the people known as Arakanese today. When their cultures clashed in the 10th Century, the Indians, who had already fused Brahmanism and Buddhism, merged their beliefs with the animism of the Pyus to form a unique mystical syncretism.

At the time of the dominance of the First Burmese Empire, Arakan was forced to pay tribute to the rulers of Pagan. Because of its geographical isolation, however, the land was able to retain its autonomy. King Anawrahta attacked Arakan and intended to take the Maha Muni for his capital, but the project was abandoned because of the transportation problems it would have entailed.

Preceding pages, modern Myohaung in the morning mist; left, the Myohaung market; and below, a 17th Century depiction of Mrauk-U.

A more immediate threat to Arakan was Mohammedan Bengal, which borders it on the northwest. The Islamic world had been pushing its frontiers east from Arabia for centuries—yet could make no inroads upon the bulwark of Buddhism and Brahmanism put up by the Arakanese. By the late 13th Century, Islam had bypassed mainland Southeast Asia entirely, instead establishing an initial foothold on the island of Sumatra.

Islam didn't entirely fail in Arakan. Many of the state's people today are, in fact, Moslems. In medieval times, Bengal was a strong supporter of Arakan: when Arakan was incorporated into the Shan kingdom of Ava for a short time in the 15th Century, it was with Bengal's assistance that it was able to break away. After that time, all of Arakan's kings, even though Buddhist, bore an Islamic title.

Mrauk-U was founded in 1433 by King Minsawmun, and until the decline of the Arakan empire 3½ centuries later remained the region's capital and cultural center. The city had thrived for nearly a century by the time the first Europeans— Portuguese pirates—appeared in the Bay of Bengal in 1517. These seafarers based themselves on the Arakan coast at

Dianga, 20 kilometers (12½ miles) south of Chittagong in present-day Bangladesh. Their coastal raids were far more successful than a miscalculated siege on the impregnable citadel of Mrauk-U; it wasn't long after that failure that the Portuguese put their ships and cannons at the disposal of the Arakan kings.

The early 17th Century was Arakan's Golden Age. In 1599, King Razagyi returned from a campaign in Pegu—then Burma's most powerful kingdom—with a white elephant, regarded as one of the seven symbols of the "universal monarch." It remained with his successors.

Elixir of Immortality

Razagyi's grandson, Thiri-thudhamma (ruled 1622–1638), was the most respected king in Arakan's history. He saw himself as a future "universal monarch" and sought immortality. According to detailed accounts by the Augustan Father Manrique—who came to Mrauk-U in 1629 as the ambassador from Portuguese Goa—Thiri-thudhamma had a famed Mohammedan doctor brew him an "immortality elixir" containing the essence of the hearts of

2,000 white doves, 4,000 white cows and 6,000 humans. It didn't work, of course, and he was poisoned by another elixir concocted by court enemies.

After Thiri-thu-dhamma's death, the situation in Arakan became more chaotic. The Portuguese in Dianga switched allegiance, supported the Mogul chief Aurangzeb, and broke Arakan's dominance at sea. In the court at Mrauk-U, Afghan and Turkish archers, who had been serving as legionnaires, assumed power. In the first half of the 18th Century, there was such turmoil in the government that the average ruler held power for only 2½ years.

In 1761 and 1762, Arakan was struck by a pair of exceptionally strong earthquakes. The epicenters of both were near Mrauk-U. The city survived, but along the coast sections of land rose by as much as seven meters (23 feet). Buddhists, of course, saw the quakes as an indication of major changes to come.

And come they did. In 1784, King Bodawpaya, on a campaign from central Burma, used Arakan's confused political situation to annex the territory to his empire. It wasn't a military conquest; he took Mrauk-U by betrayal, with support from an Arakanese populace tired of perpetual civil war. Not satisfied with the popular acclaim, however, Bodawpaya assured his success by making off with the Maha Muni—thus turning its fabled magic powers to his own ends.

Today, two centuries after Bodawpaya, Arakan remains a part of greater Burma. But many of its people still see themselves as a separate entity. In particular, the Moslem minority along the border of Bangladesh has a military arm— the Mujahid—which still makes serious trouble for Burma's central government. It is this continuing conflict that is the major reason for Burma's reluctance to allow tourists into northern Arakan.

Arakan's Capital

Akyab (Sittwe), the capital of Arakan, is one of these off-limits locales. Founded in 1826 by the English general Morrisson, who moved his troops from Mrauk-U to the Kaladan River mouth to escape the inland humidity during the First Anglo-Burmese War, there is today not much of interest to visitors. A seemingly endless stretch of beach, lying north of the city, is a minor attraction.

A mosque, left, and a Buddhist shrine at Akyab.

Of far greater interest, and under different political conditions a "must see" tourist destination, is **Myohaung**. (The name means "old city," a label it was given when the British relocated Arakan's administrative headquarters from Mrauk-U to the coast.)

By Jungle Boat to Mrauk-U

Arakan's medieval capital lies 80 kilometers (50 miles) inland from the Kaladan's mouth, occupying a rocky plateau between the Kaladan and the Lemro River. It's a six- or seven-hour voyage from Akyab, aboard a boat reminiscent of Bogart's *African Queen*. The craft travels first up the Kaladan, then along several small creeks until the settlement of **Aungdet** is reached. From there, it's a short saunter to Myohaung, built atop and amidst what was once **Mrauk-U**.

King Minsawmun constructed Mrauk-U to replace the "unlucky" royal city of Launggyet, and thereby placate his citizenry. The king's Brahman astrologers warned him, however, that he would die within the year if he moved his capital; and it wasn't long after the move was made that the prophecy was fulfilled.

It was a fine capital city, though. Natural barriers, walls and artificial lakes—the dams of which could be opened to repulse the enemy—helped make the town virtually unconquerable. Bengalis, Manipurians, Portuguese and Burmans all tried at one time or another to capture the city, and all went down to defeat.

Father Manrique, in the 17th Century, left a vivid description of the city's formidable appearance. Surrounded on all sides by high rocky mountains, its thoroughfares were waterways navigable by large and small vessels alike.

"The greater number of houses in the city are made of bamboo," Manrique wrote. "The houses are built in accordance with the rank and position of the builder, and the amount he wishes to spend. Much ingenuity and labour are spent on making for the houses mats of the finest material and of many colours, which are very neat and handsome.

"Even the buildings of the Royal Palace are made of these ... materials, and they have great wooden pillars of such length and symmetry that one is astonished that trees so lofty and straight can exist. Such palace buildings also contain rooms made of fragrant woods such as

A 1920s map of Myohaung environs, still usable today.

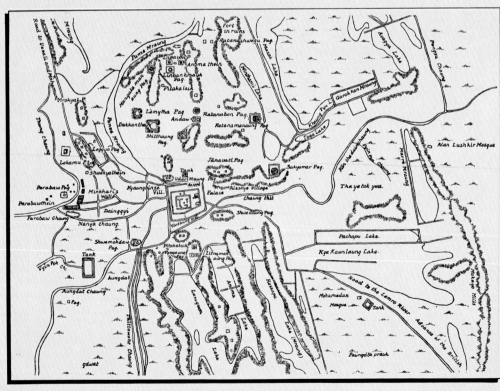

white and red sandalwood, which thus please the sense of smell by their own natural fragrance."

Manrique's description of Mrauk-U's market at the time of King Thiri-thu-dhamma's coronation is a portrait of a true metropolis:

"So numerous were the different classes of dress and language, such the varied customs at that capital, that the eye was kept busy trying to distinguish different nationalities by their apparel.

"In the shops were being sold in abundance, diamonds, rubies, sapphires, emeralds, topazes, gold and silver in plates and bars, tin and zinc. Besides these articles, there was much copper, fine brass ambergris, musk, civetscent, fragrant resin, essence of almonds, incense, camphor, red lead, indigo, borax, quicksilver, saltpetre, opium, tobacco and lac..."

Mrauk-U, indeed, was a major city, and a cosmopolitan one at that. The remnants of a 30-kilometer (19-mile) long fortification which surrounded the settlement can still be found today. In the center of the city was the **Royal Palace**, looming high over the surrounding area like an Asian Acropolis. Three layers of

square-shaped stonework are all that remains. Where the king of Arakan once had his private chambers and reception rooms, now there is only a platform from which to view the hilly landscape.

North of the palace site, hidden behind a series of low hills, are the most important religious shrines of medieval Mrauk-U. But then, everywhere one looks within Mrauk-U's city wall—in every field, and upon each and every hill—are Buddha images, temples or pagodas. Some of those on the hilltops are in active use even today, whitewashed by their devotees to keep them sparkling. Other structures are in various stages of decay, shrouded in the jungle vegetation and crumbling at the mercy of the green vines.

Temple of 80,000 Buddhas

The visitor must walk for at least eight kilometers (five miles) over the hills and through overgrown fields to reach some of the more important edifices. Unlike buildings elsewhere in Burma, these sacred structures were intended to be fortifications as well as shrines. Among the most beautiful is the **Shitthaung Temple**, located atop a small hill. Erected in the

A dhow-like sailing boat on the Lemro River.

16th Century after the unsuccessful Portuguese attack on the city, it is known as "the temple of 80,000 Buddhas." This may be an allusion to the number of statements found in the Buddha's speeches to his followers. But one is left to wonder if it isn't the actual number of Buddha images and reliefs enshrined here, many of them gracing the temple's courtyard and outside wall. Other figures out of Buddhist and Brahman mythology are also represented here.

Not far distant is the **Htukkan-thein**, an ordination hall. It has a bell-shaped stupa, and the entire structure is built upon a series of high terraces. In its courtyard are several images which exhibit clothing popular in the 16th Century.

Numerous sitting Buddha figures can also be found in the **Andaw Temple.** One of the Buddha's teeth, reported to have come from Ceylon, is in the Andaw's sanctuary. King Minbin, who built this shrine, also is believed to have founded the **Lemyethna Temple** and the **Shwedaung Pagoda**; both contain frescoes which give visitors a detailed pictorial account of daily life in the Mrauk-U court.

Virtually all of Mrauk-U's temples have carved reliefs. There are several thousand in all, depicting Hindu and Mahayana Buddhist religious scenes as well as glimpses of 17th Century royal life. Armed only with a strong flashlight, the visitor can stroll for hours through the dimly lit corridors and continually be surprised by new stories, new gods, new mythological animals.

Between these temple corridors, standing back-to-back in the light arches, are hundreds of Buddha figures. Buddha images, in fact, are to Myohaung as trees are to a forest. They are everywhere, in all sizes, all shapes and all materials. Very often they are broken, a legacy of times when Arakan had no stable government and the citizens' morale was low. Strewn about as if worthless, these Buddhas could doubtlessly fetch hundreds of dollars apiece on the antique markets of the world. But here at Mrauk-U, they are too commonplace to arouse curiosity.

South of the old royal palace, still within the old city walls, are the three large artificial reservoirs once used to flush out approaching enemies. Today, they are an inviting place for the tired, dust-covered visitor to take a swim.

Despite its former cosmopolitan nature and its great historical importance,

On the way to the rice mill in Myohaung.

Mrauk-U today is a quiet destination. Today's visitor, if permission for a trip here is granted, will find himself flanked only by his guide, the chairman of the township council, three soldiers, and a half-dozen curious Myohaungians.

Other Ancient Capitals

Although it is 5½ centuries old, Myohaung/Mrauk-U is the youngest of all the cities between the Lemro and Kaladan rivers. Within easy traveling distance of the "old city" are **Launggyet**—the capital before Mrauk-U—and **Vesali**, which dates to the 4th Century A.D. Both of these cities have fewer visible remains than those of Mrauk-U, but their hills, too, are studded with pagodas and Buddha images.

At Vesali, wherever topsoil is removed, the ground consists of red tiles. The peasants who reside here have innumerable ancient images of all kinds in their bamboo huts. These images once adorned the walls and walkways of a palace which today is buried beneath the peasants' huts; the figures are now regarded as the guardians of trees and springs. The Burmese government archaeological department cannot take them away because of the peasants' strong religious attachment to them.

Several other former royal cities—**Hkrit, Parein, Pyinsa** and **Thabeiktaung** among them—await excavation. The same is true of **Dhannavati,** some 30 kilometers (19 miles) north of Myohaung near present-day **Thayettbin.** The capital of Arakan between the 6th Century B.C. and 350 A.D., it was here that the famed Maha Muni image is believed to have been cast in the 2nd Century A.D.

To reach this site, one must return to Akyab and take another boat, this time traveling up the Kaladan as far as **Kyauktaw,** about five kilometers (three miles) from Dhannavati and **Sirigutta Hill.**

If one climbs Sirigutta Hill with the knowledge that it was once the center of Buddhist devotion for all of Arakan, there is a certain sadness in finding it as it is today. While still the most venerated site in the entire Myohaung area, it is but a shadow of its former self. The pagoda on the hill was rebuilt in Pagan style after being destroyed by the Pyus in 957. Three walls enclose a series of courtyards around the structure. In the outer court-

Mrauk-U's Shitthaung Temple.

yard are a library and a well; in the middle one are statues of 12 Hindu gods who served as guardian spirits of the Maha Muni, and who therefore symbolize the Brahman deities' submission to Buddhist thought. The pagoda itself stands in the inner courtyard, flanked by the legendary **Yattara Bell.**

Signs of Superstition

The bell—actually a duplicate of the original—is covered by astrological signs and runes of great importance to the superstitious Arakanese of medieval times. Their alchemists wove a magic spell that is difficult to understand today. But an inscription gives 20th Century man an insight into the thought of earlier times:

"To prevent the inroads of the enemies from foreign towns and villages, let offerings of flowers, parched corn and lamps be made day and night at the . . . pagodas.

"To cause the rulers of the towns and the villages in the four cardinal directions to be panic stricken, let a pagoda provided with four archways be constructed . . .

"And let the Yattara Bell be hung and struck at the eastern archway, and the

enemies of the east will be panic stricken and quit by flight. . . . Let also the Yattara *bidauk* drum be struck at the relic chambers of Buddha. By these means foreign invaders will be seized by fear and take to flight."

Modern observers might be skeptical of the claim that these methods could singlehandedly, as it were, fend off enemy attacks. But the fact remains that as long as the Maha Muni stood beside the Yattara Bell on Sirigutta Hill, Arakan remained an independent land.

The Beach at Sandoway

Visitors to Burma are usually drawn here by the country's cultural and historic attractions. Few are aware of the fact that one of Southeast Asia's most beautiful beaches is located along the southern Arakan coast—and is open to tourism except during the rainy season. **Sandoway** is the central community of this beach district, and can be reached from Rangoon by air. Formerly just one of several Burma beaches popular among British colonial officials, today it is the only seaside resort with suitable tourist accommodation. Because the beach is very popular today among Burmese, advance hotel bookings are recommended. Best of the accommodations is the Sandoway Strand Hotel.

Perhaps the most popular beach in the vicinity is at the neighboring village of **Ngapali.** Visitors who have carried equipment with them will find the water ideal for scuba diving and snorkeling. The community is thought to have received its name during the First Anglo-Burmese War from Italian mercenaries, who said the stretch of sand reminded them of their Naples home.

In ancient times, Sandoway was an important port of call for Indian merchants and seafarers on the route between their homeland and the Malay Peninsula. It was then known as Dvaravati, a name taken from a city of *Jataka* myth: when attacked by enemies, it could rise into the sky and hover until the siege had ended.

The Buddha is said to have lived three of his 547 previous lives in Sandoway. Local pagodas enshrine the evidence: there is the tooth of a cobra in the **Andaw Pagoda,** the rib of a partridge in the **Nandaw Pagoda,** and a yak hair in the **Sandaw Pagoda.** Tradition says Gautama lived these incarnations as he made his way along the path to enlightenment.

Two faces of Arakan religion: Hindu love scene in the Htukkanthein, left; and an orthodox Moslem at Akyab.

DAILY LIFE FROM BIRTH TO DEATH

There are few countries in the world today in which tradition has such a strong influence on everyday life as it has in Burma. The colonial period did not pass without affecting the Burmese; rationalism, science and realism profoundly altered commerce and national affairs. But everyday life is still dominated by old values.

Let us follow a Burmese on his life's path:

Childhood Years, From Birth to Marriage

Seven days after birth, the baby's parents invite friends to a naming ceremony. The youngster is given a name based on astrological calculations, and it need bear no relation to that of the parents.

The child is sent to school at the age of five. However, despite a system of compulsory education and strenuous efforts by the government since independence to ensure education for all, there are still areas with no state schools. In these places, the local *kyaung* (monastery) takes charge of the child's elementary education.

When a boy is nine years old, his *shin-pyu* takes place. This is an initiation ceremony marking the end of his childhood and the beginning of a period of monkhood. Girls of the same age participate in an ear-piercing ceremony called the *nahtwin*, which also symbolizes a farewell to the unburdened life of the child.

Some social psychologists see this abrupt transformation from childhood to adulthood as the cause of the characteristic Burman excitability—quickly passing, but ever present. However, as two-thirds of the population still works on the land, the transition from school to adult life is relatively easy for most young people: during their school years, they help with the harvest in their parents' fields.

Burmese tend to get married relatively young. The marriage itself requires no religious or civil ceremony, although it should be registered for the purpose of any future division of property.

Women, despite their lower status in Buddhist doctrine, have a secure place in society. Their rights almost always have been equal to those of men, and are guaranteed by an uncomplicated divorce law. A woman does not change her name when married. If her marriage does break up, she can return to her parents at any time.

Traditional Dress: Longyi and Gaung-Baung

Burmans emphasize their feeling of national identity through the clothes they wear. Most evident is the *longyi*. Similar to the Malayan sarong, it consists of a kilt-like piece of cloth worn from the waist to the ankle. Together with the *eingyi*, a transparent blouse which is also worn with a round-collared, long-sleeved jacket, the *longyi* takes the place of Western garments.

The traditional headgear of the men, the *gaung-baung*, today is seen only on special occasions. During the colonial period, it was wrapped around the head like a turban, with different styles and colors according to one's social position. Nowadays, it has been superseded by a ready-made cap, still with the typically prominent points.

Burmese women attach great importance to jewelry. As rubies, sapphires, jade and pearls are found in great quantity in Burma, it is common at festivals to see peasant women richly adorned with precious stones. The Burmese still regard the purchase of gems as the safest form of investment.

'Crossing the River' To Old Age and Death

Not many young Burmese remain in the monkhood for more than a few months or years after their *shin-pyu*. Some become *pongyis* and devote their entire lives to meditation and the teachings of the Buddha. To most adult Burmese, however, the Sangha is not merely a religious brotherhood. It is also an institution providing social insurance and old-age support.

Death has a different meaning for a Buddhist than it has for a Christian. When a Burmese dies, he is either buried or cremated. A coin is put in his mouth so he can pay the "ferryman" who transports him "across the river" into the next existence. All persons close to the deceased are invited to the funeral. It is generally accepted that the dead person himself takes part in these rites, and that his spirit remains in his family's house for a week afterward.

Preceding pages, a calendar peddler in Rangoon; ebullient children at a street festival; and sweet-hearts on the Rangoon University campus. Left, a Buddha.

HOT AND SPICY: BURMESE FOOD

The menu in a standard restaurant in Burma is dominated by Indian curries and Chinese noodle and rice dishes. That isn't really surprising, given that Burma is located on the ancient India-China trade routes, and immigrants from both countries have influenced Burma with their famed cuisines.

There *are* traditional Burmese dishes, although they are a bit harder to find. In Rangoon, the **Burma Kitchen**, the **Bamboo House** and the **Karaweik Restaurant** cater to the more affluent, which of course includes Westerners. Otherwise, one must befriend a Burmese and get invited home for a truly native-style dinner.

Burma's geographic and cultural seclusion has contributed to a culinary tradition all its own. Because the people are not stock breeders, beef is not a major element in the diet, and milk is used only sparingly. However, the rivers and long coastlines have made fish the most important source of protein.

Rice and Curry With 'A Fish-Like Smell'

Large quantities of rice are the core of any Burmese meal, usually prepared with a curry. But the meal will invariably be served with *ngapi* or *nganpayay,* fermented fish or shrimp paste with a reputation as the "national dish." Because of its strong smell, *ngapi* is not ordinarily served to Westerners. Kipling described it as "fish pickled when it ought to have been buried long ago," and Sir James George Scott said: "An old herring barrel smells strong, but there is nothing in nature that more than nga-pee hath an ancient and a fish-like smell." Used in small quantities, however, it is not unpleasant.

Another typical dish is *mohinga,* a soup with fish and rice noodles, eaten mainly at breakfast and lunch. More common at dinner, perhaps, is *hingyo,* a clear soup served with green vegetable leaves.

Fish or prawns, and frequently chicken, constitute the main course, along with the rice. Especially popular is *kaukswe,* a chicken and noodle dish prepared with coconut milk. In the Irrawaddy Delta, it is normally fixed with onions, ginger, garlic and chilies. Tastes vary regionally, however, and on the Shan Plateau it is likely to be prepared in a very different fashion.

A variety of delicious fruits are available in Burma, as any visitor to a market will quickly attest. Bananas, oranges, limes, mangoes, papayas and pomeloes (Chinese grapefruit) are easily found; other fruits, such as the highly-prized mangosteen and the notorious durian, are shipped to the capital from Moulmein and Tenasserim. (Of the durian, Scott once wrote: "Some Englishmen will tell you that the flavour and the odour of the fruit may be realized by eating a 'garlic custard' over a London sewer; others will be no less positive in their perception of blendings of sherry, delicious custards, and the nectar of the gods. . . .")

On street corners in all larger cities, small food stalls hawk shrimp chips, sweet pancakes, fried pumpkin, Shan sausage, and—for the strong of stomach—fried grasshoppers. Ice cream should be avoided, and likewise water unless it has been thoroughly boiled, but sugar cane juice, soft drinks and tea are easily obtainable. (Most Westerners find Chinese tea preferable to Burmese.) Coffee is becoming more popular. It is one of the true pleasures of travel to get to know a country through one's taste buds.

The main protein source in the Burmese diet is fish (left), often made into a strong-smelling paste called *ngapi* ; chilies (right) are in every dish.

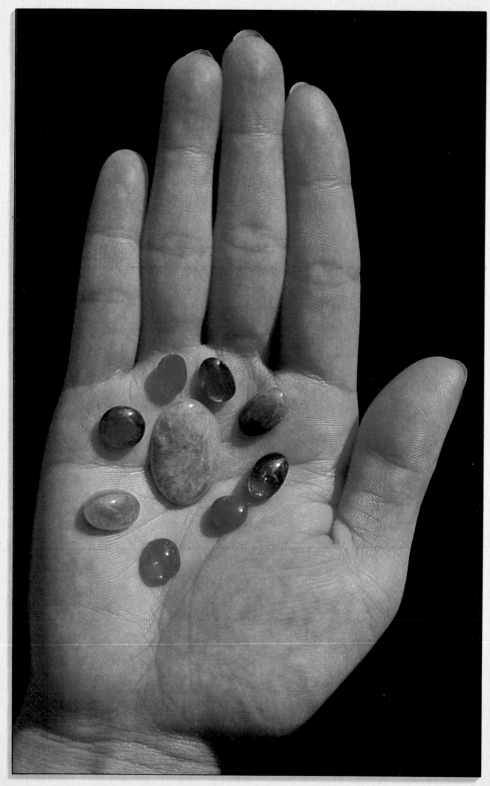

LAND OF RUBIES AND JADE

The first mental image many Westerners have of Burma is of precious stones—gems sparkling green, red and purple in the midday sun.

The reputation is not undeserved. From the northern mines of Mogok and Mogaung come large quantities of rubies, jade, sapphires and other stones.

Ludovico di Varthema, an Italian merchant who visited Burma in 1505, was the first European to report this wealth to the West. "The sole merchandise of this people is jewels," wrote di Varthema. "Large pearls and diamonds are worth more there than with us, and also emeralds." Of the King of Pegu, he wrote:

... He wears more rubies on him than the value of a very large city, and he wears them on all his toes. And on his legs he wears certain great rings of gold, all full of the most beautiful rubies; also his arms and his fingers are all full with rubies. His ears hang down half a palm, through the great weight of the many jewels he wears there, so that when the person of the king is seen by a light at night, he shines so much that he appears to be the sun.

Di Varthema was also the first Westerner to become rich through dealing in gems in Burma. He presented the king some corals, and was rewarded with 200 rubies—worth about 100,000 ducats (perhaps US$150,000) in Europe at that time.

Pigeon-Blood Rubies
And 'Trustworthy' Generals

Today, it is not so easy to become rich in the gem market. But every February, hundreds of gem dealers from all over the world gather in Rangoon for the annual "Gems and Pearls Emporium" at the Inya Lake Hotel. There, invited guests can visit special showrooms to buy what Upper Burma's soil contributes to the wealth of the country.

Most prized of all are the rubies, a stone on which Burma holds a virtual monopoly on the world market. Those rubies the color of pigeon blood, apparently unique to Burma, fetch the highest prices.

Would-be buyers must beware, however, of synthetic rubies of this color. Tourists are frequently approached by "trustworthy" retired army generals who claim a "personal link" to the ruby pits of Mogok and offer a good deal on pigeon-blood rubies. These generals can make a Westerner feel as buoyantly greedy as di Varthema might have felt after his deal with the King of Pegu.

But it doesn't require an alchemist's recipe to produce a fake. False rubies can be created in a flame fusion process from purified ammonia alum and small amounts of chrome alum, with a dash of chrome oxide tossed in for the deep color. These synthetic stones, deceptively labeled, are popular attractions at markets wherever tourists congregate. Only an expert in gems should make a purchase.

Mogok, where Burma's largest ruby mines are situated, lies about 110 kilometers (70 miles) northeast of Mandalay as the crow flies. In earlier times, the kings of Burma confiscated the wealth recovered here, leaving the miners only with small stones of lesser value.

When the British annexed Upper Burma in 1886, a year of frenzied digging ensued, as the Burmese were now unhindered by royalty. But the colonials were able to occupy the Mines District in 1887, and the London firm of Messrs. Streeter & Co. received sole buying rights for whatever the ground yielded. That made the company's shareholders and the government revenue office rich. Today, the mines have been nationalized, and export revenue has been reduced.

In the far north, west of Myitkyina in the Kachin State, is the town of Mogaung, center of a jade-mining district. The rich soil of this region was well known to the Chinese as long ago as 2000 B.C. The Chinese considered the jadeite of northern Burma to be superior in quality to the nephrite found in their own soil. To them, the stone was a mirror of virtues worthy of an emperor: hardness suggestive of sound intellect, polish indicative of purity, and visible flaws symbolic of sincerity. So this "Imperial Jade" was imported to China from Mogaung. Today, most of the priceless jade artifacts on display in Peking's Forbidden City Museum and in Chinese art exhibits elsewhere are made of Mogaung jade.

Rubies and jade are only the most evident examples of Burma's precious mineral wealth. Star, blue and colorless sapphires, Oriental aquamarine and emeralds, topaz, amethysts, and lapis lazuli are among other stones for which buyers flock to the annual Inya Lake emporium.

From the ruby pits of Mogok and the jade mines of Mogaung come the precious gemstones which Burma has exported for countless centuries.

From Rangoon's Bogyoke Aung San Market to Mandalay's Zegyo Market, and at all local bazaars beyond and between, the visitor to Burma finds a remarkable variety of native handicrafts.

Stalls display lacquerware, metalwork, brass and marble sculpture, wood carvings, embroidered textiles and more. The craftsmen of Burma may not have achieved the same international renown as artisans of other parts of Southeast Asia, but they are no less skilled at their specialties.

Burmese handicrafts run the gamut from brass Buddhas and carved, hand-painted *nat*

In times past, extraordinarily fine lacquerware bowls were produced around cores of horsehair and bamboo, or even pure horsehair. This gave such great flexibility that one could press opposite sides of the bowl's rim together, without the bowl breaking or the lacquer peeling off.

Today, two other techniques of manufacture prevail. Inferior products have a gilded lacquer relief on a wooden base. Better quality wares have a core of light bamboo wickerwork, assuring elasticity and durability.

This basic structure is coated with a layer of lacquer and clay, then put in a cool, airy place

figures to fine lacquerware pieces requiring months in production.

Lacquerware

Lacquerware in particular has developed into an art form of refined quality. Its history can be traced to China's Shang dynasty (18th to 11th centuries B.C.). The craft reached the area of present-day Burma in the 1st Century A.D. by way of the Nan-ch'ao Empire (modern Yunnan), and is believed to have been carried to Pagan during King Anawrahta's conquest of Thaton in 1057. Today it thrives in northern Thailand and Laos as well as in Burma.

Raw lacquer is tapped from the *thitsi* tree *(Melanorrhoea usitatissima)* in the same way as latex is taken from the rubber tree. As soon as the sticky-gray extract comes in contact with the air, it turns hard and black.

to dry. After three or four days, the vessel is sealed with a paste of lacquer and ash, the fineness of ash determining the quality of the work. It may come from sawdust, paddy husk or even cow dung. After this coating dries, the object is polished smooth. Over a period of time it is given several successive coats of lacquer to eliminate irregularities.

At this stage, the ware is black. But the artist isn't finished: ornamental and figurative designs must still be added. Cheaper articles are simply painted. The more expensive ones are embellished by means of engraving, painting and polishing. A similar effect can be produced with colored reliefs, painted and partially polished. Red, yellow, blue and gold are the colors usually used. The production of a multi-colored lacquerware vessel takes about

The gold-leaf manufacturer of Mandalay (left) and the *nat*-image maker of Rangoon (right) practice age-old arts with roots in religious devotion.

six months, as it must go through 12 or more stages of production.

Pagan and Prome are Burma's main lacquerware centers. There, visitors can purchase quality vases, jewel boxes, dinnerware sets and other items.

Metalwork

Perhaps the most frequently seen evidence of Burmese metalwork is gold leaf, pasted by Buddhist devotees on pagodas and Buddha images all over the country. The industry is especially prevalent in Mandalay.

mains a major cottage industry in Mandalay for about 300 families. Pegu is another center. Buddha images, orchestral gongs, bells for pagodas and monasteries, and small cattle bells are in constant demand.

Buddha images made of marble are also very popular. Good quality marble is taken from a quarry at Sagyin, 34 kilometers (21 miles) north of Mandalay. It is then transported to a district in southern Mandalay city, where carvers use chisel, mallet and file to create their works of religious art.

Wood carving is among the most ancient of Burmese handicrafts, although evidence of

The gold comes from the north of Burma in nuggets, which are flattened on a slab of marble until paper-thin. These sheets are then alternately cut and pounded between layers of leather and copper plate until they are almost transparent. Then they are picked up with pincers, placed between sheets of oiled bamboo paper, and packaged in two-centimeter-long stacks of 100 leaves for sale at pagodas and bazaars. One ounce of gold can produce gold leaf with a total surface area of about 10 square meters (almost 12 square yards).

Burmese silverwork dates to the 13th Century, when palace bowls, vases and betel-nut boxes were made from this metal, as well as daggers and sheaths. Today, work done at Ywataung village near Sagaing rivals the earlier silverwork.

Whereas silverwork is not as prominent as it once was, work in copper and brass has never seriously declined in importance. It re-

ancient artisans has been destroyed. Significant 19th Century works still remain in Mandalay, particularly in the ornamentation of monasteries. Today, *nat* images are among the objects most commonly made. The artisan sketches in charcoal and chalk on a solid block of wood the figure he wishes to carve. He shapes the rough outline with chisel and saw, and completes details with knives and other fine instruments.

Embroidery, on the other hand, is a highly respected art form. Fine gold thread, silver sequins and colored glass (imitation jewels) traditionally were stitched into cotton or wool garments for royalty and other dignitaries. Today, silk *longyis* often display peacock figures or broad belts of floral design; appliqué work of colored cloth cuttings on black velvet are sold as pictures. Blankets and shoulder bags woven by tribal groups are popular souvenir items.

THE LIVELY ART OF BURMESE THEATER

The description of the Burmese as a happy and smiling person is borne out on the stage more than one would think possible.

—James R. Brandon, *Brandon's Guide to Theater in Asia,* 1976

To the people of Burma, a festival or fair of any kind means a *pwe.* It is a time to gather the entire family and go to watch a marvelous mixture of dance, music, comedy and re-creation of epic drama.

Burmese theater has its audience by turns shrieking, sobbing and rolling with laughter. Lively, carefree dancers, as resplendent as tropical birds in their dazzling plumage, leap and whirl before the awed eyes of spectators of all ages. Clowns cavort across the stage, their antics and acrobatics inspiring fits of happy hysteria. An orchestra of drums and gongs beats out a strange melody, as the stage becomes "a fairyland peopled by ravishingly handsome princes and vivacious princesses," in the words of Asian theater authority Brandon. Certainly, no one in Burma between November and May should miss an opportunity to take in at least one form of the Burmese performing arts.

There are several types of *pwe.* Most popular is the *zat pwe,* the ultimate melange of music, dance and dramatics. *Anyein pwe* is a more "folksy" theatrical form presenting episodes from everyday life, along with dancing and story telling. *Yein pwe* is pure dance, solos alternating with group numbers. *Yokthe pwe,* or marionette theater, is a uniquely Burmese theatrical form not often seen today. *Nat pwe* is ritual spirit-medium dance, never performed in public except at animistic festivals, and rarely seen by Westerners.

Among other forms of theater, *pya zat* is frequently seen preceding *zat pwe* performances. A dance-play with a mythical theme, it is generally set in a fantasy world where a heroic prince must overcome the evil-doings of demons and sorcerers.

From the mid-18th to the mid-19th centuries, a masked dance-drama called *zat gyi* flourished in royal courts under the patronage of Burmese kings. Today, public performances are rare, although papier-mâché replicas of *zat gyi* dance masks can be purchased as souvenirs at stalls along the stairs leading to the Shwedagon Pagoda. (Marionettes and orchestral drums and gongs are also sold.)

Burma has a National Theater, a company of 14 dancers and musicians who made a highly acclaimed tour of the United States in late 1975. Other troupes are trained in the State Schools of Music and Drama in Rangoon and Mandalay. But there are countless more troupes as well, traveling from village to village, from pagoda festival to pagoda festival, throughout the rural countryside during the dry season.

These troupes present their time-proven repertoire to village throngs in temporary bamboo structures, under a makeshift awning or (more often than not) in the open air. Audiences of hundreds or even thousands sit on mats spread in front of the stage. Many bring their children and babies, as well as food and

beverage in baskets, bowls and jugs. Performances often last from sunset to sunrise; many spectators doze off for a couple of hours in the middle of the show, hoping to be nudged awake for their favorite dance sequence or story.

The history of Burmese dance troupes dates to 1767, when King Hsinbyushin returned to Ava after his conquest of the Thai capital of Ayutthia. Among his captives were the royal Siamese dancers. It was from these exquisitely trained performers that the Burmese developed the dance movements which prevail on stage today.

A Burmese actor smiles (left) during a break in a *pwe* performance, and a classical dancer (right) re-enacts traditional stories of most popular *nats.*

During the dominance of Pagan in the 11th through 13th centuries, a form of dance more closely approximating Indian dance had been popular at pagoda festivals and royal audiences. This had disintegrated into popular drama after the fall of Pagan, and took a back seat to the highly refined Thai classical dance. But it still wielded some influence in shaping a uniquely Burmese dance form.

Burmese dance reached its zenith in the late Konbaung dynasty era in Mandalay. Although the leaps and turns of Western ballet were introduced and assimilated during the years of British colonial rule, enthusiasm for dance went into a period of decline. Only since independence has Burma's government made efforts to revive the theater arts. The program has been quite successful.

To the unknowledgeable Westerner, Burmese dance appears awkward, even double-jointed. Wrists, elbows, knees, ankles, fingers and toes are bent in stylized directions with seeming effortlessness.

Setting the mood is an orchestra, called the *saing,* akin to the Javanese *gamelan* and dominated by percussion instruments. Its centerpiece is a circle of 21 drums, the *patt-waing.* (Smaller orchestras have only nine drums.) Around this are a gong section *(kye-waing),* a single large drum *(patt-ma),* cymbals *(lingwin),* bamboo clappers *(wah let khok),* an oboe-like woodwind *(hne),* a bamboo flute *(palwe),* and a bamboo xylophone *(pattala).*

Occasionally, an orchestra will employ the most delicate of all Burmese instruments, the 13-stringed harp. Shaped something like a toy boat covered in buffalo hide, with silk strings attached to a curved wooden "prow," it is a solo instrument usually played by a woman, unlike other musical instruments. When used in *pwe,* it accompanies solo singing.

Burmese music lacks a chromatic scale, or even chords. But the melody pounded out on drums and gongs is mellowed by the other instruments, and love songs are as touching as they would be on violins.

Traditionally, the Burmese compare their music to the rustling of the wind through the leaves of the rose-apple tree, and the splash of its fruit falling into a sacred river. Legend explains that King Alaungsithu of Pagan, who reigned from 1112 to 1167, encountered Thagyamin, king of the *nats,* under the shade of a rose-apple tree "at the end of the world," and here he was told the secret of the Burmese tonal system.

Legendary Performances

Legend permeates all aspects of the theater in Burma. Nearly all performances, for example, are based on either the Hindu epics, especially the *Ramayana,* or on the *Jataka* tales of the Buddha's 550 prior incarnations. The *Ramayana* is the best known saga in all of South and Southeast Asia; it tells the story of the capture of the beautiful princess Sita by the demon king Dasagiri, and of her heroic rescue by her husband, Prince Rama. The *Jatakas,* meanwhile, are familiar to every Burmese schoolchild. They relate, in quasi-historical moral fashion, how the Buddha overcame the various mortal sins to earn his final rebirth and enlightenment. The 10 tales of incarnations immediately preceding Buddhahood are regarded as especially important.

Because the stories are generally well known beforehand, it is up to the troupe and its individual dancers to bring them to life for audiences. The highlight of a *zat pwe* performance usually comes about 2:30 in the morning, when the stars of the show let go with a breathtaking exhibit of their song-and-dance skills. The more imaginative an actor or actress can be during a performance, the more the crowd will roar its appreciation.

An exception to all other forms of theater is the *yokthe pwe,* or marionette theater. A single puppeteer manipulates 28 separate doll figures, some with as many as 60 strings for different dances and gestures (although most require but 20 strings). He presents the dia-

Yokethe-pwe marionettes are nowadays found more often in dealers' windows than on stage. These remnants of a dying theater art form were hanging above a stall at a Shwedagon bazaar.

logue simultaneously, while getting help from only two stage assistants.

Puppet theater in Burma had its foundation not long after Hsinbyushin's return from Ayutthia with the Siamese dancers. The king's son and successor, Singu Min, created a Ministry for the Fine Arts in his court, and gave the minister, U Thaw, the specific task of developing a new art form.

In 18th Century Burma, and to some extent even today, modesty and standards of etiquette forbade the depiction of intimate romantic scenes on the stage. Further, many actors refused to portray the future Buddha in the *Jātaka* tales, considering this to be sacrilegious. U Thaw saw a way around these obstacles. What human beings could not do in public, wooden figures could do without

(in order) a parakeet, two elephants, a tiger and a monkey come on stage.

The imagination of the audience is stirred with the entrance of two giants, plus a dragon and a *zawgyi* (sorcerer), who always flies on stage. These figures prepare onlookers for the magical world of Brahman-Buddhist culture, which provides the plot for almost all puppet plays.

According ·to traditional Buddhist belief, each organism consists of 28 physical parts. U Thaw, seeking to be consistent with this teaching, directed that there be precisely 28 marionettes. All of them are 2½ to 3 feet high, faultlessly carved and with costumes identical to the originals U Thaw prescribed. Each of the figures derives from some mythological figure. In addition to those previously men-

prohibition. And so the *yokthe pwe* was born.

More than any other Burmese dramatic form, *yokthe pwe* has been standardized. The stage setting is always the same: a throne on the left for court scenes, a primeval forest of branches on the right, and a sofa in the center, with all action taking place in front of a monochrome wall.

The order of the various scenes is likewise predetermined. The orchestra opens with an overture to create an auspicious mood. Then two ritual dancers appear, followed by a dance of various animals and mythological beings to depict the first stage in the creation of the universe. Next to make its appearance alone is the horse, whose heavenly constellation brings order to the primeval chaos. Then

tioned, the puppets include a king, two older princes, four ministers, an old woman, a Brahman priest, a hermit, two clowns and two heavenly beings. The two principal figures are a prince and princess—Mintha and Minthami—around whom the romantic plot always revolves.

It is sad that the *yokthe pwe* is disappearing in modern Burma. Few puppet masters remain to perpetuate the art, and there are no established texts—only a prescribed order of events. It can be seen occasionally at temple festivals, including the Shwedagon Pagoda festival in Rangoon.

A one-man percussion orchestra awaits the start of a dance performance in a Mon State village.

SHIN-PYU: BECOMING A DIGNIFIED HUMAN BEING

The most important moment in the life of a young Burmese boy is that of his *shin-pyu,* his initiation as a novice in the order of monks.

Until a Buddhist has gone through the *shin-pyu* ceremony, he is regarded as no better than an animal. To become "human," he must for a time withdraw from secular life, following the example set forth by the Buddha when he left his family to seek enlightenment, and later by the Buddha's own young son, Rahula.

Unlike his illustrious predecessors, the novice monk probably will carry his alms bowl only a short time—maybe a few weeks or less, perhaps as long as several months—then re-

turn to his normal lifestyle. But his time spent as a monk, studying Buddhist scriptures and strictly following the code of discipline, makes him a dignified human being.

Some time between his ninth and twelfth birthdays, a boy is deemed ready to don the saffron-colored robes of the Sangha and become a "son of the Buddha." If his parents are very pious, they may arrange to have the *shin-pyu* staged on the full moon day of *Waso* (June/July), the beginning of the Buddhist Lent, so that the novice can remain in the monastery throughout the entire rainy season, until Lent ends with the Festival of Light in October.

Once the ceremony has been arranged, the boy's sisters announce it to the whole village

or neighborhood. Everyone is invited, and contributions are collected for a festival which will dig deep into the savings of the boy's parents.

Traditionally, a *shin-pyu* is a time of extravagance. The boy is dressed in princely garments of silk, wears a gold headdress, and has a white horse. Musicians are hired to entertain guests. These objects are meant to symbolize the worldly goods that the novice monk must renounce in accepting the rules of the Sangha. Not all families can afford this, however, and many *shin-pyus* are more modest.

The night before a *shin-pyu* is a busy one. A feast is prepared for all the monks whose company the young boy will join, and they are elaborately fed early on the morning of the ceremony. Next, all men invited to the festivities are fed, and finally women can eat.

Later in the morning, the novitiate monk's head is shaved in preparation for his initiation. The boy's mother and eldest sister hold a white cloth to receive the falling hair, and later bury it near a pagoda. This head-shaving is a solemn moment; when completed, the boy already looks like a "son of the Buddha."

In the weeks before the ceremony, the lad has been familiarized with the language and behavior befitting a monk. He has learned how to address a superior; how to walk with decorum, keeping his eyes fixed on a point six feet in front of him; and how to respond to the questions put to him at the novitiation ceremony. He has also learned the Pali language words he must use in asking to be admitted to the Sangha.

His instruction serves him well when the time for the ceremony arrives. His request to enter the monkhood is approved, and he prostrates himself three times. Then he is robed. Now he is ready to walk the path of perfection first trodden by the Buddha. If he is steadfast enough, he might even reach nirvana.

At the moment that the *sayadaw*—the abbot who has presided over the ceremony—hangs the novitiate's *thabeit* (alms bowl) over his shoulder, innocent childhood is behind the boy. He has now been accepted as a monk.

During the time he spends in the monastery, the boy's parents must address him in honorific terms. He will call them "lay sister" and "lay brother," the same names he calls others who are not in the monkhood.

A boy's *shin-pyu* begins with head-shaving in front of his anxious mother (left); but little more than an hour after the ceremony begins, he is independent, a full-fledged novice in the Sangha (right).

WHEN THE MOON IS FULL, IT'S FESTIVAL TIME

The Burmese are a hard-working people. But when festival time rolls around, they are also a hard-playing people.

Whenever the moon waxes full, there is an all-night celebration. Its nature varies from season to season: frivolity during the water dousings of the New Year in April, solemnity as Buddhist Lent begins in July, joyousness during the October Festival of Light.

Thingyan: The Changing Over

The year's biggest party is the *Thingyan* festival in the month of *Tagu* (March/April). This is when the Burmese celebrate their New Year. For three or four days (the length of the celebration is determined annually by *ponnas,* or Brahmin astrologers), farm labor, business and government come to a virtual standstill.

Thingyan is best known as the "water throwing festival." The old year must be washed away and the new year annointed with water. No one, Burmese or foreign visitor, is safe from the deluges which seem to appear from nowhere out of the hot blue sky. From the sweet-smiling maiden carrying her water pot on her head to the skinny street cleaner laboring with his bucket, everyone is a potential prankster who might at any moment drench you from head to toe. For those without buckets or pots, water pumps and hoses are set up everywhere at roadside stalls.

Thingyan begins when Thagyamin, king of the *nats,* descends to earth to bring blessings for the new year. He also carries two books with him: one bound in gold to record the names of children who have been well behaved in the past year, and one bound in dog skin to write the names of naughty children.

Thagyamin comes riding a winged golden horse and bearing a water jar, symbolic of peace and prosperity in Burma in the coming year. Every house greets him with flowers and palm leaves at their front doors. Guns fire in salute and music resounds from all corners of the land. Decorated floats parade up and down the streets of the cities and larger towns.

Yet there are times of tranquility in the midst of this exuberance. All revelers find a quiet moment each day to make offerings at pagodas and at the homes of their elders. Buddha images are given a thorough washing on this holiday by devout elderly women.

In medieval times, *Thingyan* was observed with a public hair-washing by the Burmese king, a ritual purification.

The Day of Buddha

Kason (April/May) is a month of anticipation, for the annual monsoon could break at any time. On the full moon, the birth, enlightenment and death of the Buddha is celebrated. Citizens join in a procession of musicians and dancers to the local pagoda. There, they pour scented water not over each other, but over the roots of the sacred Bodhi tree, under which the Buddha gained enlightenment.

In addition to this annual occasion, Buddha Day observances are held once a month at local temples on the day of the new moon.

The Scriptures Exam

During the full moon day of *Nayon* (May/June), after the rains have at long last begun and the hot dry months are at an end, Burmese students are tested on their knowledge of the *Tripitaka,* the Buddhist scriptures. *Sayadaws* lecture before large crowds of people, schools operated by monasteries are opened to the public, and the best scholars exhibit their knowledge and win public acclaim.

The Beginning of Lent

For the next three months, the country will be soaked in water, as the monsoons gain strength. This is the beginning of the Buddhist Lent season. On *Dhammasetkya,* the full moon day of *Waso* (June/July), the people of Burma celebrate the Buddha's conception, his renunciation of worldly goods, and his first sermon after enlightenment. A majority of *shin-pyus* are staged at this time, and full ordination of those who wish to devote their lives to the Sangha takes place.

During the following three months, all members of the Sangha go into deep retreat for study and meditation. Monks are not permitted to travel, and all devout Buddhists enter a period of fasting.

The 'Draw-a-Lot' Festival

Since no marriage or other secular celebration is permitted during the lenten season, the full moon of *Wagaung* (July/August) is observed as a festival of food offering. This is a purely religious time for merit-making. The name of each member of the local Sangha is

A dervish-like nat dancer twirls through a Rangoon street during annual Union Day festivities.

written on a piece of paper, which is then rolled up and deposited in a large basket. A representative from each household of the community draws a paper from the basket, and the next day elaborately feasts the *pongyi* named on the paper he has chosen. One layman will draw a paper containing the name of the Gautama Buddha. He is the most fortunate of all, for he will have the opportunity to host the Buddha.

The Boat Racing Festival

By the time of *Tawthalin* (August/September), Burma's rivers are full and flowing majestically. Throughout the land, boat races are held in rivers and lakes. At Inle Lake, the Phaung Daw U Festival is held this month or next, with leg-rowing competitions and the voyage of a re-created royal *karaweik* barge.

The Festival of Light

Buddhist Lent comes to an end with the long awaited arrival of the full moon of *Thadingyut* (September/October), indicating the approach of clear skies and pleasant temperatures of the cool season.

On this full moon night, the Burmese celebrate the descent of the Buddha and his followers to earth from *Tavatimsa* heaven where, according to legend, he traveled to preach the doctrine to his mother. Just as the Buddha's return to this plane was illuminated by his radiance, millions of candles and lamps now light up monasteries, pagodas, houses, even trees. Everyone tries to stay awake until dawn, and an air of joyousness pervades the country. Especially happy are engaged couples, who can marry now that the taboo of the lenten season is over.

The Weaving Festival

In the month of *Tazaungmone* (October/November), the Weaving Festival is held. Unmarried girls sit under the full moon in the pagoda grounds, engaged in weaving competitions as they make new robes for the monks. In the early morning hours, their finished products will be ceremoniously presented to the *pongyis* in the nearby *kyaung*.

The Month of Nat Festivals

During *Nadaw* (November/December), most *nat* festivals take place. When the full moon arrives, nearly every village dedicates a celebration to the spirit world.

National or regional *nat* festivals, however, are held in other months over a period of several days before, during and after the full moon. Among the most important are the Mount Popa Festival in *Nayon* (May/June), the Taungbyon Festival north of Mandalay in *Wagaung* (July/August), the Manao Festival in Myitkyina in *Pyatho* (December/January), and the Shan Festival in Kyaukme in *Tabaung* (February/March).

The Month of Temple Festivals

Pyatho (December/January) formerly was a time when Burmese royalty displayed its strength with military parades. Nowadays, however, this time is reserved mostly for local pagoda festivals.

These local festivals are religious affairs, with gifts presented to monks and offerings made for temple upkeep. But even moreso, they are occasions for merrymaking lasting three or more days. A wide-ranging bazaar, boat and pony races, magic acts and side shows, and evening *pwe* performances are common activities. The full assortment of Burmese culinary delicacies are offered.

A few major temple festivals are held in *Pyatho*. The Ananda Temple festival in Pagan falls at this time, and the Shwedagon Pagoda festival in Rangoon is held either in *Pyatho* or in *Tabaung* (February/March). Other important festivals are at Bassein's Shwemokhpaw Pagoda in *Kason* (April/May), Pegu's Shwemawdaw Pagoda in *Tazaungmone* (October/November), Nyaung U's Shwezigon Pagoda in *Nadaw* (November/December), and Prome's Shwenattaung Pagoda in *Tabaung* (February/March). These nationally known celebrations can last as long as four weeks.

The Harvest Festival

When the month of *Tabodwe* (January/February) arrives, it is time to harvest the paddy and celebrate the harvest festival. As in every land where farming is the mainstay of the population, this is a time of joy. After the first harvest is offered to the monastery, elaborate meals are prepared, and Burmese women have a chance to show off their cooking prowess to neighbors and monks. The celebration is named *Htamane* after a food offering of rice, sesame, peanuts, ginger and coconut fixed at this time.

The Month of Serenity

Tabaung (February/March), the last month of the Burmese year, is a time of romance and quiet thoughts. On the full moon day, Burmese travel to tranquil lakes or rivers, where they can relax under the stars and spend the evening playing music, singing and reciting poetry. It is a fitting close to the year, a display of the simple joys of life by a people well off the main roads of Western influence.

The Festival Calendar

The Burmese calendar subscribes to the solar year but the lunar month, making it necessary to insert an intercalary 30-day 13th month every second or third year. The next such month will be added to the month of *Waso* in July 1983. Tourists should keep this in mind when planning their visit to Burma, and consult the Burmese embassy to synchronize their schedule with the Burmese calendar. If possible, one's Burma visit should be timed to coincide with the full moon.

on this day is returned to Rangoon amidst the roar of hundreds of thousands of people from throughout the nation.

Peasants Day, March 2, and Workers Day, May 1, honor Burma's working population. They are days which more than any other demonstrate the country's socialist structure.

Resistance Day, March 27, commemorates the World War Two struggle against the Japanese. It is celebrated with parades and fireworks. Ironically, Burma spent most of the war on the Japanese side fighting Allied forces, but switched allegiance in early 1945.

Martyrs Day, July 19, is a memorial to Burma's founding father, Aung San, and his cabinet ministers who were assassinated on this day in 1947. Special ceremonies take place at the Martyrs Mausoleum in Rangoon.

The Holiday Schedule

In addition to the festival schedule, there are several secular and public holidays during which all offices are closed. The dates for these holidays follow the calendar in use in the Western world.

Independence Day is observed on January 4, commemorating the date in 1948 that Burma left the British Commonwealth and became a sovereign independent nation.

Union Day is celebrated on February 12, marking the date in 1947 that Aung San concluded an agreement with Burma's ethnic minorities at Panglong in the Shan State. The Union of Burma flag, which has been carried by runners to each of Burma's state capitals,

Non-Buddhist Religious Holidays

Because of Burma's policy of religious freedom, various minority groups celebrate important holidays which do not fall into the Burmese calendar. These include the Hindu festival *Dewali* in October, the Islamic observance of *Bakri Idd* in late November, the Christian holidays of Christmas (December 25) and Easter (late March or April), and the Karen New Year Festival about January 1.

Monks' food is specially prepared by a devout Sagaing family at a religious festival, above. Following pages, in pre-modern times as today, Burmese peasants looked forward to occasions to climb on the "festival cart" and display their hidden wealth.

449
BURMESE FESTIVAL CART
P. KLIER - RANGOON

So much to explore with so little time.

Travellers of Asia wish they can have more than a week to explore Burma. A country that's so rich in legends and relics of its 2,000 year culture.

Inspite of the 7 day visa limit, you can still enjoy a lot of what Burma has to offer in a week. Provided you plan your trip.

Decide ahead of time how much time you have and what you want to see. If you want to cover a lot in even less than a week, then the planning is even more important. Have somebody that knows Burma take care of your basic travel needs so that you can spend more time doing what you've come to Burma for.

And choosing the right agent that knows the country is also important to you. Diethelm Travel has helped thousands of Burma visitors get the most out of their trip. The experience we have gained in Burma over the years has given us the reputation as being the guide of choice to the unusual places.

GUIDE IN BRIEF

Traveling to Burma

By Air

Probably 99 percent of Burma's visitors arrive by air at Rangoon's Mingaladon Airport. Situated 19 kilometers (12 miles) northwest of the capital, it is the nation's only airport handling international flights. Two dozen flights arrive from and depart for overseas destinations each week.

The largest number of overseas flights connect Rangoon and Bangkok. Burma's national carrier, the Burmese Airways Corporation (BAC), operates daily flights between Rangoon and Bangkok. Thai International flies the same route three times a week, and Biman, the national carrier of Bangladesh, flies a weekly Dacca-Rangoon-Bangkok and return route on Sundays.

BAC also operates regular routes to Calcutta, Kathmandu and Singapore, as well as Dacca. The Civil Aviation Administration of China (CAAC) has a weekly flight between Rangoon and Kunming (Yunnan), and Aeroflot runs a weekly route through Rangoon, from Vientiane and Ho Chi Minh City (Saigon), via Tbilisi to Moscow.

Travelers from the United States, Australia, Europe and other locations probably will find it easiest to reach Burma via Bangkok. Some 30 international airlines connect Bangkok with other world capitals.

By Sea

The only option to traveling to Burma by air is to arrive by ship. Freighter travel, however, is not recommended, due to the limited visa period and to the required proof of onward passage before the Burmese government will grant visas. Information is available from shipping lines. The Burma Five Star Corporation, 132/136 Theinbyu Street, Rangoon, is the agent for all foreign lines calling in Burma.

But Not By Land

Burma's frontiers have long been closed to overland international travel, due primarily to the continuing rebellions by various ethnic groups in border areas. Until such time as conditions permit otherwise, there is no legal access to Burma by road. Neither are there international rail connections. Theoretically, it should be possible to travel from Singapore through Burma to India—and, if political turmoil ceases in Afghanistan and Iran, on to Europe.

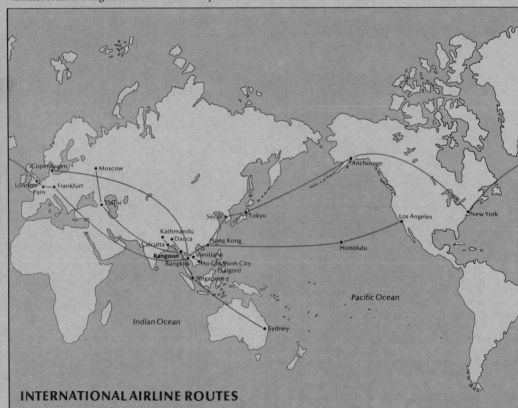

INTERNATIONAL AIRLINE ROUTES

Travel Advisories

Immigration

Visitors to Burma must present a valid passport and a tourist visa obtained at one of Burma's overseas embassies or consulates. Transit visas are good for 24 hours, and tourist visas are limited to seven days. There has been talk of increasing the length of tourist visas to 10 days or two weeks, but there is no indication that a change will be forthcoming soon. Visas for longer stays, for business, educational or diplomatic purposes, can be obtained only with a considerable amount of difficulty. Children over seven years of age, even when included on their parents' passport, must have their own visas. Any person who arrives in Burma without a visa is refused admission, and is deported on the next available flight.

While most Burmese embassies require two weeks to process tourist visas, the embassy in Bangkok will issue visas within 24 hours of application. Cost is 100 baht (US $5), and three passport photos must accompany the application. The visa is valid for three months from date of issue.

Health officials require certification of immunization against cholera, and against yellow fever if you arrive within nine days after leaving or transiting an affected area. Proof of smallpox vaccination is no longer required.

The Union of Burma has overseas embassies in the following cities:

North America—Washington, D.C., Ottawa, New York (mission to the United Nations).

Europe—Belgrade, Berlin, Bern, Bonn, London, Moscow, Paris, Prague, Rome.

Asia—Bangkok, Calcutta (consulate), Colombo, Dacca, Hanoi, Hong Kong (consulate), Islamabad, Jakarta, Kathmandu, Kuala Lumpur, Manila, New Delhi, Peking, Singapore, Tokyo, Vientiane.

Middle East—Tel Aviv, Cairo.

Australia—Canberra.

Customs

Tourists are allowed duty-free import of limited quantities of tobacco—200 cigarettes, 50 cigars, or eight ounces of pipe tobacco—as well as one liter of alcoholic beverage, and a one-half liter bottle of perfume or eau de cologne.

You will be required to fill out a customs form declaring your camera, jewelry, tape recorder, radio, typewriter and similar effects. This declaration must be returned to customs officials upon departure to assure that you haven't sold any of these items on Burma's black market. Artifacts of archaeological interest cannot be taken out of the country, nor can any precious stones—unless they've been purchased from the government Diplomatic Shop, the airport duty-free shop, or with special government permission. There is no enforced restriction on the export of souvenirs of genuine tourist interest.

Formalities both on arrival and departure can be tiresome and time-consuming. Officials normally make a thorough search of all baggage. Be sure not to lose the various official forms you are given on entry, so as to avoid problems on departure.

When you leave Mingaladon Airport, there is a 15-kyat airport tax.

Currency

Among the required documents is a currency form. There is no limit to the amount of foreign currency you can bring into Burma, as long as it is declared upon entry. However, the import and export of Burmese kyats is forbidden, and the export of foreign currency is limited to the amount declared upon entry.

The currency form must be presented whenever money is converted, and again when you leave the country. Customs officials will then reconvert up to one-fourth of the currency converted to kyats during your stay in Burma. If you are using travelers cheques, only a quarter of the amount of the last check cashed will be changed back. Therefore, it's a good idea to spend most of your leftover kyats before heading for the airport.

Custom officials will probably also double-check to see that the foreign currency you declared coming into the country is accounted for upon your departure. Whenever you change your money at a bank or pay your hotel, train or plane bills with foreign exchange (as required), you'll have an entry made on your currency form. This is the Burmese government's way of preventing visitors from changing their money on the black market for a rate three times the official currency exchange rate. It has been said that at the official rate of exchange, Burma is one of the more expensive countries to visit in Asia, but at the black market exchange rate, it is one of the cheapest.

You can make your first official currency exchange at the state bank counter at the airport. Thereafter, foreign currency officially can be exchanged only at the Foreign Trade Bank (in Rangoon, it's on Barr Street; in Mandalay, on B Road at 82nd Street), or at major hotels. Travelers cheques will bring a slightly better return than cash. Only the following currencies will be accepted for exchange, however: the U.S. dollar, British pound, German mark, French franc, Swiss franc, Australian dollar, Singapore dollar, Malaysian dollar, Hong Kong dollar and Japanese yen.

It is possible to obtain kyats before entering Burma from the Indian and Chinese money dealers on Bangkok's New Road, Singapore's Change Alley and Hong Kong's Nathan Road. You will get a very good rate of exchange here. Remember, though, that it is illegal to take kyats into or out of Burma, and the government appears to be stiffening its controls. Tourists have sometimes circumvented the system with a scheme to which Burmese officials traditionally have turned a blind eye: they buy cigarettes and liquor at an airport duty-free shop before flying into Rangoon, and sell them upon arrival.

Burmese coins come in a variety of interesting sizes and shapes. They are in denominations of 1, 5, 10, 25 and 50 pyas and 1 kyat. Notes are in denominations of 1, 5, 10, 25 and 100 kyats, marked with both Arabic and Burmese numerals.

As of January 1982, the official exchange rate of the kyat was 7.35 to the U.S. dollar, 13.79 to the

British pound, 3.20 to the German mark, and 1.25 to the French franc.

Credit cards

American Express cards are accepted at Tourist Burma offices, the Diplomatic Shop in Rangoon, and at the large state-owned hotels.

Time conversion

Burma Standard Time is 6 hours, 30 minutes ahead of Greenwich Meridian Time. Coming from Bangkok, that means you would set your watch back a half-hour upon arrival in Rangoon. International time differences are staggered as follows:

Burma	12 noon today
Bangkok	12:30 p.m. today
Hong Kong	1:30 p.m. today
Tokyo	2:30 p.m. today
Sydney	3:30 p.m. today
Hawaii	7:30 p.m. yesterday
San Francisco	9:30 p.m. yesterday
New York	12:30 a.m. today
London	5:30 a.m. today
Paris	6:30 a.m. today
Bonn	6:30 a.m. today
New Delhi	11 a.m. today

Climate

Like all countries in South and Southeast Asia's monsoonal region, Burma's year is divided into three seasons. The rains begin in May, and are most intense between June and August. This is a time of high humidity—especially intense in the coastal and delta regions—and of daily afternoon and evening showers, as monsoonal winds carry the moisture in off the Indian Ocean. The central inland is drier than other parts of the country, but is still subject to considerable rain during this season.

In October, the rains let up. The ensuing winter "cool season" (November through February) is the most pleasant time to visit Burma. The average mean temperature along the Irrawaddy plain, from Rangoon to Mandalay, is between 21°C and 28°C (70°F and 82°F), although in the mountains on the north and east, the temperature can drop below freezing and snow can fall.

During the months of March and April, Burma has its "dry season." Temperatures in the central Burma plain, particularly around Pagan, can climb to 45°C (113°F).

Annual rainfall along the rainshadow coasts of Arakan and Tenasserim ranges from 300 to 500 cm (120 to 200 inches). The Irrawaddy Delta gets about 150 to 200 cm (60 to 100 inches), while the central Burma region, between Mandalay and Pagan and surrounding region, averages 50 to 100 cm (20 to 40 inches) of rain each year. In the far north, the melting snows of the Himalayan foothills keep rivers fed with water.

What to Wear

Dress in Burma is casual but neat. Unless you are conducting business in Rangoon, you won't be expected to wear a tie. Long pants for men and dress or long skirt for women, lightweight and appropriate to the prevailing climatic conditions, is the generally accepted mode of dress for Westerners. Quick-drying clothes are a good idea for visits during the rainy season or *Thingyan* (the "water festival"). There is no law against shorts or mini-skirts, but this type of clothing is not respected by the Burmese. A sweater or jacket should be carried if you plan a visit to the hill stations or Shan Plateau, especially in the cool season. Open footwear, such as sandals, is certainly acceptable, but remember to remove footwear when entering religious monuments. Sunglasses are a practical accessory to pack. If you forget your umbrella and arrive during the rainy season, a worthwhile investment would be one of the highly-colored hand-painted Burmese umbrellas.

Medical Advice

All visitors to Burma should take appropriate anti-malarial precautions before entering the country, and should continue to take medication throughout their stay. The risk is highest at altitudes below 1,000 meters (3,000 feet) between May and December. Most hotels have mosquito nets, but they're worthless if they have holes in them. It can be a worthwhile investment to carry your own mosquito net and pack mosquito coils to burn while you sleep.

Perhaps the two most common hazards to Burma visitors are sunburn and "Delhi Belly." The best way to prevent sunburn, especially if you're not used to the intense tropical sun, is to stay under cover whenever possible at midday—and if you do go out, wear a hat or carry an umbrella. You'll see many Burmese, especially women and children, with yellow *thanaka*-bark powder applied to their faces to help shut out the sun. If you find yourself sweating a lot and feeling weak or dizzy, sit down (in the shade!) and eat some salt, either in tablet form or by mixing salt in a soft drink or tea.

North Americans sometimes know "Delhi Belly" as "Montezuma's Revenge." No matter what it's called, sooner or later, nearly every Westerner traveling in Asia and eating local food comes down with diarrhea. This can be uncomfortable and inconvenient. A good solution is to carry Lomotil tablets. Another solution is to stay away from less familiar foods when possible.

Health standards in much of Burma are still relatively low. Under no circumstances should you drink water unless you *know* it has been boiled. All fruit should be carefully peeled before being eaten, and no raw vegetables should be eaten. Amoebic dysentery is a danger to those who are not careful.

In the event that you get sick in spite of all precautions, several hospitals in Rangoon can cater to Westerners' medical needs. These include:

Diplomatic Hospital *(Kandawgyi Clinic)*, Kyaikkasan Road, Tel. 50149.

Rangoon General Hospital, Bogyoke Aung San Street, Tel. 81722.

Infectious Diseases Hospital, Upper Pansodan Street, Tel. 72497.

Eye, Ear, Nose and Throat Hospital, Signal Pagoda Road, Tel. 72311.

University Hospital, University Avenue, Tel. 31541.

Photography

You would be well advised to carry plenty of film into Burma with you. With the exception of the Diplomatic Store in Rangoon, which sometimes has Fuji print film (but never 35-millimeter slide film) in stock, there is no official import and sale of photographic film. It is common, therefore, for visitors to be approached on the streets of Rangoon and Mandalay by Burmese offering to buy spare rolls of film. Kodak, Agfa, Fuji and other imported films can frequently be found in the night markets on Rangoon's Merchant Street, and at Madalay's Zegyo Market. But the price is always high, and the expiration date stamped on the box of film has often passed.

Electricity

When it's in working order, electricity is 220-volt, 50 hertz.

Weights and Measures

Burma has retained many of the old weights and measures in use during the British colonial period. Conversion is as follows:

1 viss *(peith-tha)*	1,633 grams, 3.6 pounds
1 tical	16.33 grams
1 cubit *(tong)*	.457 meters, 18 inches
1 span *(htwa)*	0.23 meters, 9 inches
1 *lakh*	100,000 (units)
1 *crore*	100 *lakh*

The *tin*, or basket, is used to measure quantities of agricultural export goods. The kilogram equivalent differs for rice, sesame, and other goods.

Business hours

Most government offices, including the post office, Tourist Burma and the Burma Airways Corporation, are open 9:30 a.m. to 4 p.m. Monday through Friday, and 9 a.m. to noon Saturday.

Banks are open to the public 10 a.m. to 2 p.m. weekdays and 10 a.m. to noon Saturday. The Central Telegraph Office stays open from 8 a.m. to 9 p.m. weekdays, and from 8 a.m. to 8 p.m. Sunday and holidays.

Most restaurants close by 10 p.m., although some tea and coffee shops will stay open later. Drug stores have staggered days off, so that shops dealing in medicine are always open somewhere.

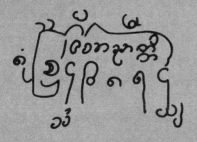

Tourist Information

The Burmese government's Hotel and Tourist Corporation, better known as Tourist Burma, has full information on all activities the government feels ought to be of interest to tourists. The Tourist Burma office is located in downtown Rangoon at 77-79 Sule Pagoda Road, and is open normal government business hours. There are branch offices in the other three tourist destinations actively promoted by the government—Mandalay, Pagan and Taunggyi.

Other destinations within Burma fall into two classes: those forbidden for travel, and those accessible but not encouraged.

Forbidden areas are the rebel-held regions of Burma's north, northeast and south. There, civil war continues between the rebellious ethnic minorities and government troops. Military roadblocks mark the end of areas of government control; beyond there, anyone could step on unmarked land mines or fall prey to an ambush.

However, there are many places which, although not on the list of routes actively promoted by Tourist Burma, are not actually "prohibited." These include towns like Bassein, Prome, Toungoo and Moulmein. In going to these destinations, it is best not to ask Tourist Burma to make arrangements. You won't be told that travel to these areas is prohibited; but you will likely be told there is no transportation or accommodation available at the time you plan your journey. Nonetheless, if you make your own arrangements, you will encounter few obstacles. Taxi, bus, boat or train are all open to travelers, and there are no special controls. The Burmese government cannot watch every step of every foreign visitor.

Official Registration

Officially, as a foreign tourist you must register either with immigration authorities or police whenever you move around the country. This obligation is automatically fulfilled by staying overnight at any tourist hotel. An overnight stay at a monastery, pagoda or private home—especially if it is not in a principal tourist region—presents complications. The travelers' rule of thumb in Burma is this: don't ask, or you'll create more problems.

Tourist Burma and the Burma Airways Corporation both operate four to eight-day group tours through the country. Aside from the usual Rangoon-Pagan-Mandalay-Taunggyi-Rangoon circuit, Tourist Burma offers a package tour to Sandoway, the beach resort on Arakan's Bay of Bengal coast, during the dry season (November to February). While not a likely destination for a first-time visitor to Burma on a one-week visa, Sandoway is an attractive alternative. Occasionally, especially if called for by a group of Japanese war veterans, Tourist Burma will arrange a tour to Moulmein. Excursions to Mount Popa, the Pindaya Caves, and other off-the-beaten-track locations can also be arranged. Special pilot tours have been run to Arakan, and it is possible these will become more regular at some time in the future.

Tourist Burma also conducts half-day tours of Rangoon city, and full-day excursions to Pegu and Syriam from Rangoon.

Outside of Burma, the best tour arrangements can be made through Diethelm Travel of Thailand (544 Ploenchit Road, Bangkok). A four-day tour of Rangoon, Mandalay and Pagan, and a six-day trip including an excursion to Inle Lake, depart weekly from Bangkok.

Essentially, as a visitor to Burma you have two choices within the context of your one-week visa. You can travel through the country, taking in as many sights as possible; or you can dawdle in one or two locations, soaking up the culture and atmosphere. One option to consider is a return to Bangkok when your visa expires. You can obtain a new visa overnight at the Burmese embassy in Bangkok, and immediately return to Burma for another week.

Generally speaking, groups have an easier time of traveling in Burma than individuals. Tourist Burma pre-plans all group travel, including hotels and flight arrangements. The individual traveler(s), however, will better be able to absorb the "lost, old-time travel feeling" of which Somerset Maugham stories are a reminder. Financially, the individual's trip won't be as costly as that of the group traveler, but there will be complications in finding accommodation and transportation, and in shuffling through the network of government bureaucracy.

Transportation

Airport Transportation

There are two ways to get from Mingaladon Airport to downtown Rangoon, a distance of 19 kilometers (12 miles), and one is much easier than the other. Before you're even out of the terminal doors, taxi drivers will besiege you, offering to carry you into the city in their huge 1950s conveyances for exorbitant sums. You shouldn't have to pay more than 30 *kyats,* and might be able to bargain them down another five *kyats* or so below that. The option is to hike about a kilometer to the road leading past the airport. You can catch a crowded bus into Rangoon from here for about 1 *kyat.*

Technically, the BAC is supposed to provide a bus to city hotels for incoming flights, but this service is often not available. When you're returning to the airport from your Rangoon hotel, however, things become much easier. BAC's bus picks you up at your hotel and transports you to the airport for only five *kyats.*

Domestic Air Travel

The BAC, until recently known as the Union of Burma Airways (UBA), controls an intricate network of air routes to 45 localities within Burma. The airline's fleet consists of three Fokker F-28 jets, seven Fokker F-27s, and nine Haviland Twin Otter aircraft for routes into smaller airstrips. Western tourists, however, will see few of these airports. The BAC will sell foreigners tickets only to Mandalay,

Pagan (Nyaung U), Taunggyi (Heho), and on rarer occasions Sandoway and Moulmein, plus return flights to Rangoon. Tickets to other destinations are impossible to obtain without special government permission.

Tickets for BAC domestic flights can be purchased overseas, but it is probably better to wait until you arrive in Burma. Tickets may be cheaper overseas, but because the BAC is not a member of the International Air Transport Association (IATA), it is not bound to honor tickets sold at those prices. Therefore, upon arrival at Rangoon's Mingaladon Airport, you should book air passage to your next destination; and upon reaching that destination, you should confirm—in person at a BAC office—your return flight.

Visitors can purchase domestic flight tickets (with foreign exchange only) at Tourist Burma offices. The main offices are located at 73 Sule Pagoda Road, just south of the pagoda itself and across the street from Maha Bandoola Park. There are other Tourist Burma offices in Pagan, Mandalay and Taunggyi, but Rangoon is most reliable.

Despite all precautions, it is still possible that you might get bumped from your seat on the plane. The Burmese government runs an unofficial but nevertheless rigid priority list which can disrupt flight bookings right up to the last minute. Burmese VIPs, of course, have first priority. Behind them, in order, come tour parties, individual foreign visitors, foreign expatriate residents, and—last and least—native residents of Burma.

Railways

The Union of Burma Railways—like all other important means of transportation, run by the state—has a network of more than 4,000 kilometers (2,500 miles) of track. Rangoon's Central Railway Station, of course, is the nation's hub. By day and night, express trains, mail trains and local trains depart on journeys of varying length.

Ordinary (second class) and Upper Class (first class) seating is available on all trains. Upper Class seats cost almost three times Ordinary Class. Sleepers are not readily available for overnight trips. Foreigners must purchase their tickets through Tourist Burma, advisably 24 hours in advance if possible. The tourist office has a quota on tickets available during its business hours.

The line most often used by tourists is the **Rangoon-Mandalay Line.** This is the country's finest railway and is highly recommended for the varied view of Burmese village life it offers from its windows. Passengers must be willing to put up with a little bump and grind; however, the journey conforms roughly to European expectations.

There are three services daily between Rangoon and Mandalay. The fastest is the 7 a.m. express, which covers the 621 kilometers (386 miles) in 12½ hours, making only four stops (Pegu, Toungoo, Pyinmana and Thazi) along the way and arriving in Central Burma's metropolis at 7:30 p.m., in time to find a room and a meal. Other trains leave Rangoon at 11:45 a.m. (arriving Mandalay at 4:45 a.m. the next day) and 7 p.m. (arriving Mandalay at 9 a.m. the next day).

The return schedule from Mandalay to Rangoon is much the same, with an identical 7 a.m. express. The 11:45 a.m. from Mandalay arrives in Rangoon at 5:05 a.m. the next day, and the 7:15 p.m. from Mandalay reaches Rangoon at 9:15 a.m. the next day.

These times, however, are only those listed on Burmese timetables, which are not always strictly adhered to. Problems of climatic, technical or bureaucratic nature often cause long delays in rail journeys. Nevertheless, the Rangoon-Mandalay service is certainly the most reliable in Burma.

From Mandalay, there are train connections to the hill station of Maymyo, 61 kilometers (38 miles) east. The five-hour rail journey is twice what the trip takes by Jeep collective, however.

Other rail trips of interest to tourists might include the following:

Rangoon-Thazi Line. Leaves Rangoon 3:35 p.m. daily, arriving Thazi 4:55 a.m. Local trains connect Thazi with Shwenyaung, the nearest rail terminus to Taunggyi and Inle Lake; there are also buses which travel west to Pagan from Thazi. The southbound train leaves Thazi 7:50 p.m., arriving Rangoon 8:15 a.m. Passengers can disembark the Rangoon-Mandalay express here, but to board the main line in Thazi might be more difficult: it is usually full.

Rangoon-Pyinmana Line. Leaves Rangoon 8:07 a.m., arriving Pyinmana 8:45 p.m. Local trains cover the 225 kilometers (140 miles) between Pyinmana and Kyaukpadaung. Buses connect Kyaukpadaung with Pagan, about 50 kilometers (31 miles) further west. This rail and bus link is not suggested, however: it is an exceedingly slow trip that can last up to 36 hours. The southbound train leaves Pyinmana at 4:10 a.m., arriving Rangoon at 6 p.m. The Rangoon-Mandalay train makes a stop in Pyinmana.

Visitors to Toungoo can disembark at that town when any of the three above-mentioned lines stops at the Toungoo station.

Rangoon-Martaban Line. Express leaves Rangoon 6 a.m., arriving Martaban 12:20 p.m. Local trains leave Rangoon 7:20 a.m., arriving Martaban 5 p.m.; and 6:30 a.m., arriving Martaban 3:25 p.m. A train ferry across the Salween River carries travelers from Martaban to Moulmein on the opposite bank. The most direct return train from Martaban to Rangoon leaves at 1:50 p.m., arriving in the capital 8:10 p.m. Other trains depart Martaban 7:20 a.m., arriving Rangoon 4:20 p.m., and 8:45 a.m., arriving Rangoon 7:10 p.m.

Stops can also be made in Kyaik-to or Thaton on this line. This and all previously mentioned lines pass through Pegu, and day trippers can disembark there as well.

Rangoon-Prome Line. Leaves Rangoon 2:30 p.m., arriving Prome 8:15 p.m. Return train leaves Prome 6 a.m., arriving Rangoon 11:50 a.m. A local train also departs from Rangoon's Kemendine Station 8:45 a.m. daily, arriving Prome 7:50 p.m.; the southbound local leaves Prome 7:15 a.m., arriving Kemendine 6:55 p.m..

Long-distance rail travelers in Burma will find vendors pushing fruits, curries and soft drinks through the windows of the train at every stop. Burmese trains don't have diners, with the excep-

tion of the daytime Rangoon-Mandalay express. Therefore, you would be well advised to carry your own food and beverage with you, especially during the dry season.

Journeys outside of the normal tourist areas are not expressly forbidden by government edict. However, they are in practice quite difficult to undertake. Station masters are not allowed to sell tickets to foreigners without special authorization, and Tourist Burma makes tickets available only on certain routes. For one foreigner's experience in bucking the Burma Railways Corporation, see Paul Theroux's *The Great Railway Bazaar*.

Rangoon city has a suburban local train service which connects to the national routes. Of greatest interest to the visitor is the **Circular Line**, running both clockwise and counter-clockwise through Rangoon Central Station to Insein and Mingaladon in the north, and stopping at all smaller stations in between. The route takes about three hours to complete, but should be avoided during rush hours. Tickets are less than two *kyats* for the full circle trip.

Inland Boat Travel

Burma's rivers provide more than 8,000 kilometers (5,000 miles) of navigable routes, and as a result shipping is the most important means of transportation for much of the country.

The Irrawaddy River, Burma's lifeline, is navigable from its delta to Bhamo throughout the year, and all the way to Myitkyina during the rainy season. The Twante Canal links the Irrawaddy to Rangoon. The Chindwin River—the Irrawaddy's most important tributary, joining it a short distance above Pagan—is navigable in shallow-bottomed boats for another several hundred kilometers.

In the east, the Salween River is suitable for shipping only as far as 200 kilometers (125 miles) from its mouth near Moulmein. Strong currents funneling through its narrow chasm block further progress. In Arakan, the Kaladan River and its tributaries are the most important routes of transportation.

The red-and-black-colored passenger vessels and cargo steamers of the Inland Water Transport Corporation, therefore, are a common sight throughout Burma. Still, the government network is only a little more than half of what it was under the British-owned Irrawaddy Flotilla Company prior to 1948. Equipment is antiquated, and timetables offer only the roughest idea of when boats will arrive and depart.

The most interesting river route of tourist interest (under present political conditions) is the stretch of Irrawaddy between Mandalay and Pagan. A boat leaves Mandalay daily except Monday at 5 a.m., arriving in Pagan about 24 hours later—or more, if the boat becomes stranded on a sandbar, as occasionally happens. (You may wish to disembark in Nyaung U and cover the last few miles to Pagan by horse-drawn cab.) You can travel deck class on the boat, sharing open quarters with monks, soldiers, nursing mothers, chicken and fruit baskets; or you can step up to the "first class" section—a cabin in the prow of the upper deck with four wooden benches and a table. Either way, you should outfit yourself with a blanket or sleeping bag, especially during the winter months, and with mosquito netting or repellent.

The sheer romance of this particular river journey is enough to repay the loss of comfort in triplicate. But the return voyage to Mandalay should be avoided for two reasons: first, one cannot afford to spend too much time afloat given the limited visa period; and second, the journey upriver takes an extra night, and thus is longer than the trip to Pagan.

It is theoretically possible to continue downriver from Pagan to Prome, and from there take the train to Rangoon. But this would require several days of travel, and is impractical with a seven-day visa. A round-trip river journey between Rangoon and Mandalay would take 21 days.

Considerably less time is needed, however, to make the voyage from Rangoon to Bassein via the Twante Canal. An express steamer leaves Rangoon at 4:30 p.m. daily from the Mawtin Street Jetty, arriving in Bassein at 8 a.m. the next day. The return boat departs Bassein at 4:30 p.m., reaching Rangoon about 8 a.m. Thus a visitor can leave Rangoon on a Monday afternoon, spend Tuesday in Bassein, and be back in Rangoon by Wednesday morning, having spent two nights aboard the boat.

Ferry service between Rangoon's Htinbonseik Jetty and Syriam operates on a commuter basis. Once an hour between 5:30 a.m. and 9:45 p.m., triple-deck boats shuttle back and forth across the Pegu River at its confluence with the Rangoon River. The trip takes about 45 minutes.

Another popular ferry trip for tourists is the one across the Irrawaddy between Mandalay and Mingun. Boats leave from Mandalay's B Road Jetty at 7:30 and 8:30 a.m. every day for the one-hour voyage.

The Burma Five Star Line manages all overseas routes. Four smaller company ships also link Rangoon to coastal towns between Mergui (Tenasserim) and Akyab (Arakan).

Buses

Bus travel is not recommended for long-distance journeys. Most roads are poor, vehicles are overcrowded, and in the event a bus breaks down, it can be hours before mechanical assistance becomes available. However, there are a few routes with which tourists should be acquainted.

The longest journeys are aboard the Road Transport Corporation vehicles that ply regular routes from Rangoon to Mandalay and to Magwe via Prome. Connections to Pagan can be made from either route.

Pagan via Kyaukpadaung, but that's a tedious 16-hour trip. Preferable would be the 10-hour bus ride to Pagan from Mandalay. Buses depart at 4 a.m. daily from the corner of 29th Road and 82nd Street.

It's also possible to travel by bus to Taunggyi, capital of the Shan State, from both Pagan and Mandalay. In both cases, it's a fatiguing 12-hour journey. The Taunggyi bus leaves Mandalay between 4 and 5 a.m. daily, and leaves Pagan at the same time from near the Tourist Burma office. In addition, buses leave hourly for Taunggyi from the

rail junction at Thazi, and direct service between Pagan and Taunggyi is available. Check with Tourist Burma.

Visitors to Mandalay can reach the ancient capitals of Amarapura and Ava by taking the No. 8 bus south from the city.

From Rangoon, buses run the 80 kilometers (50 miles) to Pegu on a regular half-hourly basis. The terminal is on 18th Street, near the Chinese quarter west of downtown.

Rangoon city is served by an extensive network of local buses. There are 17 routes operated by three separate agencies as follows:

All Bus Lines Control Committee

Route 1: South Okkalapa to Kemendine via Tamwe.

Route 3: Thaketa to Kemendine via Lower Pazundaung and Anawrahta streets.

Route 4: Thaketa to 1st Street via Lower Pazundaung and Anawrahta streets, with a turnabout at 1st Street and a return to Thaketa via Maha Bandoola Street.

Route 7: South Okkalapa to Rangoon via Yankin Road or Kanbe.

Route 13: Thingangyun to Mawtin.

Route 14: South Okkalapa to Mawtin via Thingangyun.

Route 15: South Okkalapa to Mawtin via Tamwe.

Route 16 (loop line): Lansdowne (below Inya Lake)-Tamwe-Shwegondine Road-Kemendine-Kamayut-University Avenue-return to Lansdowne.

Route 17: Insein to Rangoon with a turnabout on Maha Bandoola Street.

Road Transport Board

Route 2: South Okkalapa to Kemendine via Bolane Road and Theinbyu Street.

Route 5: North Okkalapa to Rangoon via Kaba Aye Pagoda Road.

Route 8 (36-passenger): Insein to Rangoon to Lansdowne. Route 8 (24-passenger): Thamaing to Bandoola Square.

Route 9: Mingaladon to Rangoon.

Route 10 (loop line): Botataung to Kandawgyi and back to Botataung via Shwedagon Pagoda Road.

Route 11: Ah Lone Road to Thuwunne via Strand Road.

Route 12: Lansdowne to Kemendine.

Cooperative System

Route 6: North Okkalapa to Rangoon via Thamaing Link Road and Prome Road.

Taxis

Cab drivers wait in front of all the big tourist hotels in Rangoon, anxious to carry visitors to their destinations. Private vehicles are largely oversized remnants of American autos of the 1950s; government-owned taxis are newer Japanese models. Although Tourist Burma has fixed rates for most regular routes, you'll probably have to haggle with the drivers to bring their rates down to a reasonable level. Still, taxis are probably the best way to explore the countryside surrounding Rangoon, especially if one is able to split the cost of the fare with other riders.

Other Local Transport

Bicycle trishaws are the most popular means of getting around the city streets of Rangoon. Plentiful and cheap, they take their passengers—who sit back to back—anywhere in the city they want to go.

For longer trips in the vicinity of Rangoon, Mandalay and other large population centers, jeep collectives or "pick-ups"—not unlike the *collectivos* of Latin America—do yeoman's work carrying large numbers of riders. They don't follow a set schedule; instead, they take off whenever the last seat is taken. For journeys from Rangoon to Pegu and from Mandalay to Maymyo, this is a cheap, fast means of transportation.

In Burma's dry central plain, especially in the areas of Mandalay and Pagan, there are many horse-drawn cabs, or *tongas*. They are slow moving, but are particularly well-suited for sightseeing trips. In smaller towns and villages, high-wheeled ox carts often are counted upon for transportation.

Accommodations

The hotel situation in Burma is rapidly improving. Previously, there has been a lack of ample tourist-class accommodations. But in late 1981 the new Kandawgyi Royal Lake Hotel opened in Rangoon, and by 1983 there will be new hotels in Mandalay (the Mya Mandalay), Maymyo (the Nan Myang Hotel), and at Inle Lake (the Yaunghwe Sakhanth Hotel). Long-range plans call for additional new hotels at Tavoy, Meiktila, Pindaya, Mon-Ywa and another at Inle Lake by 1985.

Travelers should book well in advance if they wish to stay in better hotels. Even then, there's no guarantee that a room will be available. Written confirmation is unusual; and as with airplane bookings, there is a priority list putting Burmese VIPs and tour parties ahead of individual travelers.

In the following list of accommodations, you can expect to pay up to US $25 a night (double) at luxury hotels, about half that at first-class hotels, and as little as US $2 or $3 a night at lesser hostelries.

RANGOON
Luxury
Inya Lake Hotel, Kaba Aye Pagoda Road, Tel. 50644. Restaurant, cocktail lounge, swimming pool, tennis, putting green, barber shop, beauty salon, conference facilities. Opened 1961.
Kandawgyi Royal Lake Hotel, Lake Road. Opened 1981; details unavailable. On lakeshore; located on site of former Museum of Natural History and Orient Boat Club.

First Class
Strand Hotel, 92 Strand Road, Tel. 81533. Restaurant, bar. Opened 1901.
Thamada (President) Hotel, 5 Signal Pagoda Road, Tel. 71499. Restaurant, bar. Opened 1972.

Second Class
Dagon (Orient) Hotel, 256 Sule Pagoda Road, Tel. 71140. Restaurant, bar, swimming pool.
Garden Guest House, Sule Pagoda Road, South Block, Tel. 71516. Opened 1979.

Golden City Hotel, 199 Sule Pagoda Road.
There are several other small hotels in the area of the railway station.

Third Class
YMCA (men and women), 263 Maha Bandoola Street. Opened 1965.
YWCA (women only), 119 Brooking Street. Opened 1900.

PEGU
Third Class
Pegu Circuit House.

MOULMEIN
Third Class
Government Rest House.
A new 50-room hotel was scheduled to open in 1981.

MANDALAY
First Class
Mandalay Hotel, corner 26th Road and 3rd Street, Tel. 22499. Restaurant, bars, beer garden, bakery.

Second Class
Tun Hla Hotel, 27th Road, Tel. 21283. Restaurant, bar, beer garden, swimming pool.

Third Class
Sabai Rest House, corner 25th Road and 84th Street.
Bandoola Guest House, corner 26th Road and 81st Street.
Man Shwe Myo, 31st Road between 80th and 81st streets.
Man San Dar Win, 31st Road between 80th and 81st streets.
Man Yatanar, corner 29th Road and 82nd Street.
Man Myo Daw, 80th Street between 30th and 31st roads.
Aye Thaw Dar, B Road near the Mingun jetty.
There are a number of other small guest houses in Mandalay as well. During the winter season, it is often difficult to find a room in Mandalay, as the Mandalay and Tun Hla hotels are frequently filled by tour parties. Individual travelers often must search some time before finding a room.

MAYMYO
Second Class
Candacraig Hotel (Maymyo Government Rest House), East Ridge Road, Tel. 47. Restaurant, bar.

Third Class
Thin Sabai Guest House.
U Ba Han Guest House.
Shwe Ye Ma Guest House.
YMCA.

PAGAN
First Class
Thiripyitsaya Hotel, Tel. 28. Restaurant, bar, gardens, conference facilities.

Second Class
Irra Inn, Tel. 24, near Bupaya Pagoda.
Cooperative Inn, Tel. 40, near Gawdawpalin Temple.

Third Class
Moe Moe Noodle Inn, near Gawdawpalin Temple.
Soe Soe Inn, at junction of main road and road to Irra Inn.
Pagan Room, near Mimalaung-kyaung Temple.
Zar Nee Rest House, near Mimalaung-kyaung Temple.

Aung Mahaya Lodge and Restaurant, near Shwegugyi Temple.

Burma Rest House, near BAC office.

If all of the above hostelries are full, in an emergency you can get a room for the night at the Buddhist monastery near the Ananda Temple.

TAUNGGYI
Second Class
Taunggyi (Strand) Hotel, Tel. 21127. Restaurant, bar.

Third Class
Shan States Hotel.
Khan Bawzia Hotel.
Thee Thant Hotel.
San Pya Inn.
May Kyu Inn.
Myo Daw Guest House.

INLE LAKE
Third Class
Inle Inn, Yaunghwe.

KALAW
Third Class
Kalaw Hotel.
Railway Rest House.
Accommodation is also available with Father Angelo de Meio, Catholic priest in Kalaw.

AKYAB
Third Class
Sun and Moon Rest House.

SANDOWAY
Second Class
Sandoway (Strand) Hotel, Tel. 27. Restaurant, bar, cottages, golf course.

Others
Burma Railway Corporation Hotel.
Sea Breeze Beach Hotel.

Any traveler moving off the normal tourist routes should always carry a sleeping bag or blankets, as pagodas, temples and monasteries will usually make floor space available for a night or two. The proverbial hospitality of the Burmese may also come to the rescue: it isn't all that unusual for Burmese to invite a total stranger to spend the night in their home.

Many towns that served as regional administrative centers during the period of British rule have "circuit houses." Then as now, these are primarily reserved for traveling state officials. However, if the tourist has been granted official permission to travel outside the normal tourist areas, there is a good chance of finding overnight accommodation at these inns.

Dining Out

Chinese, Indian and European food—and, of course, the spicy curries and fish dishes typical of Burmese cuisine—are available at restaurants throughout the country. Here's a listing of some of them:

RANGOON
Burmese
Karaweik Restaurant, east shore Royal Lake, Tel. 52352.
Burma Kitchen, 141 Shwegondine Road, Tel. 50493.
Bamboo House, 3 Thapye Nyo Street.
U Than Maung Daw Dwe May, 33-12th Street.
Danubyu, Anawrahta and 28th streets.
Kyaiklat (*mohinga* shop), Myenigone, West Rangoon.
There are also street stalls selling Burmese food at numerous locations throughout Rangoon.

European
Strand Hotel, 92 Strand Road, Tel. 81533.
Inya Lake Hotel, Kaba Aye Pagoda Road, Tel. 50644.

Chinese
Thamada Hotel, 5 Signal Pagoda Road, Tel. 71499.
Cozy Restaurant, East Racecourse Road.
Star Garden, Wingate Road.
Chung Wah Restaurant, 162 Sule Pagoda Road.
Palace Restaurant, 84-37th Street.
Hai Yuan Restaurant, 29 University Avenue.
Nam Sin Restaurant, 120 Prome Road, 8th Mile.
Kan Bow Za Restaurant, 120 Sule Pagoda Road.
Nan Yu Restaurant, 81 Pansodan Street.
Kwan Lock Restaurant, 67-22nd Street.
Hwan Chyu Restaurant, 98 Kaba Aye Pagoda Road.
Wah Min Restaurant, 79 Godwin Road.
New Oi Hkun Restaurant, 75 Latha Street.

Indian
Dagon (Orient) Hotel and Restaurant, 256/260 Sule Pagoda Road, Tel. 71140.
Mya Nanda Restaurant, Lewis Street opposite Strand Hotel.
Hotel de City, 232 Anawrahta Street.
Also, the Indian quarter has many small restaurants and food stalls. Try the biryani chicken shop on the street level of the Surathi Mosque in Mogul Street.

Snack Shops
People's Patisserie, 345 Bogyoke Aung San Street, Tel. 76579.
Yatha Confectionary, 458/460 Maha Bandoola Street, Tel. 70281.
Mya Sabe Cafe, 71 Pansodan Street.

MANDALAY
Burmese
Nyaung Bin Yin, 278-29th Road.
European
Mandalay Hotel, corner 26th Road and 3rd Street, Tel. 4.
Chinese
Tun Hla Hotel, 27th Road, Tel. 283.

Shwe Wah, 80th Street between 32nd and 33rd roads.

Kin Kyi Restaurant, 189-29th Road.
Meiktila Parker, 191-29th Road.
Shan Pin Restaurant, 199-29th Road.
Kanbawza Restaurant, 502-80th Street.
Shanghai Restaurant, 172-84th Street.

Snack Shops

Nylon Ice Cream Bar, 83rd Street between 25th and 26th roads.

Olympic Cafe, 83rd Street between 25th and 26th roads.

MAYMYO
European
Candacraig Hotel, East Ridge Road, Tel. 47.
Chinese
Shanghai Restaurant, Mandalay-Lashio Road.
Lay Ngoon Restaurant, Mandalay-Lashio Road.

PAGAN
European
Thiripyitsaya Hotel, Tel. 28.
Mixed Asian
National Restaurant, Sarabha Gate.
Cooperative Restaurant, opposite museum.
Moe Moe Noodle Inn, near Gawdawpalin Temple.
Aung Mahaya Restaurant, near Shwegugyi Temple.
OK Restaurant, next to village market.

TAUNGGYI
European
Taunggyi (Strand) Hotel, Tel. 21127.
Chinese
Tha Pye Restaurant.
Lyan You Restaurant.

Drinking Establishments

Western-style nightlife is nonexistent in Burma. But most of the better hotels make it possible for visitors to imbibe in spirits, both domestic and imported, and to sample Mandalay Beer from the People's Brewery.

In Rangoon, the Inya Lake Hotel has a formal cocktail lounge, while the Strand, Thamada and Dagon hotels have pleasant bars. The Nanthida Pub, adjacent to the Strand, has a beer garden, and the Win Bar, across the street from the Dagon Hotel, also serves drinks.

In Mandalay, and in other provincial cities, beer and spirits are sold only through government hotels (although some guest houses buy from the bigger hotels and resell to their patrons for a higher price).

In addition to the local beer, there is also rum, whisky and gin made in Burma. You'll see bottles of many imported liquors, particularly Scotch whisky, for sale in night markets, but this is considerably more expensive here than if you were to buy it outside of the country.

Communications

Mail

The **Rangoon General Post Office** is located on Strand Road at the corner of Bo Aung Gyaw Street. All post offices in Burma are open 9:30 a.m. to 4 p.m. Monday through Friday, and 9:30 a.m. to 12:30 p.m. Saturday. They are closed Sunday and public holidays.

The only exception is the Mingaladon (Rangoon) Airport mail sorting office. It is open round-the-clock daily, including Sunday and holidays, for receipt and dispatch of foreign mail. Ordinary letters and postcards will be accepted here at any time. Registered letters can be taken at the airport postal counter only during normal government working hours.

Foreign postage rates are:

Aerograms, 1.25 *kyat* to all destinations.

Postcards, 85 *pyas* to Asia, 1.30 *kyat* to Europe and Australia, 1.60 *kyat* to North America.

Letters up to one ounce, 1.25 *kyat* to Asia, 2.15 *kyats* to Europe and Australia, 2.70 *kyats* to North America.

For parcels and other postal rates, the post office should be consulted for a complete rate schedule.

Inland postage is negligible. Letters are 15 *pyas* for the first half-ounce, 10 *pyas* for each additional half-ounce; postcards are a standard 10 *pyas*.

Mail for the Americas (via New York) and for Europe (via London) goes out twice a week, on Monday and Friday nights. There are two mailings a week to Australia as well (mid-day Tuesday and Saturday morning), with dispatches to most of Asia three times a week.

Standard Burmese postage stamps feature the country's eight major ethnic groups—Burman, Kachin, Kayah, Karen, Chin, Mon, Arakanese and Shan—in traditional costume. An earlier series of stamps depicted the nation's birds. Commemorative stamps are occasionally issued. All can be purchased at Rangoon's GPO.

The Posts and Telecommunications Corporation operates the post office.

Telephone

You can make international telephone calls from Burma, but the rate is not cheap. There is a trunk-call line available from Rangoon. Call 101 for an overseas or inland booking between 7 a.m. and 7 p.m., and the operator will call you back at your hotel (or wherever else you may be) when the trunk line is open for your call.

You can call North American between 9 a.m. and 2:30 p.m. any day but Sunday, for a cost of 85.50 *kyats* for the first three minutes and 28.50 *kyats* for each additional minute. Times and rates to other locations vary considerably. It's 68.40 *kyats* to Frankfurt (8 to 10:30 a.m. daily except Sunday), 61.10 *kyats* to Zurich (4:30 to 7 p.m. any day), 85.50 *kyats* to Sweden (8 to 10:30 a.m. daily except Sunday), and 65.10 *kyats* to London. (According to the official Burmese government schedule, you can telephone the United Kingdom between 9 a.m. and

2:30 p.m. daily except Sunday, but calls to England are permitted only between 4:30 and 7 p.m.—on any day, including Sunday.)

Calls to Australia are 69.85 *kyats* (9 a.m. to 2:30 p.m. daily except Sunday), and to Singapore 27.40 *kyats* (8 to 10:30 a.m. daily except Sunday). For further information, call the information line, Tel. 103, or the trunk supervisor, Tel. 72001.

Telegrams

The **Central Telegraph Office**, located one block east of the Sule Pagoda on Maha Bandoola Street, is open from 8 a.m. to 9 p.m. Monday through Saturday, and from 8 a.m. to 8 p.m. Sunday and public holidays.

If you encounter any problems with any of the communications systems, direct your queries to the Posts and Telecommunications Corporation, 43 Bo Aung Gyaw Street, Tel. 85499.

Media

Cinemas

The Burmese love movies. There are more than 50 "cinema halls" in Rangoon, about a third of them in the downtown area. In addition to Burmese language films, the Motion Picture Corporation shows carefully selected foreign features on a regular basis, including movies from North America, Europe, India and Japan.

The following seven cinema halls present English-language and other foreign films on a regular basis:

Bayint, 321 Bogyoke Aung San Street, Tel. 75368.

Gon, 223/229 Sule Pagoda Road, Tel. 72982.

Pa Pa Win, Sule Pagoda Road, Tel. 72270.

Thamada, 5 Signal Pagoda Road, Tel. 70282.

Waziya, 327 Bogyoke Aung San Street, Tel. 73468.

Wizaya, 224 U Wisara Road, Tel. 30660.

Yei Yint, corner Sule Pagoda Road and Bogyoke Aung San Street, Tel. 70945.

Theaters

The best place to view Burmese *pwe* is on the city streets or pagoda grounds at festival times. For those whose visit doesn't coincide with a festival, however, there are three public theaters in Rangoon which have irregular performances of various types. They are:

Jubilee Hall, Shwedagon Pagoda Road, associated with the State School of Music and Drama.

Open-Air Theatre, Lanmadaw (Godwin) Road.

Garrison Theatre, U Wisara Road.

The Press

Rangoon has six daily newspapers, four of them Burmese-language papers and two of them in English. The *Working People's Daily* (212 Theinbyu Road), with a circulation of 20,000, and the *Guardian* (392/396 Merchant Street), with a circulation

of 13,000, provide extensive coverage of international news. Most of their information is drawn from major Western and Asian news agencies. Papers are generally available at major hotels and from booksellers.

Radio

The **Burma Broadcasting Service** is on the air 16 hours, 45 minutes a day—including 2½ hours of daily English-language programming. Half-hour news programs are broadcast in English at 8:30 a.m. (42.14 and 314 meters) and 1:30 p.m. (30.85 and 314 meters); there is also an hour-and-a-half of English-language programming from 9 to 10:30 p.m. daily (59.52 and 314 meters).

Of interest to the linguist might be the "nationalities program" presented daily from 5 to 9:15 p.m. on 63.49 meters Short Wave. Broadcasts in Kachin, Kayah, Sgaw Karen, Pwo Karen, Chin, Mon, Burman, Arakanese and Shan are made during this time slot.

The BBS has its headquarters in Rangoon on Prome Road near Kamayut.

Television

Television was introduced in Burma in 1981. A national channel presents overseas programs for about two hours each evening. Many of these programs are in the English language. But TV sets are few and far between.

Libraries

The **Sarpay Beikman Public Library,** 529 Merchant Street at the corner of 37th Street, has more than 11,000 English-language books among its 35,000 volumes. Of particular interest here are contemporary Burmese books translated into English.

Burma's largest library is the **University Central Library** on the Rangoon University campus. Some 170,000 books in Burmese, English and many other languages are kept here. Visitors cannot check books out (that privilege is reserved for students and faculty), but can peruse the books in the library.

The library at the **International Institute of Advanced Buddhistic Studies,** Kaba Aye Pagoda, has a large selection as well. Among its holdings are more than 10,000 volumes in English. The collection also includes about 9,000 sets of ancient palm-leaf manuscripts and 2,412 museum objects.

The **National Library** in the Rangoon City Hall houses an interesting collection of rare books and palm-leaf manuscripts.

There are libraries in the **United States Embassy,** 581 Merchant Street, and at the **British Embassy,** 80 Strand Road. Both carry current magazines as well as a variety of books.

In addition, the **Information and Broadcasting Department** operates 110 libraries and reading rooms throughout the country. Many of them, especially in major towns, have English-language literature. The department's headquarters in Rangoon, near the Strand Hotel on Pansodan Street, has a wide selection of newspapers and periodicals, as well as official publications.

Booksellers

Sarpay Beikman, the public library at 529 Merchant Street, also has a book sales section. This is probably the best place to find contemporary Burmese works in English.

Paperbacks and foreign journals can generally be found at two shops operated by the Paper, Stationery, Books and Photographic Stores Trading Corporation. They are located at 232 Sule Pagoda Road and 98 Pansodan Street. The corporation also has shops dealing in general literature at the corner of Merchant and Pansodan streets, and in medical literature at 181/189 Sule Pagoda Road.

Rare book collectors will find it worthwhile to browse the many book stalls set up along main streets in both Rangoon and Mandalay. Long-sought, out-of-print books can often turn up in odd locations like these. In addition, there are two outstanding used book shops in Burma. In Rangoon, book collectors should seek out the **Pagan Bookshop,** 100–37th Street. And in out-of-the-way Taunggyi, a charming surprise is the **Myoma Book Stall,** 390 Main Road.

Customs and Lifestyle

The National Flag

The Burmese national flag is red in color with a dark blue canton in the top left corner. Within the blue field are a white pinion and ears of paddy rice, surrounded by 14 white stars. The pinion represents industry, the rice symbolizes agriculture, and the stars correspond to the 14 administrative districts of Burma. According to the Burmese government, the color white signifies purity, truth and steadfastness. Dark blue denotes the goal of peace, while red indicates courage, determination and unity.

Government

The Socialist Republic of the Union of Burma (in Burmese, *Pye Daung-Su So-She-Lit Thammada Myanma Nainggan-Daw*) is a one-party state with an elected People's Assembly *(Hluttaw).* The chairman of the Burma Socialist Program Party, Ne Win, was also president of Burma until his resignation in November 1981. The new president is U San Yu. The prime minister since 1977 has been U Maung Maung Kha.

Administrative Regions

Burma has seven minority-dominated states: Arakan, Chin, Kachin, Karen (Kawthule), Kayah, Mon and Shan. There are seven regions populated mainly by Burmans: Irrawaddy, Magwe, Mandalay, Pegu, Rangoon, Sagaing and Tenasserim.

Statistical Data

Burma has a population of 33.6 million (1979 estimate), of whom 80 percent are rural dwellers and 20 percent urban. Population density is 46.9 per square kilometer, or 123 per square mile. Annual population growth rate is 2.4 percent. Life expectancy is 50 years; infant mortality rate is 56.3 per 1,000.

Burma's gross national product is US $5,160 million (1979), a per capita GNP of US $154. The national labor force numbers 12.6 million, of whom 67 percent are employed in agriculture and 13 percent in industry. The literacy rate is 70 percent.

Burmese Names

Unlike Western culture, there are no family names in Burmese usage. Men and women, parents and children, married couples and single people, cannot be differentiated by their names. Women keep their maiden names upon marriage, and a child can have a name which bears no relation whatsoever to its parents' names.

A Burmese has a name of one, two or three syllables, given to him (or her) shortly after birth at a naming ceremony. Parents consult an authority in astrology and supernatural knowledge—perhaps a monk, a soothsayer or a spiritual medium—in selecting the name. While this practice does not follow Buddhist doctrine, it is customary throughout the country.

In contrast to Western tradition, a Burmese can change his name as often as he likes. If he feels he can bring success to a new enterprise or change his fortune by doing so, he will change his name. Small children are often given unpleasant names to ward off illness and evil; when they have grown up, they change their names to something more pleasant.

Only through mode of address can one tell the sex or social status of a Burmese.

For example, a Burmese named Kau Reng, if a man, might be addressed as "U Kau Reng," "Ko Kau Reng" or "Maung Kau Reng." The title "U" says that the person being addressed is a superior in social or official position or in age. "Ko" is commonly used among men of similar standing in addressing each other. "Maung" generally is used toward persons who are younger or of an inferior status; it also is commonly used among children and teen-aged boys. Sometimes the dual title "Ko Maung" is used if the Burmese has a monosyllabic name.

A woman named Kau Reng would be addressed either as "Daw Kau Reng" or "Ma Kau Reng." "Daw" implies social status or greater age; it can suggest that the woman is married, although this is not necessarily so. "Ma" is applicable to Burmese women regardless of social status, and is the most commonly used female title, even for married women. It is very discourteous to address any woman in Burma without the use of one of these titles.

Within the family circle, there are several other titles with finer shades of meaning. Wives often address their husbands as "Eing Ga Lu" or "Ein Thar," meaning "Good man of the house." An elder brother is called "Ko Ko." An uncle is "U Lay," "U Gyi" or "Ba Gyi." Similar terms of affection are directed towards women. "Ma Ma" and "A Ma Gyi" refer to an elder sister, and "Daw Daw" is an aunt.

Superiors are often addressed "Ah Ko Gyi," "Ko

Gyi" or "Saya" (teacher). "Saya" is also used in reference to medical doctors. Monks are called "Sayadaw" ("Venerable"), "Ashin" ("Reverend") or "Kodaw" (Your Reverence), the latter used most frequently by a layman addressing a monk. Military officers are addressed as "Bo."

It is particularly difficult for a Burmese to address a Westerner only by his Christian name, even when they are close friends. Thus Ko Kau Reng will never call his friend "Ronnie," but will address him as "Ko Ronnie" or "Maung Ronnie." Similarly, Nancy would be called "Ma Nancy." Ko Kau Reng expects that he, too, will be similarly addressed.

Tipping

Tipping is not a common practice in Burma. It is becoming less unusual in Rangoon at major tourist hotels; but even there, a waiter might come running after you to return the change you had intended to leave as a tip. If you wish to show your appreciation for some small service, a gift such as a ballpoint pen or a cigarette lighter will be more readily accepted, and perhaps more appreciated, than a monetary tip.

The Eras

Burmese date their years by four different systems. Most frequently seen is the calendar based on the Christian Era, but you may see any of these other three as well:

The Buddhist Era began in 544 B.C. with the death of Gautama. According to this system, the Christian year 1982 is the Buddhist year 2526.

The Prome Era began in 78 A.D. A large amount of epigraphical data of interest to archaeologists is dated by this system. The year 1982 would be 1904 of the Prome Era.

The Pagan Era is considered to have begun in 638 A.D. Linked to Burmese royalty, it is rarely in use today. The year 1344 of the Pagan Era would be 1982 of the Christian Era.

Places of Worship

Despite its heavy emphasis on Buddhism, Burma is a country of great religious freedom. The following list of non-Buddhist places of worship in Rangoon is indicative.

CHRISTIAN
Roman Catholic
St. Augustine's Church, 64 Inya Road, Tel. 30620. Sunday masses at 7 and 9:30 a.m.
Anglican
Cathedral of the Holy Trinity, 446 Bogyoke Aung San Street. Sunday services: communion 7 a.m., communion and sermon 8:30 a.m., church school (children) 9:45 a.m., evensong 5 p.m.

Church of the Holy Cross, 104 Inya Road, Tel. 30658. Holy communion and sermon at 8 a.m. Sunday.

Methodist
Methodist-English Church, 65 Signal Pagoda Road, Tel. 72808. Sunday school 8:30 to 9:30 a.m., morning service 9:45 a.m., Methodist youth fellowship 3:30 to 4:30 p.m. Sunday.
Baptist
Immanuel Church, corner of Maha Bandoola and Barr streets, Tel. 75905. Sunday school 8 a.m., Sunday worship 5 p.m.
Armenian
St. John the Baptist Armenian Church, 113 Bo Aung Gyaw Street at the corner of Merchant Street. Sunday service 9 to 10:30 a.m.

JEWISH
There is a Jewish synagogue in Rangoon. Call the Israeli Embassy for a current schedule of services.

ISLAM
Surathi (Sunni) Mosque, Mogul Street.
Sunni Mosque, Shwebontha Street.
Sunni Mosque, Maung Taulay Street.
Sunni Mosque, Sule Pagoda Road.
Shia' Mosque, 30th Street.
Khoja Mosque, Shwebontha Street.
Prayers are offered five times daily at all mosques.

HINDU
Sri Sri Siva Krishna Temple, 141 Pansodan Street. Open 10 to 11 a.m. and 3 to 8 p.m. daily.
Sri Sri Durga Temple, 307 Bo Aung Gyaw Street.
Hindu Temple, Anawrahta Street near Thein Gyi Zei market.

SIKH
Sikh Temple, 256 Theinbyu Road.

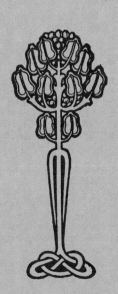

Cultural Information

How to Tell a Pagoda From a Temple

There are two principle types of Buddhist monuments in Burma—pagodas and temples.

A pagoda consists of a stupa and its surrounding enclosure. The stupa (also known as a *zedi, cetiya* or *dagoba*) is a monument of commemoration containing a relic chamber beneath (or sometimes over) the bell-shaped central structure. Burmese stupas are generally built on several terraces; these are passages on which devotees should walk in a clockwise direction.

The term "temple" is applied to Buddhist structures in Burma only because a more specific terminology does not exist in English. In Theravada Buddhism, a temple is not a place of worship of a higher being; the Buddha is not a god, and Theravada Buddhism in its pure form does not recognize any form of divine worship. The temple is instead seen as a place of meditation. The Burmese word is *ku*, derived from the Pali *guha*, which roughly translated means "cave." This word also reflects the cultural heritage of the edifice—these buildings were formerly constructed as artificial caves to be used by monks where there were no overhanging slopes.

The main feature of a *ku* is that it is dark and cool inside. This feature characterizes the Mon-style ("hollow cube") Pagan temples, into which only a little light is able to enter through the perforated stone windows. The Burman-style ("central pillar") temples are totally different: they were built with huge entrances and two tiers of windows to make the interiors bright and airy.

It is possible to trace the development of the "central pillar" type from the stupas. During festivals, it was the custom to stretch huge awnings from the stupa to the surrounding wall of the enclosure in order to give protection from rain and sun. As a result, there was a covered walkway around the central sanctuary. When this was copied in solid materials, it gave the appearance that the upper part of a stupa had been built on the roof of a temple. This is the same principle behind the multi-storied Burman-style temples.

The "hollow cube" type of temples are not actually hollow inside; they may seem to be so, but the majority have a central supporting pillar. From the outside, their pointed, bell-shaped domes resemble Gothic buildings. But the temples of Pagan could not be more different. Instead of spanning the greatest possible space, the Buddhist temple interiors consist of a multitude of walls enclosing narrow passageways and chambers, thereby satisfying the *ku's* original purpose as a sanctuary for inner peace and meditation. The exterior of these temples—white, and invariably decorated with a gold finial—can be seen to represent Mount Meru and the devout Buddhist's striving for a spiritual goal via the ever-valid Dharma, the law of life.

Temple Etiquette

A Buddhist place of worship is very unlike a similar place in the West. You might find a devout Buddhist in deep meditation on any temple platform, but you might also find whole families eating their lunches in front of a Buddha image. You will see lines of monks walking slowly and consciously around the stupa, but you also may see hordes of children running around merrily and haphazardly. The temple ground is where every Burmese village or city neighborhood congregates in the evening. But don't let the "everyday-ness" fool you. This is sacred ground, and there are certain rules you must keep to show your respect.

Throughout Burma, wherever you enter or leave religious grounds, you must remove your shoes (or sandals) and socks. Many shrines will have a sign posted to remind you: "Footwear Prohibited." You'll have to plod with naked soles over marble plates scorched by the mid-day sun, up long flights of stairs (the whole of Mandalay Hill, for example, is sacred ground), or even over thorn-studded fields if they lie within the enclosure that marks a temple ground.

You can also show your respect for Burmese religion by wearing proper clothing at a temple—especially, no short skirts for women, and no short pants. Those who come for meditation and contemplation do not want to be distracted by "shocking" Westerners: Theravada Buddhists have a strong "anti-flesh" attitude, an equally strong desire for virtue, and a refined awareness of beauty.

If you watch the pious Buddhists who climb to the terrace surrounding a stupa, or who wander through the passageways leading around a temple's central cella, you will notice that they always turn to their left. By keeping the sanctuary on the right, they follow universal "law," going the same direction as the sun goes through the sky.

At the Shwedagon Pagoda and other shrines with planetary posts on their terraces, the pilgrim walks from one season to another; by visiting monuments to the last four Buddhas, he walks through different worlds and different times. This reminds him of his smallness compared to the universe, and awakens in him pure Theravadin spirit. He may stop at planetary posts corresponding to his birthday and the current weekday; he may pause (especially at older shrines) to study the terra-cotta friezes describing the Buddha's former lives; he might make an offering of flowers or candles at a Buddha image, and perhaps wash it for additional merit. You no doubt

will see him murmur the "Three Gems": "I take refuge in the Buddha, I take refuge in the Dharma, I take refuge in the Sangha."

Pagodas and temples are always beautifully decorated, and most Burmese show great pride if you are inspired to photograph their shrine. But photos should be your only souvenirs. Although many Buddhist structures seem to have a surplus of small Buddha statues that no one appears to care about, these are still venerated images. Leave them alone. Note: See temple and site plans on pp. 320–323.

The Mudras

Just as temples and pagodas are created in different styles, so are Buddha images. The various body postures and hand and leg positions have different symbolic meanings, each of considerable importance to students of Buddhism. These various positions, called the *mudras*, are thousands of years old. As religion and art form an inseparable unity in Burmese life, they constitute the basis of dance and of the *yokethe pwe*, or marionette theater.

There are four basic body postures in which an image might appear. The **standing posture** depicts the descent of the Buddha from the *Tavatimsa* heaven where, according to legend, he traveled to preach the Buddhist doctrine to his mother.

The **walking posture** represents the Buddha's taming of the rampaging Nalagiri elephant.

The **seated posture** is the most common. It can represent any of three events: the Buddha calling upon Mother Earth to stand witness to his enlightenment; his preaching of the Sermon of the Wheel of the Law; or the Buddha in deep meditation. There are three different seated postures: legs crossed with both soles invisible; legs crossed with soles turned upward and resting on thighs, in the lotus position; and legs dangling in almost a European style of sitting.

The Buddha might also be in a **reclining posture**. If his head is pointed north, the position depicts his death and transition into nirvana. If his head is pointed any direction but north, he is sleeping.

In addition to the body and leg postures, there are six different hand gestures, each conveying a clear message. These are demonstrated in the following:

1. The Bhumisparsa Mudra

In this *mudra,* the left hand lies palm upward on the Buddha's lap, and the right hand rests palm downward across his right knee, with the fingertips touching the ground below. This is the most common *mudra*; it shows the Buddha calling upon Mother Earth to stand witness to his moment of enlightenment.

According to the Buddha legend, Mara, the god of destruction, tried to subdue the Buddha by sending his army of demons to attack the Buddha as he meditated under the Bodhi tree, and by sending his three daughters—Desire, Pleasure and Passion—to tempt the Buddha. But the Buddha called upon Vasumdarhi, the Earth goddess, to bear witness that he had found perfect knowledge. With this, the ground began to shake, and Mara took flight.

2. The Dhyana Mudra

This position, said to represent many events in the life of the Buddha, has the palm of his right hand placed flat in the palm of the left, with both hands laid in his crossed legs. Objects placed in the palms, or figures standing to the side of an image in this position, specify which event is being depicted.

3. The Dharmacakra Mudra

In this *mudra,* both of the Buddha's hands are held in front of his breast. The tips of the middle finger and thumb of the left hand are joined with the tips of the index finger and thumb of the right hand to form a circle. This gesture recalls the Buddha's first sermon (at Sarnath, India); the hand sign is said to set the Wheel of the Law in motion.

4. The Abhaya Mudra

This posture, found only in a standing Buddha, has the figure's right hand raised and the left pointed downward. It represents the promise of tranquility, protection and fearlessness given by the Buddha to his followers. It is also a reminder of the attempted assassination of the Buddha by his cousin Devadatta, who sent the Nalagiri elephant against him.

5. The Varada Mudra

The arms of the standing Buddha are half outstretched in front of the body in this pose. The palms are opened out, and the tips of the fingers point downward. This *mudra* depicts the bestowal of the Buddha's blessing on followers.

6. The Abhaya and Varada Mudras

The Buddha's right hand is in the raised position of the Abhaya Mudra, and his left hand is outstretched as in the Varada Mudra. This posture signifies protection and blessing, and at the same time recalls the Buddha's descent to earth after preaching in the *Tavatimsa* heaven.

All makers of Buddha images in Burma today must follow the specific *mudras* outlined here, as well as other strict rules. A list of 112 characteristics which all Buddha images must exhibit are laid down in the *Dikka Nikaya,* found in the Buddhist scriptures.

Monasteries

If the temples and pagodas of Burma haven't exhausted you, and you're still enthused about exploring more Buddhist buildings in Rangoon before departure from Burma, the Burmese government has compiled a list of "impressive monasteries" in Rangoon. Many of them feature ornate wood carving and fine Buddhist artifacts. Visitors should make it a point to obtain permission to enter the monasteries from their respective *sayadaws,* or abbots.

Aletawya Kyaungtaik, Boundary Road.
Bagaya Kyaungtaik, Bagaya Road, Kemendine.

Bahan Kyaungtaik, Bahan.
Kyaunggyi Kyaungtaik, Kemendine.
Mingun Tawyar, Lowis Road.
Mya Theindan Kyaungtaik, Kemendine.
Naw-man Kyaungtaik, Pazundaung.
Ngadatkyi Kyaungtaik, Ngadatkyi Road.
Payagyi Kyaungtaik, Shwegondine Road.
Pazundaung Kyaungtaik, Pazundaung.
Pyinnya Ramika Maha, Theinbyu Road.
Salin Kyaungtaik, Lower Kemendine Road.
Shin Ah-deiksa-wuntha Kyaungtaik, Pazundaung.
Theinbyu Kyaungtaik, Theinbyu Road.
U-kyin Kyaungtaik, Bagaya Road, Kemendine.
Weluwun Kyaungtaik, Kemendine.
Zeyawaddy Kyaungtaik, Kemendine.

Museums

Burma's myriad pagodas and temples are her finest museums. Countless priceless religious artifacts are contained within. The following museums have also assembled various items of historical and anthropological interest:

National Museum, Pansodan Street between Strand Road and Merchant Street, Rangoon. Contains the Mandalay Regalia from Burma's last royal court and various artifacts of ancient history. Open 10 a.m. to 3 p.m. Sunday through Thursday and 1 to 3 p.m. Saturday. Closed Friday and holidays.

National Museum and Library, 24th Road and West Moat Road, Mandalay. Contains a variety of memorabilia from many eras of Burmese history, and a fine collection of Buddhist literature.

Pagan Museum, near Thiripyitsaya Hotel, Pagan. A good indoctrination to the images and architectural styles of this ancient city.

Taunggyi Museum, Main Road, Taunggyi. Displays traditional costumes and cultural artifacts of the 30-plus ethnic groups living in the Shan Plateau region.

Sports

As in every country of the world, sports are a popular amusement and diversion in Burma. Soccer (football) is often played at Aung San Stadium in Rangoon, and on small fields throughout the country. Other sports familiar to Westerners are also played. Uniquely Burmese, however, are the sport of *chinlon* and traditional boxing.

Chinlon

Chinlon is Burma's national game. Said by some to have originated in ancient Prome in the 7th Century, its object is to keep a caneball in the air for as long as possible, using no part of the body except the feet and knees.

Although the game is played for fun by any number of people throughout the country, the All-Burma Chinlon Association has set up rules for team play that is increasing its status. A team of six players stands within a boundary circle 6½ meters (21 feet) in diameter, passing the ball back and forth among themselves. Points are scored according to the difficulty of the footwork used and the skill with which it is executed; specific point values are assigned to certain "strokes." Points are subtracted if the ball hits the ground, or if a player steps outside the boundary circle.

The *chinlon*, or caneball, is made of six leaves of sugar cane interwoven and dried, forming a circular ball with holes about an inch and a half apart. The standard-size ball is 40 centimeters (16 inches) around.

Burmese Boxing

To the unfamiliar Westerner, Burmese boxing appears to be a needlessly vicious sport. Boxers may

use any parts of their bodies in attacking their opponents, and a match is won by whoever draws first blood. But there are specific rules and courtesies which keep a match from getting out of hand, and musical accompaniment by a Burmese percussion orchestra, or *saing-waing*, lends an air of unreality to the entire event.

The following description of Burmese boxing is taken from *Forward* magazine (August 1, 1964), as quoted by author Helen Trager in her book *We, The Burmese:*

"The head is used for butting, either to stop an opponent's rush or to soften him up while holding him fast in a tight grip. The hands are used not only for hitting but also for holding. The elbows are used to parry an opponent's blow or to deliver one in the opponent's side. The knees are used for hitting an opponent who is held fast, or they may be used to deliver blows while the boxers are apart. The feet may trip an opponent or at least keep him off balance, or they may be used to stop an opponent's rush with a well-executed flying kick.

"These tactics are commonly employed by Burmese boxers. To deliver the blows effectively, however, the boxer has to master his footwork, which is also considered important in another branch of the art of self-defense, *Thaing*. A Burmese boxer has to know where to place his feet, how to advance, how to retreat, from what position to jump into the attack, and how best to evade the blows of the opponent. In close combat the Burmese boxer has to be well acquainted with techniques of wrestling.

"... To safeguard the boxers from accidents, there are rules against scratching, biting, pulling hair, and hitting or kicking an opponent in the groin. The fingernails and toenails of boxers have to be kept properly trimmed. A boxer who is down may not be kicked or hit in any way...

"The match is decided at the sign of blood. Each boxer is allowed to wipe away the blood three times before he is declared the loser. A match may also be decided when one of the boxers is too hurt to continue although he may not be bleeding."

General Information

Airline Offices

The following international airlines have offices in Rangoon:

Aeroflot, 18 Prome Road, 7th Mile, Tel. 61066. Airport Tel. 40435.
Air France, 69 Sule Pagoda Road, Tel. 74199.
Burma Airways Corporation, 104 Strand Road, Tel. 84566 or 72911. Airport Tel. 40379.
Civil Aviation Administration of China (CAAC), 67-A Prome Road, Tel. 75714. Airport Tel. 40113.
Indian Airways, 533 Merchant Street.
KLM Royal Dutch Airlines, 104 Strand Road, Tel. 74840.
Pakistan International Airways, 510 Merchant Street, Tel. 74807.
Thai Airways International, 441–445 Tavoy House, Maha Bandoola Street, Tel. 75936. Airport Tel. 40112.

Burma Airways also handles bookings for the following airlines: Air India, British Airways, Czechoslovak Airlines, Cathay Pacific, Japan Air Lines, Lot-Polish Airways, Lufthansa, Pan American, Royal Nepal and Scandinavian Airlines.

State Trade Corporations

All businesses in Burma are nationalized. The nation's economy is controlled by 11 so-called "trade corporations," recently reorganized from an original list of 22.

Many Burmese, with tongue in cheek, like to say there are actually 12 trade corporations—the 12th being the import-export business under the shady umbrella of private enterprise. It is estimated that 70 percent of Burma's international trade is accounted for by smuggling.

The 11 official trade corporations are:

Agricultural and Garden Produce, 70 Pansodan Street, Tel. 84044.
Foodstuffs and General Supplies, 11/17 Bogale Bazaar Street, Tel. 75355.
Restaurants and Beverages, 186 Maha Bandoola Street, Tel. 77399.
Textiles, 19/43 Maung Taulay Street, Tel. 77077.
Paper, Stationery, Books and Photographic Stores, 550/552 Merchant Street, Tel. 74177.
Medical Stores, 189/191 Maha Bandoola Street, Tel. 81466.
Transport Equipment and Machinery, 180/184 Bogyoke Aung San Street, Tel. 74626.
Construction and Electrical Stores, 170 Bo Aung Gyaw Street, Tel. 75522.
Hotel and Tourist Corporation (Tourist Burma), 73 Sule Pagoda Road, Tel. 77466, or 77/91 Sule Pagoda Road, Tel. 78376.
Stores Inspection and Agencies Corporation, 377 Maha Bandoola Street, Tel. 80429.
Myanma Export-Import Corporation, 34/38 Strand Road, Tel. 80266.

State Organizations

The following list provides addresses and telephone numbers of various Burmese government organizations of possible interest to businessmen, scholars or other visitors:

Agriculture Corporation, 72/74 Shwedagon Pagoda Road, Tel. 72655.

Archaeology Department, 32-D Prome Road, 6th Mile, Tel. 31699.

Bureau of Special Investigation, 67/69 Seikkantha Street, Tel. 82086.

Burma Broadcasting Service, Prome Road, Tel. 31355.

Burma Five Star Shipping Corporation, 132/136 Theinbyu Road, Tel. 80022.

Burma Historical Research Department, Culture House, Nawarat Yeiktha, Tel. 81088.

Burma Pharmaceutical Industry, Gyogon, Tel. 40099.

Burma Ports Corporation, 10 Pansodan Street, Tel. 83122.

Burmese Literary Commission, 27 Prome Road, 6½ Mile, Tel. 31068.

Central Accounts Office, 1 Pansodan Street, Tel. 84799.

Central Court of Justice, Barr Street, Tel. 82249.

Central Research Organization, Kanbe and Kaba Aye Pagoda roads, Tel. 50544.

Central Statistical Organization, Government Office Complex, Strand Road, Tel. 81166.

Cigarette Industry Management Committee, 30 Strand Road, Tel. 84028.

Civil Aviation Department, Mingaladon Airport, Tel. 74011.

Construction Corporation, 60 Shwedagon Pagoda Road, Tel. 80955.

Co-operative Department, 259/263 Bogyoke Aung San Street, Tel. 75611.

Cultural Institute Department, 42 Pansodan Street, Tel. 81321.

Customs Department, 132 Strand Road, Tel. 84533.

Department of Higher Education, Prome Road, Tel. 30611.

Directorate of Trade, 228/240 Strand Road, Tel. 84299.

Education Research Bureau, 426 Prome Road, Tel. 31522.

Electric Power Corporation, 197/199 Lower Kemendine Road, Ahlone, Tel. 85366. Rangoon Division, 503/509 Merchant Street, Tel. 72303.

Fire Services Department, 371 Ahlone Road, Tel. 72877.

Fisheries Department, 309/313 Pansodan Street, Tel. 78208.

Foreign Languages Institute, 119/131 University Avenue, Tel. 31713.

Forest Department, 62 Pansodan Street, Tel. 81367, 71624.

Health Department, 36 Theinbyu Road, Tel. 84600.

Housing Department, 228/234 Bogyoke Aung San Street, Tel. 71322.

Immigration and Manpower Department, Government Office Complex, Strand Road, Tel. 85505.

Industrial Minerals Corporation, 226 Maha Bandoola Street, Tel. 74711.

Industrial Planning Corporation, 192 Kaba Aye Pagoda Road, Tel. 50744.

Information and Broadcasting Department, 22/24 Pansodan Street, Tel. 31850.

Inland Water Transport Corporation, 50 Pansodan Street, Tel. 84055.

Internal Revenue Department, Head Office, 59/61 Pansodan Street, Tel. 83055. Income Tax and Commercial Taxes Division, 554/556 Merchant Street, Tel. 83055.

Marine Administration Department, Government Office Complex, Strand Road, Tel. 85555, 81889.

Medical Research Department, 5 Zafar Shah Road, Tel. 72033.

Meteorology and Hydrology Department, Kaba Aye Pagoda Road, Tel. 60824.

Motion Picture Corporation, 379/383 Bo Aung Gyaw Street, Tel. 81267. Documentary Films, 35-A Hermitage Road, Tel. 50194.

Myanma Bawdwin Corporation, 104 Strand Road, Tel. 75300.

Myanma Development Corporation, Kanbe Road, Yankin, Tel. 50166.

Myanma Insurance Corporation, 69 Pansodan Street, Tel. 84166.

Myanma Oil Corporation, 604 Merchant Street, Tel. 82266.

National Health Laboratory, 35 Stewart Road, Tel. 76533.

News Agency Burma, 212 Theinbyu Road, Tel. (internal news) 77665, (external news) 73013.

Pearl and Fishery Corporation, 654 Merchant Street, Tel. 78022.

People's Police Force, Director-General's Office, Duty Room, Tel. 73365. Rangoon Division, 147 Anawrahta Street, Tel. 82511. Special Intelligence, Ministers' Office, Tel. 80488.

Posts and Telecommunications Corporation, 43 Bo Aung Gyaw Street, Tel. 85499.

Printing and Publishing Corporation, 228 Theinbyu Road, Tel. 81033.

Prisons Department, Bogyoke Aung San Street, Tel. 74122.

Public Services Selection and Training Board, Government Office Complex, Strand Road, Tel. 84066.

Rangoon City Development Committee, City Hall, Maha Bandoola Street, Tel. 83988.

Religious Affairs Department, Kaba Aye Pagoda Road, 7th Mile, Tel. 31301.

Road Transport Corporation, 375 Bogyoke Aung San Street, Tel. 82252.

Social Security Board, 327/367 Maha Bandoola Garden Street, Tel. 71698.

Social Welfare Department, 17/25 18th Street, Tel. 75344.

Sports and Physical Education Department, Aung San Stadium, Tel. 81726.

Survey Department, 460 Merchant Street, Tel. 50380.

Technical, Agricultural and Vocational Department, 123 Natmauk Road, Tel. 50211.

Timber Corporation, Ahlone, Tel. 83933.

Transport Administration Department, 36 Barr Street, Tel. 83069.

Union of Burma Bank, 24/26 Sule Pagoda Road, Tel. 85300.

Veterinary and Animal Husbandry Department, 50 Shafraz Road, Tel. 75288.

Youth Affairs Department, Kyaikkasan Grounds, Tel. 51556, 51689.

Clubs

The following private clubs might be of interest to visitors, who generally will be welcomed to activities:

Burma Golf Club, Prome Road, 9th Mile, Tel. 61702.

Growers Club, Myepadethakyun, Kandawgyi, Tel. 50288.

Kokine Swimming Club, 34 Goodliffe Road, Tel. 50034.

Orient Club, 169 Shwegondine Road, Tel. 50869.

Rangoon Golf Club, Danyingone Mingaladon, Tel. 40001.

Rangoon Sailing Club, 132 Inya Road, Tel. 31298.

Useful Telephone Numbers

Ambulance, Tel. 192.

Fire, Tel. 191.

Police, Tel. 199 (emergency). Headquarters, Tel. 82511.

Red Cross (8 p.m. to 6 a.m.), Tel. 71111.

Rangoon General Hospital, Tel. 81722.

Telephone Inquiry, Tel. 100. Trunk call booking, Tel. 101. Fault complaint, Tel. 102. Time announcing machine, Tel. 150.

General Post Office, Tel. 85499.

Central Telegraph Office (inquiry), Tel. 81133.

Newspapers: The Guardian, Tel. 70150. Working People's Daily, Tel. 73202.

Customs House, Tel. 84533.

Ministry of Foreign Affairs (exchange), Tel. 83333.

Union Bank of Burma, Tel. 85300.

Railways (inquiry), Tel. 74027.

Burma Airways Corporation (booking), Tel. 74874, 77013. General manager, Tel. 82261. Freight, Tel. 40111. Traffic (inquiry), Tel. 40567, 40568.

Diplomatic Missions

Burmese Embassies

Following is a list of Burmese diplomatic and consular representatives abroad.

Australia—85 Mugga Way, Red Hill, Canberra, A.C.T. 2600, Tel. 95-0045.

Bangladesh—Plot No. 38, Road No. 11, Banani Model Town, Dacca. Tel. 30-1915, 30-1461.

Canada—116 Albert Street, Ottawa. Tel. 236-9613.

China—No. 6, Tung Chih Men Wai Street, Chaoyang District, Peking. Tel. 52-1488, 52-1425.

Czechoslovakia—Romania Rollanda 3, Bubenec 6, Prague. Tel. 38-1140, 38-1149.

Egypt—24 Mohamed Mazhar Zamalek, Cairo. Tel. 80-9154, 80-9176.

France—60 rue de Courelles, 75008 Paris. Tel. 622-5695.

Germany (East)—Niederschonhausen, Heinrich-Mann Street 36, 111 Berlin. Tel. 482-8634.

Germany (West)—Schumannstrasse 112, 53 Bonn. Tel. (0228)21-0191.

India—No. 3/50F, Shanti-path, Chanakyapuri, New Delhi. Tel. 70251. Consulate-General, Everest Building, 3rd Floor, 46C Chowringhee Road, Calcutta 16. Tel. 44-8224.

Hong Kong—Consulate-General, A.I.A. Building, Suite 106, No. 1 Stubbs Road, Hong Kong. Tel. 572-9241.

Indonesia—109 Jalan Haji Agus Salim, Jakarta. Tel. 40440, 47204.

Israel—12 Mattei Aharon Street, Ramt Gun, Tel Aviv. Tel. 78-3151.

Italy—Via Vincenzo Bellini, 20 Interno, 10098 Rome. Tel. 85-9374, 85-6863.

Japan—8-26, 4-chome, Kita Shinagawa, Shinagawa-ku, Tokyo. Tel. 441-9291.

Laos—Burmese ambassador resident at embassy to Vietnam in Hanoi.

Malaysia—7 Jalan Taman U Thant, Kuala Lumpur. Tel. 25798.

Nepal—Thapathali, Kathmandu. Tel. 13146, 14083.

Pakistan—368, Shalimar 6/3, Islamabad. Tel. 22460, 20123.

Philippines—Ground Floor, ADC Building, 6805 Ayala Avenue, Makati, Rizal, Manila. Tel. 87-2373.

Singapore—15 St. Martin's Drive, Singapore 10. Tel. 235-8763.

Sri Lanka—53 Rosmead Place, Colombo 7. Tel. 91964.

Switzerland—3 Giacomettistrasse, 3006 Bern. Tel. 43-3024.

Thailand—132 North Sathorn Road, Bangkok. Tel. 233-2237, 234-0278.

Union of Soviet Socialist Republics (U.S.S.R.)—41 Gertsena Street, Moscow. Tel. 291-0534.

United Kingdom—19A Charles Street, London W1. Tel. 629-9531, 629-4486, 629-6966, 499-8841.

United Nations—Permanent Mission of Burma to the United Nations, 10 East 77th Street, New

York, N.Y. 10021, U.S.A. Tel. (212) 535-1310.

United States of America—2300 "S" Street N.W., Washington, D.C. 20008. Tel. (202) 302-9044/6.

Vietnam—Hotel Thong Nhat, Hanoi. Tel. 52784, ext. 368.

Yugoslavia—72 Kneza Milosa, Belgrade. Tel. 645-420, 645-128.

Foreign Embassies in Rangoon

Australia—88 Strand Road, Tel. 80711.

Bangladesh—340 Prome Road. Tel. 23818, 32900.

Belgium—18B Inya Road. Tel. 32775.

China—1 Pyidaungsu Yeiktha. Tel. 82087, 80841.

Czechoslovakia—326 Prome Road. Tel. 30515.

Egypt—81 Pyidaungsu Yeiktha.

France—102 Pyidaungsu Yeiktha. Tel. 82122.

Germany (East)—60 Golden Valley. Tel. 30837, 30933.

Germany (West)—32 Natmauk Street. Tel. 50477, 50603.

Hungary—84 Inya Road. Tel. 31687.

India—545/547 Merchant Street. Tel. 82933.

Indonesia—100 Pyidaungsu Yeiktha. Tel. 81714, 83515 (after office hours).

Israel—49 Prome Road.

Italy—3 Lewis Road, Golden Valley. Tel. 30966, 30474.

Japan—100 Natmauk Road. Tel. 52288, 52640.

Korea (North)—30 Tank Road.

Korea (South)—591 Prome Road. Tel. 30497, 30655.

Malaysia—65 Windsor Road. Tel. 31031, 31677.

Nepal—16 Natmauk Yeiktha. Tel. 50633.

Norway (consulate)–48A Komin Kochin Road. Tel. 50011.

Pakistan—18 Windsor Road.

Philippines—11A Windermere Road. Tel. 32087 (consular section).

Poland—31 Aung Minggaung Avenue. Tel. 31562, 32617.

Romania—71 Mission Road.

Spain (consulate)—26 Prome Road, 7th Mile, Kaba Aye Post Office. Tel. 60723.

Sri Lanka—34 Fraser Road.

Sweden (consulate)—48A Komin Kochin Road, P. O. Box 1088. Tel. 50011.

Thailand—91 Prome Road.

Union of Soviet Socialist Republics (U.S.S.R.)—52 Prome Road.

United Kingdom—80 Strand Road. Tel. 81700.

United States of America—581 Merchant Street. Tel. 82055.

Vietnam—40 Komin Kochin Road. Tel. 50361.

Yugoslavia—39 Windsor Road. Tel. 30127, 30399.

Other Diplomatic Missions to Burma

Afghanistan—9A Ring Road, Lajpat Nagar III, New Delhi 24, India. Tel. 622161.

Austria—Maneeya Building, 3rd Floor, 518 Ploenchit Road, P. O. Box 27, Bangkok 5, Thailand. Tel. 252-8327, 525-9781.

Bulgaria—House No. 12, Road No. 127, Gul-shan Model Town, Dacca 12, Bangladesh.

Canada—11th Floor, Boonmitr Building, 138 Silom Road, P. O. Box 2090, Bangkok, Thailand. Tel. 234-1561/8.

Cuba—34 Ward Place, Colombo 7, Sri Lanka.

Denmark—10 Soi Attakarn Prasit, Sathorn Tai Road, Bangkok 12, Thailand. Tel. 286-3930.

Finland—15A Jalan Kusumah Atmaja, Jakarta, Indonesia. Tel. 34-6686, 34-5871.

Greece—16 Sundar Nagar, New Delhi, India. Tel. 61-7800.

Iran—65 Golf Links, New Delhi, India. Tel. 69-9521.

Iraq—169/71 Jor Bagh, New Delhi, India. Tel. 61-8011.

Laos—193 Sathorn Tai Road, Bangkok, Thailand. Tel. 286-0010.

Mongolia—No. 2, Hsiu Shui Pei Chien, Chien Kuo Men Wai, Peking, China.

Netherlands—6/50-F, Shantipath, Chanakyapuri, New Delhi, India. Tel. 69-9271.

New Zealand—P. O. Box 2003, Kuala Lumpur, Malaysia.

Nigeria—1 Panchsheel Marg, Chanakyapuri, New Delhi, India. Tel. 37-4454.

Norway—16 Surasak Road, off Silom Road, G.P.O. Box 81, Bangkok, Thailand. Tel. 31889, 30271.

Singapore—129 South Sathorn Road, Bangkok, Thailand. Tel. 286-2111, 286-1434, 286-9971.

Spain—12 Prithviraj Road, New Delhi, India. Tel. 37-5892.

Sweden—AIA Building, P. O. Box 239, Kuala Lumpur, Malaysia.

Switzerland—35 North Wireless Road, G.P.O. Box 821, Bangkok, Thailand. Tel. 252-8992/4.

Turkey—27 Jor Bagh, New Delhi, India. Tel. 61-1921.

International Organizations in Rangoon

Burma maintains membership in a large number of international organizations. Several of them have offices in Rangoon:

United Nations Program for Drug Abuse Control, Burma (UNPDAC), 557A Prome Road. Tel. 32301.

United Nations Childrens Fund (UNICEF), 132 University Avenue. Tel. 31107, 31895, 31287.

United Nations Development Program (UNDP), 24 Manawhari Road, Tel. 82144.

United Nations Information Center (UNIC), 24 Manawhari Road. Tel. 81037.

World Health Organization (WHO), 11 Goodliffe Road. Tel. 51673.

Shopping

Burma's markets and bazaars are the most interesting, and at the same time the most reasonable, places to shop for native arts and crafts. In Rangoon, the **Bogyoke Aung San Market** is open from 9:30 a.m. to 4:30 p.m. Monday through Saturday; other markets, including Mandalay's **Zegyo Market**, generally open early in the morning and remain open until dark. There are also separate night markets which set up on specified streets after dark; the best ones are in Rangoon's Chinese and Indian quarters, and in Mandalay on 84th Street between 26th and 28th roads.

Bazaars and markets thrive in Rangoon city. There are open-air markets across Bogyoke Aung San Street from the Bogyoke Market; at the corner of St. John's Road and Prome Road; and east of the Botataung Pagoda. The **Thein Gyi Zay** Indian market is just off Anawrahta Street, and there's a Chinese market at the corner of Maha Bandoola Street and Lanmadaw Road.

The entrances to the **Shwedagon Pagoda** are also bazaars—of some length, in fact, covering both sides of the stairways. The bazaar at the east entrance is possibly the most interesting: among the items frequently sold are puppets, drums, masks, toys, brassware, and metal goods including swords. The bazaar at the pagoda's south entrance is notable for wood and ivory carvings.

Wood carvings are also sold in quantity and quality at the **New Carving Shop**, 20 University Avenue. For other types of art work, try the **Loka Nath Art Gallery**, 62 Pansodan Street, or the **Aung Zeya Art Gallery**, 90 Kaba Aye Pagoda Road; and **Curio de City**, 35 Bahan Road, for antiques. In Mandalay, a variety of art work is sold during exhibitions at the **State School of Fine Arts, Music and Drama**.

A pricey selection of all types of Burmese handicrafts is always for sale at the **Diplomatic Shop**, 143–144 Sule Pagoda Road in Rangoon. Open 10 a.m. to 4 p.m. Monday through Friday and 10 a.m. to 1 p.m. Saturday, the Diplomatic Shop will accept only foreign exchange in its transactions.

There are gift shops at the Inya Lake and Strand hotels. Both are open 9:30 a.m. to 5 p.m. daily except Sunday.

Language

The Burmese language is a member of the Tibeto-Burman language family, which is in turn a subgroup of Sino-Tibetan. While 80 percent of Burma's diverse peoples speak this language, there remain more than 100 distinct languages and dialects spoken in different parts of the country. The great variation in cultural histories of the ethnic groups can be seen in their languages.

Burmese is thought to have originated in the Burmans' ancestral central Asian homeland. The language spread rapidly among Burma's Thai (Shan) and Mon-Khmer peoples during the 19th Century, when the last Mon Empire had declined and the Irrawaddy Delta was opened to rice cultivation, attracting many hill Karens.

Burmese script has an origin quite different than the written tongue. It derives from the Pali language of south India, and has strong similarities with the Telugu written language. The Mons had adopted the script during their interactions with Theravada Buddhist priests from south India, and the Burmans absorbed it after King Anawrahta's conquest of the Mon capital of Thaton in the 11th Century.

The Burmese alphabet consists of 44 letters: 32 consonants, eight vowels and four diphthongs. It is written and read from left to right, top to bottom.

The Burmese numerical system, although written in typically Burmese script, is based upon the Arabic and decimal systems in common use in the West.

Burmese Numerals

The Burmese Alphabet

Survival Burmese

The Burmese language is tonal, like Chinese. The way in which a word is pronounced affects its meaning: a single syllable, given different kinds of stress, may carry several distinctly different meanings.

In the following list of words and phrases, the following accent marks are used:

(no mark)	low even tone
(:)	long falling tone
(.)	short falling tone
(')	glottal stop or creaky tone

Transliteration into English is given according to William Cornyn's *Beginning Burmese*. A rendering into phonetic English is also given.

(Transliteration)	(Phonetic)	(English)
Numbers		
ti'	tit	one
hni'	nit	two
thoun:	thone	three
lei:	lay	four
nga:	ngar	five
hcau'	chak	six
hkun-ni'	kun nit	seven
hyi'	shit	eight
kou:	ko	nine
ta hse	ta sair	ten
hse. ti'	sair tit	eleven
hse. hni'	sair nit	twelve
hnahse	na sair	twenty
thoun:ze	thone sair	thirty
lei:ze	lay sair	forty
nga:ze	ngar sair	fifty
hcau'hse	chak sair	sixty
hkun-nahse	kun na sair	seventy
hyi'hse	shit sair	eighty
kou:ze	ko sair	ninety
ta ya:	ta yar	one hundred
ta taun:	ta taung	one thousand
Conversation		
nei kaun: the la:	Nay gaun the lah?	How are you?
nei kaun: ba de	Nay gaun ba day.	I am well.
nei ma kaun: ba bu:	Nay magaun ba boo.	I am not well.
be lou le:	Be low lay?	How's it? (informal)
kaun: de	Kaun day.	That's good.
na: le the la:	Na lay the lah?	Do you understand?
na: le ba de	Na lay ba day.	I understand.
na: male ba bu:	Na malay ba boo.	I do not understand.
hkamya	Kamyah.	Yes (male).
hyin	Shin.	Yes (female).
hou'ke.	Hout ke(t).	Yes (polite).
hou'ba de	Hout bah day.	Yes, that's right.
ma hou'ba bu:	Ma hout bah boo.	No, that's not so.
ba pyo: the le:	Bah pyaw the lay?	What are you saying?
pyan pyo: ba quon:	Byan pyaw ba own.	Please repeat.
pyei pyei pyo: ba	Byay byay pyaw bah.	Speak clearly.
ba hpyi' lou le:	Bah pyit lou lay?	Why?
nei ba zei	Nay bah zay.	Never mind.
kei' sa ma hyi ba bu:	Keit sa ma shi bah boo.	It doesn't matter.
ba le:	Bah lay?	What is it?
bama lou da' the la:	Bamah lou dat the lah?	Do you know Burmese?
ne: ne: be: da' ba de	Neh neh beh dat ba day.	Only a little.
kaun: kaun: da' te	Gaun gaun dat day.	He speaks well.
qin: ga lei' la:	Ing gah lay lah?	Are you English?
qin: ga lei' ma hou' ba bu	Ing gah lay ma hout ba boo.	No, I'm not English.
be ga la the le:	Beh gah lah the lay?	Where do you come from?
qameiyika pyei ga la de	Amay yi kah pyay gah lah day.	I come from America.
cei: zu: pyo: ba	Jay zu pyaw bah.	Please.
qamya: gyi: cei: zu: tin ba de	Amyah ee jay zu tin ba day.	Thank you very much.
thwa: me	Thwa may.	Goodbye.

Eating

ba htamin: sa: jin the le:	Bah tamin sah jin the lay?	What do you want to eat?
____hyi. the la:	____shee the lah?	Is there ____?
____sa: me	____sah meh.	I'll eat ____.
we' tha: hin	Wet that hin	Pork curry
ce' than: hin	Chet thah hin	Chicken curry
qame: tha: hin:	Amay thah hin	Beef curry
nga: hin:	Ngah hin	Fish curry
bazun hin:	Bazoon hin	Shrimp curry
ce' qu.	Chet oo	Egg
ce' qu. jo	Chet oo jaw	Fried egg
ngapi. jo	Ngapee	Shrimp paste
hkau'hswe	Kaut sway	Noodles with curry soup
hin: thi hin: ywe'	Hin thee hin youwet	Vegetables
thi' thi:	Thit thee	Fruit
ma sa: jin ba bu:	Ma sah jin ba boo.	I don't want to eat.
ba thau' ma le:	Bah thaut ma lay?	What will you drink?
____thau' me	____that may.	I'll drink ____.
kahpi	Kahpee	Coffee
lahpe	Lapay	Black tea with milk and sugar
lahpe yei jan:	Lapay yay john	Plain green tea
yei nwei	Yay nway	Hot tea
yei	Yay	Water
biya	Beeyah	Beer
zi: hpyo yei	Zee pyaw yay	Plum juice soda
hin: jou	Hin joe	Hot soup
ba hma. ma thau' ba bu:	Bah hmat ma thaut ba boo.	I don't want to drink.

Directions

____ ba hma le:	____ beh hmah lay?	Where is the ____?
be kou thwa: ma le:	Beh gou thwa melay?	Where are you going?
mi: yahta: youn	Mee yatah yown	Railway station
hsei: youn	Say yown	Hospital
you' hyin bwe	Yout shin bwe	Theater
ho te	Ho tay	Hotel
sa dai'	Sah daik	Post Office
ban dai'	Ban daik	Bank
hsabin hnya'thama:	Sabin hnyat the mah	Barber
be do thwa: ma le:	Beh daw thwa me lay?	When will you go?
be qachein pya. me le:	Beh a chain pyat me lay?	When will it start?
be qachein htwe' ma le:	Beh a chain twet ma lay?	When will it leave?
tana-yi	Ta nai yee.	One o'clock.
hnana-yi	Na nai yee.	Two o'clock.
thoun:na-yi	Thone nai yee.	Three o'clock.
be lau' le:	Beh laut lay?	How much is it? (price)
taja' nga:pya'	Ta jat ngar byaz.	One kyat five pyas.

An-ah-deh

Every language contains some expressions which don't lend themselves to translation. Burmese is no exception.

The noble art of Burmese courtesy and persuasion lies behind the principle of "an-ah-deh." This entails never using the word "No," and never putting anyone else in the position of having to use it. At the same time, "an-ah-deh" allows a Burmese to convince another person that the thing that person wants but cannot achieve is, in fact, not worthy of aspiration.

"An-ah-deh" must be learned and felt inwardly. It is a true art to meet another person at a halfway point where neither side will lose face in the confrontation.

There is a difference between a lie and a statement that is not exactly true. Drawing the fine line in the right place is, for the Burmese, indicative of good manners and upbringing.

Because this principle is integral to the Burmese social graces, the people of Burma find it difficult to exclude foreign visitors from "an-ah-deh." It is indicative of Burma's deep-rooted culture—an expression of a view of life both tolerant and compromising, often the very antithesis of the West's "down-to-earth" mentality.

In the Westerner's dealings with Burmese officialdom, he will often encounter this "an-ah-deh" approach to problems, coupled with a marked aversion for making decisions. In some cases, this can be very frustrating and lead to considerable delays. The Westerner simply must be patient and try to understand the underlying reason for the Burmese behavior.

Suggested Readings

General Interest

Bixler, Norma. *Burma: A Profile*. New York: Praeger, 1971. A well done general survey.

Burma Research Society. *50th Anniversary Publication* (two volumes). Rangoon: 1961. Highlights of 50 years of scholarly writings.

Collis, Maurice. *Lords of the Sunset*. New York: Dodd Mead, 1938. A tour of the Shan States.

Donnison, F.S.V. *Burma*. New York: Praeger, 1970. The country from a patronizing British standpoint.

Enriquez, C.M.D. *A Burmese Loneliness*. Calcutta: Thacker, Spink 1918. Travels in the Shan States.

Esche, Otto von. *Burma: Land und Leute*. Leipzig: Brockhaus, 1963.

Henderson, John W., and others. *Area Handbook for Burma*. Washington, D.C.: American University Foreign Area Studies, 1971. An overview.

Kessel, Joseph. *Mogok: La Vallée des Rubis*. Paris: Gallimard, 1955.

Keyes, Charles F. *The Golden Peninsula: Culture and Adaptation in Mainland Southeast Asia*. New York: Macmillan, 1977. An anthropologist studies changes in the region's Buddhist societies.

Kipling, Rudyard. *Letters From the East*. London: 1889. The author's travels through Asia.

Maring, Joel M. and Ester G. *Historical and Cultural Dictionary of Burma*. Metuchen, N.J.: The Scarecrow Press, 1973.

Maugham, Somerset. *The Gentleman in the Parlour*. Garden City, N.Y.: Doubleday, Doran & Co., 1930. Subtitled: A Record of a Journey From Rangoon to Haiphong.

Nash, Manning. *The Golden Road to Modernity: Village Life in Contemporary Burma*. New York: Wiley, 1965. A study of peasant agricultural society.

Scott, Sir James G. *Burma: From the Earliest Day to the Present Day*. New York: Alfred A. Knopf, 1924.

Shway Yoe (Sir J.G. Scott). *The Burman: His Life and Notions*. London: Macmillan, 1882. Two volumes. A gold mine of cultural information from a 19th Century British colonial official.

Storz, H.U. *Birma: Land, Geschichte, Wirtschaft*. Wiesbaden: Otto Harrassowitz, 1967. German-language survey.

Theroux, Paul. *The Great Railway Bazaar: By Train Through Asia*. New York: Random House, 1975. Insightful, amusing account of the author's railway adventures.

Trager, Helen G. *We the Burmese*. New York: Praeger, 1969. Burmese life and culture through its people's eyes.

General History

Bennett, Paul J. *Conference Under the Tamarind Tree*. New Haven, Conn.: Yale University Southeast Asian Studies, 1971. Three essays on Burmese history.

Cady, John F. *A History of Modern Burma*. Ithaca, N.Y.: Cornell University Press, 1958. The standard history of Burma since the 18th Century.

Hall, D.G.E. *Burma*. London: Hutchinson's University Library, 1960. A brief but complete history.

Hall, D.G.E. *A History of Southeast Asia*. New York: St. Martin's Press, 1968. Third edition. The most comprehensive book yet published about this exotic region.

Harvey, Godfrey E. *History of Burma*. London: Longmans, Green, 1925. Reprinted 1967. A detailed treatment from ancient times to 1824.

Htin Aung. *A History of Burma*. New York: Columbia University Press, 1967. A Burmese view of the nation's history.

Phayre, Sir Arthur P. *History of Burma*. London: Trübner, 1883. Reprinted 1967. The first formal history of Burma by a Westerner.

Trager, Frank N. *Burma From Kingdom to Republic*. New York: Praeger, 1966. A historical and political analysis.

Ancient History

Htin Aung. *Burmese History Before 1287*. Oxford, England: Asoka Society, 1970. "A defence of the Chronicles."

Humble, Richard. *Marco Polo*. New York: G.P. Putnam's Sons, 1975. Easy-reading survey of the travels of Polo.

Luce, Gordon H. *Old Burma—Early Pagan*. Ascona, Switzerland: Artibus Asiae, 1970. Three volumes. The crowning achievement of a lifetime of study of the art and architecture of 10th to 12th Century Pagan.

Pe Maung Tin and Gordon H. Luce. *The Glass Palace Chronicle of the Kings of Burma*. Oxford, England: Oxford University Press, 1923. Also, Rangoon: Burma Research Society, 1960. English translation of the royal chronicle of Burma, first written in 1829.

Yule, Sir Henry. *The Book of Ser Marco Polo*. London: John Murray, 1929. Polo's journal edited by Yule.

European Contact

Anderson, John M.D. *English Intercourse With Siam in the 17th Century*. London: Kegan Paul, Trench, Trübner, 1890.

Cox, Hiram. *Journal of a Residence in the Burmahn Empire, and more particularly at the Court of Amarapoorah*. London: John Warren and G. & W.B. Whittaker, 1821. Establishes a pattern of anti-Burmese writing by British authors.

Collis, Maurice. *The Land of the Great Image*. New York: Alfred A. Knopf, 1943. The experiences of Friar Manrique of Arakan.

Dalrymple, A. *Oriental Repository*. London: Ballantine and Law, 1808. The East India Company in Burma, 1695 to 1761.

Fitch, Ralph. "The Voyage of Mr. Ralph Fitch, Merchant of London, to Ormuz & so to Goa in the East Indies, 1583 to 1591." In Volume IX of John Pinkerton, editor, *A general collection of the best*

and most interesting voyages and travels ...,
London, 1808–1814.

Hunter, W. A. *A Concise Account of the Kingdom of Pegu*. Calcutta: John Hay, 1785. From the East India Company viewpoint.

O'Connor, V. C. Scott. *Mandalay and Other Cities of the Past in Burma*. London: Hutchinson, 1907.

Sangermano, Father Vicentius. *Description of the Burmese Empire*. Westminster, England: Archibald Constable, 1893. Third Edition. (First published in Rome in 1833.) A Barnabite missionary in Burma, 1783 to 1803.

Symes, Michael. *An Account of the Embassy to the Kingdom of Ava sent by the Governor-General of India in 1795*. London: W. Bulmer, 1800. Keen observations on all aspects of Burmese life.

Symes, Michael. *Journal of his Second Embassy to the Court of Ava in 1802*. London: George Allen and Unwin, 1955.

Yule, Henry. *A narrative of the mission sent by the Governor-General of India to the Court of Ava in 1855*. London: Smith, Elder, 1858. An intelligence report with excellent plates and sketches.

The British Colonial Era

Anderson, John M.D. *Mandalay to Momein*. London: Macmillan, 1876. Reprinted 1979. Subtitled: A narrative of the two expeditions to western China of 1868 and 1875 under Col. Edward B. Sladen and Col. Horace Browne. Good data about Shan and Kachin areas.

Banerjee, A.C. *Annexation of Burma*. Calcutta: A. Mukherjee, 1944. British policy toward Burma.

Bigandet, Father Paul A. *An Outline of the History of the Catholic Burmese Mission From the Year 1720 to 1887*. Rangoon: 1887. A good study by a French missionary.

Bird, George W. *Wanderings in Burma*. London: Simpkin, Marshall, Hamilton, Kent, 1897. British travel book.

Browne, Horace A. *Reminiscences of the Court of Mandalay*. Woking, England: Oriental Institute, 1907. Extracts from the diary of England's last resident at the Court of Mandalay.

Bruce, George. *The Burma Wars, 1824–1886*. London: Hart-Davis MacGibbon, 1973. A review of the three Anglo-Burmese wars.

Chong, Siok-hwa. *The Rice Industry of Burma 1852–1940*. Kuala Lumpur: University of Malaya, 1968. Scholarly treatment of the industry's growth.

Collis, Maurice. *Into Hidden Burma*. London: Faber and Faber, 1953. Autobiography of a British colonial administrator.

Cooler, Richard M. *British Romantic Views of the First Anglo-Burmese War, 1824–26*. DeKalb, Ill.: Northern Illinois University, 1977. Catalogue of prints for an Asian exhibition.

Crawford, John. *Journal of an Embassy From the Governor-General of India to the Court of Ava in 1827*. London: Henry Colburn, 1829. Narrative with ethnic and social commentaries.

Crosthwaite, Sir Charles. *The Pacification of Burma*. London: Edward Arnold, 1912. The end of Burma's traditional village governments.

Foucar, E.C.V. *Mandalay the Golden*. London: Dennis Dobson, 1963. First published in 1946 as *They Reigned in Mandalay*. The city's royal era.

Furnivall, J.S. *Colonial Policy and Practice*. New York: Cambridge University Press, 1948. How the British ran Burma.

Fytche, Albert. *Burma Past and Present*. London: Kegan Paul, 1878. Two volumes. Burma during the British era.

Gouger, H. *A personal narrative of two years imprisonment in Burma 1824–1826*. London: John Murray, 1860. A British merchant's account.

Hall, Gordon L. *Golden Boats from Burma*. Philadelphia: Macrae Smith, 1961. The life of Ann Hasseltine Judson, the first American woman in Burma.

Htin Aung. *The Stricken Peacock*. Den Haag: Martinus Nijhoff, 1965. Anglo-Burmese relations between 1752 and 1948.

Moscotti, Albert D. *British Policy in Burma, 1917–1937*. Honolulu: University Press of Hawaii, 1974.

Orwell, George. *Burmese Days*. London: Secker and Warburg, 1934. Reprinted 1975. Bittersweet novel about British colonial rule.

Rawson, Geoffrey. *Road to Mandalay*. New York: Harcourt Brace and World, 1967. A popular account of the end of Burmese royalty and the British takeover.

Singhal, D.P. *The Annexation of Upper Burma*. Singapore: Eastern Universities Press, 1960.

Stewart, A.T.Q. *The Pagoda War*. London: Faber, 1972. Subtitled: "Lord Dufferin and the fall of the Kingdom of Ava, 1885–86."

The Second World War

Collis, Maurice. *Last and First in Burma*. London: Faber and Faber, 1956. An account of the country during and after the war.

Fellowes-Gordon, Ian. *Amiable Assassins: The Story of the Kachin Guerrillas of North Burma*. London: Robert Hale, 1957. Freedom fighters against the Japanese.

Jesse, Tennyson. *The Story of Burma*. London: Macmillan, 1946. A wartime account.

Kinvig, C. *Death Railway*. London: 1973.

Morrison, Ian. *Grandfather Longlegs*. London: Faber and Faber, 1946. The biography of Major H.P. Seagrim, who stayed behind Japanese lines in Burma.

Nu, Thakin. *Burma Under the Japanese*. London: Macmillan, 1954. An important account of the occupation.

Seagrave, Gordon S. *Burma Surgeon*. New York: W.W. Norton, 1943. An important work about the life of a wartime doctor.

Seagrave, Gordon S. *Burma Surgeon Returns*. New York: W.W. Norton, 1946. More of the same.

Slater, Robert. *Guns Through Arcady: Burma and the Burma Road*. Madras, India: Diocesan Press, 1943. An account of events leading to the Japanese invasion.

Slim, W.J. *Defeat Into Victory*. London: Cassell, 1956. A good autobiographical account of the war, by the British military leader.

Stilwell, Joseph. *The Stilwell Papers*. Edited and arranged by Theodore H. White. New York: William Sloane Associates, 1948. "Vinegar Joe" in his own words.

Takeyama, Michio. *Harp of Burma*. Tokyo: Charles E. Tuttle, 1966. First published in Japanese in 1949. Novel about the Japanese experience in wartime Burma.

Tuchmann, Barbara W. *Stilwell and the American Experience in China, 1911–1945*. New York: Macmillan, 1971. A very important history and biography.

Williams, J.H. *Elephant Bill*. Garden City, N.Y.: Doubleday, 1950. An autobiography by the commander of a World War Two elephant brigade.

Contemporary Burma

Butwell, Richard. *U Nu of Burma*. Stanford, Calif.: Stanford University Press, 1963. Second edition, 1969. A political biography.

Maung Maung, editor. *Aung San of Burma*. Den Haag: Martinus Nijhoff, 1962. Collected writings by and about the nation's founding father.

Maung Maung. *Burma and General Ne Win*. Bombay, India: Asia Publishing House, 1969. A Burmese interpretation of the nationalist movement.

McAlister, John T. Jr., editor. *Southeast Asia: The Politics of National Integration*. New York: Random House, 1973. A collection of 30 interpretive essays, several specifically on contemporary Burma.

McCoy, Alfred W. *The Politics of Heroin in Southeast Asia*. New York: Harper & Row, 1972. A fascinating expose of the web of international involvement in the Golden Triangle.

Nu, U. *U Nu: Saturday's Son*. New Haven, Conn.: Yale University Press, 1975. The former prime minister's autobiography.

Pye, Lucian W. *Politics, Personality and Nation Building: Burma's Search for Identity*. New Haven, Conn.: Yale University Press, 1962. An analysis of events in postwar Burma.

Silverstein, Josef. *Burma: Military Rule and the Politics of Stagnation*. Ithaca, N.Y.: Cornell University Press, 1977. An analysis of Ne Win's politics.

Silverstein, Josef, compiler. *The Political Legacy of Aung San*. Ithaca, N.Y.: Cornell University Press, 1972.

Sitte, Fritz. *Rebellenstaat im Burma-dschungel*. Graz, Austria: Verlag Styria, 1979. A German-language study of Burma's ethnic rebellions.

Tinker, Hugh. *The Union of Burma*. London: Oxford University Press, 1967. Fourth edition. A study of Burma's first years of independence.

Ethnic Minorities

Cochrane, Wilbur W. *The Shans*. Rangoon: Government Printing Office, 1915. Reprinted 1978. A missionary's account.

Colquhoun, Archibald R. *Amongst the Shans*. New York: Schribner and Welford, 1885. Reprinted 1970. Of historical interest.

Enriquez, C.M.D. *A Burmese Arcady*. London: Seeley, Service, 1923. Reprinted 1978. An account of the Burmese hill tribes.

Enriquez, C.M.D. *Races of Burma*. Calcutta: Government of India Central Publication Depart-

ment, 1924. Reprinted 1978. Descriptive account for British military recruiting purposes.

Gilhodes, Charles. *The Kachins: Religion and Customs*. Calcutta: Catholic Orphan Press, 1922. Strong on folklore and mythology.

Hanson, Ola. *The Kachins, Their Customs and Traditions*. Rangoon: American Baptist Mission Press, 1913. A missionary account.

Head, W.R. *Handbook of Haka Chin Customs*. Rangoon: Government Printing Office, 1917.

Leach, Edmund R. *Political Systems of Highland Burma*. Cambridge, Mass.: Harvard University Press, 1954. A study of Kachin social structure. An anthropological classic.

Leber, Frank, Gerald C. Hickey and John K. Musgrave. *Ethnic Groups of Mainland Southeast Asia*. New Haven, Conn.: Human Relations Area File Press, 1964. Standard reference volume.

Lehman, Frederick Y. *The Structure of Chin Society*. Urbana, Ill.: University of Illinois Press, 1963. Contemporary anthropological study.

Marshall, Harry I. *The Karens of Burma*. London: Longmans, Green, 1945.

McCall, Anthony G. *Lushai Chrysalis*. London: Luzac, 1949. A study of the Chins of the Indian border region.

McMahon, A.R. *The Karens of the Golden Chersonese*. New York: 1978.

Milne, Leslie. *The Home of an Eastern Clan*. New York: Clarendon Press, 1924. Reprinted 1978. A study of the Palaungs of the Shan States.

Milne, Leslie. *Shans at Home*. London: Murray, 1910. Reprinted 1970. Descriptive account.

Scott, Sir James G. *Burma: A Handbook of Practical Information*. London: Daniel O'Connor, 1921. Third edition. Reference book on ethnic minorities.

Yegar, Moshe. *The Muslims of Burma*. Wiesbaden: O. Harrassowitz, 1972.

Religion

Appleton, George. *Buddhism in Burma*. London: Longmans, Green, 1943.

Bigandet, Father Paul A. *The Life or Legend of Gautama, the Buddha of the Burmese*. Two volumes. London: Kegan Paul, Trench, Trübner, 1911. Reprinted 1978.

Bode, Mabel Haynes. *The Pali Literature of Burma*. London: Royal Asiatic Society, 1909. Reprinted 1965.

Fielding-Hall, H. *The Soul of a People*. London: Macmillan, 1909.

Htin Aung. *Folk Elements in Burmese Buddhism*. London: Oxford University Press, 1962.

King, Winston L. *A Thousand Lives Away: Buddhism in Contemporary Burma*. Oxford, England: Bruno Cassirer, 1964. One of the best modern studies, by an American scholar.

Lester, Robert C. *Theravada Buddhism in Southeast Asia*. Ann Arbor, Mich.: University of Michigan Press, 1973. Good basic survey.

MacGregor, Allan. *Die Religion von Burma*. Breislau, Germany: 1911. (Reprinted as *The Religion of Burma and Other Papers* by Ananda Maitreya. New York: 1978.)

Mahasi Sayadaw. *Mahasi Abroad*. Rangoon: 1979.

Mendelson, E. Michael. *Sangha and State in*

Burma. Ithaca, N.Y.: Cornell University Press, 1975. Relations between the government and Buddhist monks.

Pe Maung Tin. *Buddhist Devotion and Meditation*. London: Pali Text Society, 1964.

Ray, Nihar-ranjan. *Brahmanical Gods in Burma*. Calcutta: University of Calcutta Press, 1932. Study of iconography by a Sanskrit scholar.

Ray, Nihar-ranjan. *An Introduction to the Study of Theravada Buddhism in Burma*. Calcutta: University of Calcutta Press, 1946. Reprinted in 1978. Historical treatment.

Ray, Nihar-ranjan. *Sanskrit Buddhism in Burma*. Calcutta: University of Calcutta Press, 1936.

Sarkisyanz, Emanuel. *Buddhist Backgrounds of the Burmese Revolution*. Den Haag: Martinus Nijhoff, 1965.

Smith, Donald E. *Religion and Politics in Burma*. Princeton, N.J.: Princeton University Press, 1965. Excellent study of the impact of Buddhism on the nationalist movement.

Soni, R.L. *A Cultural Study of the Burmese Era*. Mandalay: Institute of Buddhist Culture, 1955. Burmese history from the viewpoint of Buddhist cosmology.

Spiro, Melford E. *Buddhism and Society*. New York: Harper and Row, 1970. Scholarly treatment.

Spiro, Melford E. *Burmese Supernaturalism*. Englewood, N.J.: Prentice-Hall, 1967. Expanded edition, 1977. A fascinating study.

Temple, Sir Richard C. *The 37 Nats*. London: W. Griggs, 1906. Interesting work, especially valuable for its illustrations.

Uhlig, Helmut. *Auf den Spuren Buddhas*. Berlin: Safari Verlag, 1973.

Warren, Henry Clarke. *Buddhism in Translations*. Cambridge, Mass.: Harvard University Press, 1896. Reprinted 1953, 1962, 1976. Perhaps the best translation of the most important Buddhism scriptures.

Arts and Culture

Allott, Anne. "Burmese Literature" in *A Guide to Eastern Literatures,* edited by David M. Lang. New York: Praeger, 1971.

Brandon, James R. *Brandon's Guide to Theater in Asia*. Honolulu: The University Press of Hawaii, 1976. What to see, where to go.

Franz, H.G. *Von Gandhara bis Pagan*. Graz, Austria: 1979.

Frederic, Louis. *The Art of Southeast Asia*. New York: 1965.

Griswold, Alexander B. *The Art of Burma, Korea, Tibet*. New York: Methuen, 1964.

Htin Aung. *Burmese Drama*. Calcutta: Oxford University Press, 1937.

Htin Aung. *Burmese Folk Tales*. Calcutta: Oxford University Press, 1948.

Htin Aung. *Burmese Monks' Tales*. New York: Columbia University Press, 1966.

Htin Aung. *A Kingdom Lost for a Drop of Honey and Other Burmese Folk Tales*. With Helen G. Trager. New York: Parents Magazine Press, 1968. For a young readership.

Htin Aung. *Thirty Burmese Tales*. London: Oxford University Press, 1958.

Khin Myo Chit. *The 13-Carat Diamond and Other Stories*. Rangoon: Sarpay Lawka, 1969.

Lustig, Freidrich von. *Burmese Classical Poems*. Rangoon: Rangoon Gazette, 1966.

Munsterberg, Hugo. *Art of India and Southeast Asia*. New York: H.N. Abrams, 1970.

Myint Thein. *Burmese Folk Songs*. Oxford, England: Asoka Society, 1969.

Myint Thein. *When at Nights I Strive to Sleep*. Oxford, England: Asoka Society, 1971.

Rawson, Philip. *The Art of Southeast Asia*. New York: Praeger, 1967.

Swaan, W. *Lost Cities of Asia*. New York: G.P. Putnam's Sons, 1966. A view of Kampuchea's Angkor Wat, Burma's Pagan, and three sites in Sri Lanka through art and architecture.

Thomann, Thomas H. *Pagan: Ein Jahrtausend Buddhistischer Tempelkunst,* Stuttgart: Walter Seifert, 1923. "A thousand years of Buddhist temple art." One of the few art books on Pagan.

Withey, J.A., and Kenneth Sein. *The Great Po Sein: A Chronicle of the Burmese Theater*. Bloomington, Ind.: Indiana University Press, 1965. A unique look at the *pwe* and its greatest performer.

Travel Guides

Diezmann, Dr. E. *Birma*. Pforzheim, Germany: 1979. German-language guide.

Far Eastern Economic Review. *All-Asia Guide*. 11th Edition. Hong Kong: 1980.

Hudson, Roy. *The Magic Guide to Burma*. Chiang Mai, Thailand: Hudson Enterprises, 1977.

Klein, J. *Birmanie*. Paris: 1975. French.

Le Ramier, Gabriel. *Birmanie*. Paris: 1978. French.

Moisy, C. *Birmanie*. Lausanne, Switzerland: Editions Rencontre, 1964. French.

Treichler, R. *Südostasien selbst en tdecken*. Zürich, Switzerland: 1979. German.

Wheeler, Tony. *Burma: A Travel Survival Kit*. South Yarra, Vic., Australia: Lonely Planet,

1979. Good suggestions for the shoestring traveler.

Zagorski, Ulrich. *Burma, Unknown Paradise.* Tokyo: Kodansha International, 1972. A pictorial guide.

Burmese Publications

Aung Thaw. *Historical Sites in Burma.* Rangoon: Rangoon University, 1972.

Burma Gazetteers. Rangoon: Government Printing Office, 1907 through 1967. Regional studies of Akyab, Amherst, Bassein, Bhamo, Henzada, Insein, Kyaukse, Lower Chindwin, Mandalay, Myitkyina, Northern Arakan, Pegu, Rangoon, Ruby Mines, Salween, Sandoway, Shwebo, Syriam, Tharrawaddy, Toungoo, Upper Burma and Shan States, Upper Chindwin, and Yamethin districts.

Directorate of Archaeological Survey. *The Mandalay Palace.* Rangoon: Government Printing Office, 1963.

Directorate of Archaeological Survey. *Pictorial Guide to Pagan.* Rangoon: Government Printing Office, 1963.

Directorate of Information. *The Golden Glory: Shwedagon Pagoda.* Rangoon: Government Printing Office, 1956.

Directorate of Information. *A Handbook on Burma.* Rangoon: Government Printing Office, 1968.

Directorate of Information. *Rangoon: A Pocket Guide.* Rangoon: Government Printing Office, 1956.

E Maung. *Burmese Buddhist Law.* Rangoon: New Light of Burma Press, 1937. Reprinted 1978.

Duroiselle, Charles. *Guide to the Mandalay Palace.* Rangoon: 1925. Interesting as a pre-World War Two account.

Khin Myo Chit. *Anawrahta of Burma.* Rangoon: Sarpay Beikman, 1970. Historical novel.

Lu Pe Win. *Historic Sites and Monuments of Mandalay and Environs.* Rangoon: Government Printing Office, 1960.

Lu Pe Win. *Historic Sites and Monuments of Pagan.* Rangoon: Government Printing Office.

Ministry of Union Culture. *Manao-Kachin Festival.* Rangoon: Government Printing Office.

Bibliographies

Aung Thwin. *Southeast Asia Research Tools: Burma.* Honolulu: University of Hawaii Asian Studies Program, 1979.

Trager, Frank N. *Burma: A Selected and Annotated Bibliography.* New Haven, Conn.: Human Relations Area Files Press, 1973. The most complete bibliography available.

ART/PHOTO CREDITS

Appendices

Plans of Cities and Temples

The following diagrams are intended to give the student of ancient Burma an insight into Burmese city planning and religious architecture of past centuries. They will also help the visitor meander through the maze of passageways in some temples.

(Figure 1)
Plan of Ava, circa 1837. Note lion-head design.

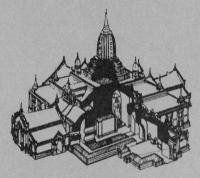

(Figure 2)
Interior plan of Ananda Temple, Pagan.

(Figure 3)
Cross-section of Ananda Temple, Pagan.

(Figure 4)
Ground plan of Ananda Temple, Pagan.

(Figure 5)
Cross-section of Thatbyinnyu Temple, Pagan.

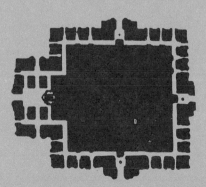

(Figure 6)
Ground plan (lower floor), Thatbyinnyu Temple, Pagan.

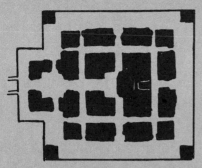

(Figure 7)
Ground plan (upper floor), Thatbyinnyu
Temple, Pagan.

(Figure 10)
Cross-section of Dhammayangyi Temple, Pagan.

(Figure 8)
Cross-section of Shwegugyi Temple, Pagan.

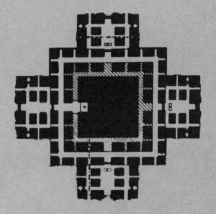

(Figure 11)
Ground plan of Dhammayangyi Temple, Pagan.

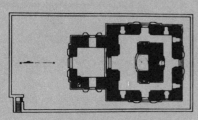

(Figure 9)
Ground plan of Shwegugyi Temple, Pagan.

(Figure 12)
Cross-section of Pitakat Taik, Pagan.

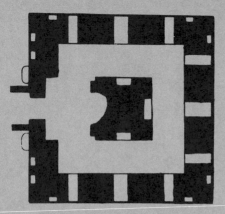

(Figure 13)
Ground plan of Nat-hlaung Kyaung, Pagan.

(Figure 16)
Cross-section of Abeyadana Temple, Pagan.

(Figure 14)
Cross-section of Nanpaya Temple, Pagan.

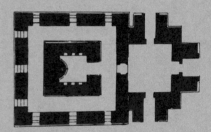

(Figure 17)
Ground plan of Abeyadana Temple, Pagan.

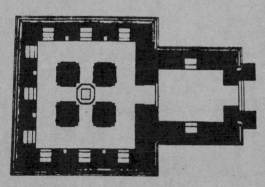

(Figure 15)
Ground plan of Nanpaya Temple, Pagan.

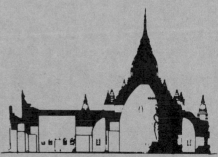

(Figure 18)
Cross-section of Nagayon Temple, Pagan.

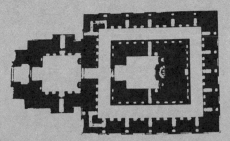

(Figure 19)
Ground plan of Nagayon Temple, Pagan.

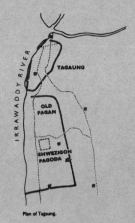

Plan of Tagaung.

(Figure 22)
Town plan of Tagaung and Old Pagan.

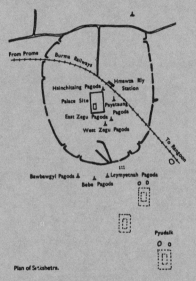

Plan of Srikshetra.

(Figure 20)
Town plan of Sri Ksetra.

(Figure 23)
Ground plan of Shittaung Temple, Myohaung.

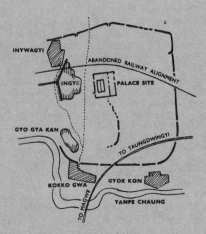

(Figure 21)
Town plan of Beikthano.

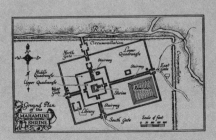

(Figure 24)
Ground plan of Mahamuni Shrine, Dhannavati.

Glossary

abhidhamma—Buddhist scriptures dealing with interpretation of the Dharma.
acheit-htamein—ceremonial *longyi*.
Airawata—white elephant on which Brahmin god Indra rides; the Irrawaddy River got its name from this.
an-ah-deh—cultural principle of never saying "No" and never forcing others to say it.
Ananda—cousin and favorite pupil of the Buddha.
anyein pwe—"folksy" theater form combining dance and story telling.
Areindama— King Anawrahta's mythical spear.
arhat—Buddhist saint.
Arimaddana—another name for Pagan.
Ari monks—separatist religious sect with Tantric beliefs who wielded great influence in ancient Burma.
Ashoka — great Buddhist king from India's Maurya dynasty (ca. 274 to 232 B.C.).
avatar—past or future incarnation of important religious figure, especially Vishnu.

Bakri Idd—Islamic religious festival in late November.
baungyit—vaulted turban in stupa architecture.
Bayingyi—a Eurasian exiled to Upper Burma in 17th Century.
bidauk—temple drum.
bo—military officer.
Bodhgaya—place in India where Gautama achieved enlightenment and Buddhahood.
Bodhi tree—tree under which the Gautama Buddha gained enlightenment.
bodhisattva—future Buddha; someone on path to enlightenment.
Boddhahu—Burmese day of Wednesday, midnight to noon.
Brahma—the "creator" of the Hindu pantheon.
bu—a gourd-like climbing plant.
Buddha—one who has achieved enlightenment and broken the cycle of reincarnation *(samsara); more* specifically, Gautama, the last Buddha.

cetiya—religious monument.
chakravarti—universal monarch; a true Buddhist king.
cheroot—a hand-rolled cigar, green or white in color.
chettyar—one of a south Indian caste of money-lenders.
chindawya—footprint of the Buddha.
chinlon—Burmese national sport, played by keeping a caneball in the air as long as possible using only the feet and knees.
chinthe—mythological leogryph (half-lion, half-griffin); temple guardian.
crore—type of measurement equal to 10 million units.

daboai—deadly poisonous snake, also known as Russel's viper.
Daw—appellation for older or superior woman.
deva—goddess.

Devadatta—cousin of the Buddha who attempted to assassinate him with an evil elephant.
Dewali—Hindu festival, usually in October.
Dhammasetkya—full-moon day of *Waso* (June/July), the beginning of Buddhist Lent.
Dharma—Buddhist doctrine (Sanskrit; *dhamma* in Pali).
dvarapala—warrior; temple guardian.

eingyi—transparent silk blouse worn with the *longyi*.

galon—mythological bird guarding Mount Meru; also known as *garuda*.
Ganesh—elephant-headed son of Shiva.
gaung-baung—traditional male Burmese head-dress.
Gautama—the historical Buddha, as he was known before his enlightenment.
Glass Palace Chronicle—Record of Burma's history, combining fact and legend, written in 1829.
Golden Triangle—opium-producing region on border of Burma, Thailand and Laos.

hamsa—mythological duck, sacred bird of Pegu dynasty; also known as *hintha*.
Hinayana—the branch of Buddhism, also known as Theravada, dominant in Burma; the "lesser vehicle."
Hluttaw—Burmese house of representatives.
hne—oboe-like woodwind, part of Burmese orchestra.
hnget pyaw bu—the "banana bud" in stupa architecture.
Htamane—February harvest festival; also, a food offering fixed at this time.
hti—the "umbrella" above a stupa or pagoda.
htwa—unit of measurement, sometimes called a span, about nine inches.

Indra—Vedic and Hindu god.

Jambudipa—southern island of the Burmese Buddhist cosmos, on which Burmese are considered to live.
Jataka—a tale about a previous life of the Buddha.

Kakusandha—one of the four most recent Buddhas.
kalasa—Indian-style pottery.
kappa—a unit of cosmological time-distance, equal to 4,320 million years, the duration of one universe.
karaweik—mythological water bird, the heraldic bird of Burmese kings.
karma—one's actions and the consequences of those actions, in this life or in reincarnation.
Kason—Burmese month falling in April/May.
Kassapa—one of the four most recent Buddhas.
kaukswe—chicken and noodle dish popular among Burmese.
khaung laung bon—the main bell of a stupa.
Ko—appellation for younger or inferior men.
Konagamana—one of the four most recent Buddhas.

Konbaung—the last Burmese dynasty, which ended in 1885.
ku—cave-temple, place of meditation; used in reference to any temple.
kvahlan—lotus-petal decoration on a stupa.
kyaik—pagoda.
kyat — primary unit of Burmese currency, 7.35 of which equal one U.S. dollar (as of January 1982).
kyaung—Buddhist monastery.
kye-waing—gong section in Burmese orchestra.
kyunpaw—a floating garden of Inle Lake's Intha people.

lakh—type of measurement equal to 100,000 units.
La Mu—the sour fruit of the *sonneratia* tree, which grows abundantly in tidal creeks.
lingwin—cymbals, used in Burmese orchestra.
longyi—sarong-like wrap-around garment, worn at ankle length by both men and women.

Ma—appellation for women of average or equal status.
maha—great.
mahaparinirvana—the Buddha's death, or transition into nirvana.
Mahayana—Buddhism's "Great Vehicle," dominant in East Asia.
mahout—elephant rider.
Maitreya—the future Buddha.
manokthiha — a king of sphinx, often a temple guardian.
manusiha — mythical half-man, half-beast.
Mara—god of pleasure, passion and death; embodiment of temptation and evil.
Maung—appellation for men of average or equal status.
Mintha and Minthani—the prince and princess characters of the *pwe*.
mohinga—popular fish and noodle soup.
Mount Meru—mythological mountain; center of the universe according to Burmese cosmology.
Mucalinda—a *naga* who protected the Buddha during a fierce storm.
mudra—a prescribed posture or gesture in which the Buddha is depicted in art.
Myanma—the official name of Burma.
myothugyi—traditional village or district administrator, generally phased out by British colonialists.

Nadaw—Burmese month falling in November/December.
naga—mythological serpent.
naga-yone—Buddha protected by a *naga*; central icon of religious cult of same name.
nahtwin—a "coming of age" ear-piercing ceremony for young women.
nat—spirit being; traditionally, there are 37 around whom a nationwide animistic worship revolves.
nat pwe—ritual spirit dance.
Nayon—Burmese month falling in May/June.
ngapi—fermented fish or shrimp paste, staple of Burmese diet.
nirvana—state of "neither existence nor non-existence", which is the ultimate goal of a Buddhist.

adi—rice.

agoda—Buddhist sanctuary, comprising a stupa and its enclosure.

ali—language of India in which *Tripitaka* was written.

alwe—bamboo flute.

andauk—Andaman redwood, an export timber.

athi—Burmese name for Moslems.

attala—bamboo xylophone.

att-me—large drum.

att-waing—circle of drums at center of a Burmese orchestra.

eith-tha—one viss, 1,633 grams.

ice—small copper coin.

itaka—one of the Buddhist scriptures; literally, "basket."

itakat taik—library; originally, a place where *pitakas* were stored.

ongyi—Buddhist monk.

onna—Brahmin astrologer.

we—Burmese dance-drama (general term).

ya—Burmese coin; 100 equal one *kyat*.

yathat—tower of a royal palace.

Pyatho—Burmese month falling in December/January.

ya zat—dance play with mythical theme.

yi-gyi-mun—royal Burmese barge.

Rahu—imaginary planet, associated with day of *Yahu* (**Wednesday p.m.**).

Rakhaing—Arakan; Indian Aryan word meaning "wild, uncivilized people."

Rama—hero of the Ramayana epic, and an incarnation of Vishnu.

saing—Burmese orchestra.

Sakka—king of the Burmese gods.

Sakya—royal family into which the Buddha was born.

Salon—sea gypsies of Tenasserim coast.

samsara—the cycle of rebirth in Buddhist belief.

Sangha—the Buddhist monastic community.

Sanskrit—ancient Indian language in which most Buddhist philosophical texts were written.

Sarnath—the place near Varanasi (Benares) where the Buddha preached his first sermon.

sawbwa—hereditary Shan or Kayah prince.

saya—teacher.

sayadaw—abbot of Buddhist *kyaung*.

seinbu—golden orb at tip of pagoda's *hti*.

shin-pyu—boy's initiation ceremony, marking his acceptance into a monastery.

Shiva—Hindu god of destruction.

sikhara — beehive-like crown atop a stupa.

sima—hall of ordination for Sangha; also called *thein*.

stupa—Buddhist place of worship and reliquary monument.

sutra—Buddhist discourse or religious reading.

Suvannabhumi—ancient Mon empire, "the land of gold."

Tabaung—Burmese month falling in February/March.

Tabodwe—Burmese month falling in January/February.

Tagu—Burmese month falling in March/April.

Tantrism—form of mystical Buddhism dominant in Tibet.

Tathagata—another name for the Buddha.

taunggya—slash-and-burn form of cultivation (also known as swidden).

Tavatimsa—the heaven to which the Buddha traveled to preach to his mother.

Tawthalin—Burmese month falling in August/September.

tazaung—pavilion (at pagoda).

Tazaungmone—Burmese month falling in October/November.

thabeik—bowl; refers to monk's alms bowl, and also to inverted bowl in stupa architecture.

Thadingyut—Burmese month falling in September/October.

Thagyamin—most venerated of the Burmese *nats*.

Thakin—originally, a title of respect for Europeans; later, title which Burmese freedom fighters gave themselves.

thanaka—tree bark from which yellow cosmetic powder of same name is made.

thein—hall of ordination for Sangha; also called *sima*.

Theravada—form of Buddhism dominant in Burma and Southeast Asia; "teachings of the elders."

Thingyan—Burmese water festival, held annually in *Tagu* (April).

thitsi—tree from which lacquer is tapped.

tical—unit of measurement equal to 16.33 grams.

tong—a cubit, approximately 18 inches.

tonga—horse-drawn cab.

Tripitaka—the holy scriptures of Theravada Buddhism; literally, "the three baskets" (Pali: *Tipitaka*).

Triratna—the three "gems" or "jewels" which all Burmese Buddhists recite, and in which they "take refuge": Buddha, Dharma (teachings) and Sangha (monkhood).

U—title of respect for older or superior men.

vinaya—rules and regulations of the Sangha.

Vishnu—one of the principal Hindu gods, also known as the protector.

Wagaung—Burmese month falling in July/August.

wah let khok—bamboo clappers, used in orchestra.

Waso—Burmese month falling in June/July.

Yahu—Burmese day lasting from Wednesday noon to midnight.

yoma—hills.

yuzena — measure of 28,000 cubits, or about nine miles.

zat gyi—masked dance-drama formerly popular in Burmese royal courts.

zat pwe—most popular form of Burmese theater, comprising music, dance and drama.

zaungdan—covered stairway, especially at pagodas.

zawgyi—alchemist, sorcerer.

zayat—resting place (at pagoda).

zedi—stupa; Buddhist monument and reliquary.

Index

327

Insight Guides

DISTRIBUTORS

AUSTRALIA: Lonely Planet Publications, P.O. Box 88 South Yarra, Victoria 3141.
BENELUX: Uitgeverij Cambium Albert Einsteinweg 41 3731 CW De Bilt Nederland
CANADA: See USA
DENMARK: Medicinsk Forlag ApS, Tranevej 2, 3650 Olstykke.
FRANCE: Librairie Armand Colin, 103 Boulevard Saint Michel, 75005 Paris.
HAWAII: APA Productions Hawaii Inc., 339 Saratoga Road, Suite 21, Hoolulu 96815.
HONGKONG: Far East Media Ltd, 1102A-1104A, Watson's Estate, Block B, 11th Floor, Watson Road, Hong Kong.
INDONESIA: N.V. Indoprom Co. (Indonesia) Ltd, SGV Building, 2nd Floor, JI Letjend S. Parman Kav. 56, Slipi, Jakarta Barat.
JAPAN: Charles E. Tuttle Co. Inc., 2-6, Suido I-chrome, Bunkyo-ku, Tokyo 112.
KOREA: Korea Britannica Corp., C.P.O. Box 690, Seoul 100.
MALAYSIA: MPH Distributors Sdn Bhd, 13, Jalan 13/6, Petaling Jaya, Selangor.
NEPAL: Tiger Tops Jungle Lodge, P.O. Box 242, Kathmandu.
PHILIPPINES: Erehwon Bookshop Inc., P.O. Box 86, Makati, Metro Manila 3117.
SINGAPORE: MPH Distributors (S) Pte Ltd., 116-D JTC Factory Building, Lorong 3, Geylang Square, Singapore 1438.
SRI LANKA: K.V.G. De Silva, 415 Galle Road, Colombo 4.
SWITZERLAND: EMA-Handel AG, 4410 Liestal, Burghade 34, Basel 40-13 308.
THAILAND: The Bookseller Co Ltd 28/1 Sukhumvit, Soi 13 Bangkok 11 Thailand
UNITED KINGDOM: Roger Lascelles, 3 Holland Park Mansions; 16 Holland Park Gardens, London W14 8DY.
USA (Mainland): Lee Publishers Group Inc 171 Madison Avenue New York 10016 New York U.S.A.
WEST GERMANY & AUSTRIA: Geo Center. Honigwiesenstrasse 25, D7 Stuttgart 80, Postface 800830, West Germany.